Beer

Beer

A History Of Suds

And Civilization

From Mesopotamia

To Microbreweries

GREGG SMITH

AVON BOOKS ◆ NEW YORK

BEER is an original publication of Avon Books. This work has never before appeared in book form.

AVON BOOKS
A division of
The Hearst Corporation
1350 Avenue of the Americas
New York, New York 10019

Library of Congress Cataloging in Publication Data:
Smith, Gregg, 1952–
   Beer : a history of suds and civilization from Mesopotamia to microbreweries / Gregg Smith.
        p.   cm.
Includes bibliographical references and index.
1. Beer—History.   I. Title.
TP577.S588   1995   95-21146
641.2'3'09—dc20   CIP

First Avon Books Trade Printing: December 1995

Contents

Contents

Beer

INTRODUCTION

What to Have

There is nothing which has yet been contributed by man, by which so much happiness is produced as a good tavern or inn.

—SAMUEL JOHNSON

Everyone's Beer History

Why write a book on the history of beer? Maybe it's connected with my earliest memory of tasting beer, at my grandmother's house. At age eight or so, this was a significant event. The beer was a Ballantine Ale from a tall green bottle, bearing their distinctive three-ring logo on the label. When offered a taste, I first looked to Dad for approval, which he gave with a bit of a smile. Tentatively reaching for the beer, it seemed as though the best approach was to imitate the adults and boldly tip back the bottle for a large swig, but I did so too abruptly. So when I brought the bottle back down, a geyser erupted from the neck and sprayed about in a terrifying foam. Although I was somewhat embarrassed, and a bit put off by the taste, there was still something intriguing in the flavor, something that would call me back. From then on, though, I would prefer a glass.

The true significance of that first swallow could only be

1

understood as I got older. It was a bond stretching back through time to ancient civilizations, a link to the Pilgrims, Washington, Adams, and Jefferson. It was an event as American as a baseball game, and as much a part of our country's heritage as Thanksgiving.

The sensation of that first taste became submerged deep in my memory, but every once in a while something would pull it to the surface. Maybe it was the fleeting smell of hops or spotting the golden colors glowing in a glass of beer, or simply the glimpse of a green bottle. My introduction to regular beer drinking occurred, as with many others, in college. It was an inexpensive mainstream beer and a weak comparison to the old Ballantine Ale. Yet I happily consumed glasses, cans, and kegs not so much as a beer enthusiast but more like a mass consumer. It was a great time, but still left me wanting something more, and the memory of that Ballantine would come back to me.

Sometimes people get to places they never intended by paths they tried to avoid. One of my missteps was a navy tour in Scotland—which led to a bar in Dunoon named the Saracen. Now long gone, it was a pub for locals, not sailors, and as such it had none of the all too familiar American brands. The owners, Mom and Pop, took the few sailors who wandered in under their wing and taught them what time spent in a pub was all about.

First there were things to unlearn. The pub didn't mean loud rock and roll while guzzling beer as fast as it could be funneled down a gullet. The pub was not the place for girl chasing, nor boisterous sports talk. There was a slot machine, as in every bar, but depositing a coin brought the reproach "Now, boys, you don't need to be wasting your money on the likes of that." Above all, the pub was not a place for sitting about and slowly getting stewed. If you had to sit and drink, it meant you had committed the sin of going beyond what you should have, which resulted in a polite but firm expulsion from the pub's friendly social circle for the night. It was an early and very effective lesson in responsible drinking.

Once you'd completed unlearning, they introduced you to a new "bar etiquette." The pub meant learning the intricacies of playing dominoes, and how to hold a hand of the white ivory pieces between the fingers of your nonplaying hand. It was the occasion for communal viewing of the news or a documentary on the "telly," which was promptly turned off at the conclusion so a quiet discussion could ensue. It meant learning the sport of darts and developing a curiosity for games like 301 and 501, wherein the best score wasn't the highest, but zero. Darts was like indoor golf and a perfect substitute for the links during the long, dark, and damp Scottish winters. Conversation always hushed as competitors made their plays. And when a throw resulted in a particularly good score, there was reserved celebration. It made for a very relaxed atmosphere.

The owners also enrolled you in the school of British ales. The education spanned subjects from how a warmed serving allowed full appreciation of the beer's character through the spectrum of styles. And should you wonder what it would be like to go back home and have an American beer, the owner would lean across the bar and gently explain, "Son, once you drink Guinness, you'll always drink Guinness."

I always found the trip home an adjustment. In the United States there was no easily secured pint of ale. And in comparison the mass-market beers seemed insipid. What was a new beer lover to do? Just when things seemed hopeless, something strange started happening on beer shelves across the country. Some who longed for the full and varied tastes of European beers decided that if they wanted that type beer in the States, they would just have to make it themselves. As interest grew in these beers, more European brands were imported. And as the shelves became more rich with possibilities, it became fun to seek out and try as many different beers as possible.

Several events broadened my interest in beer from its taste to its history. Once, over some Chinese food, a friend asked me what symbol was on the bottom of a Tsingtao bottle. Not knowing, I turned it over, and I was nothing short of shocked, for there in the center of the bottom were three interlocking rings. Later, after I became a successful homebrewer, my relatives eagerly related the exploits of my great-grandparents, who brewed their own beer during Prohibition. And once I became a beer writer, I had more and more conversations that began with, "Did you know there was once a brewery . . ." I quickly found that the history of beer made for good lead-ins when I was covering the new breweries springing up. Finally, *Yankee Brew News* asked me about writing a piece devoted to beer history.

Beginning with colonial brewing, my research led in several directions at once. With each new source, I found more information outside my original scope that was far too interesting to just let go. I tucked away each new gem in one of a growing number of files, until one day, while moving and organizing the files, I realized my article had grown into a book.

But the history of beer goes beyond a chronicle of the birth, growth, and destruction of, say, a brewhouse. It's something more personal. Certain beers make up each of our own beer histories. Mine includes a cold American lager after a day of fence mending in Idaho with brothers Rick and Karl; cheap college beers and hot dogs in Dubuque, Iowa, with Bob Hayes, Chuck Doyle, Spanky Meresman, Duane (DJ) Jaeger, and Nick Tenerelli; the first *hefe-weizen* with Scott Maxfield in New Jersey; that first rich, coffeelike Guinness Stout with John Paperniak, Dennis Jones, Brett Darr, Steve Adler, and Jim Kaiser (the 636 crew) in Holy Loch; a Winter Warmer in Arcen, Netherlands, with Jack Zahn; a certain exceptional bottle of Orval with Lisa and Michael Variano in Horsefeathers; Canadian lagers while sailing on Lake Champlain with the Wallings; and the first *Berliner Weisse* (with syrup) I bought for Carrie Getty in the Brickskeller.

Those are brands anyone could have, yet they were made special by the atmosphere in which they were consumed. Beer is perhaps the most social of beverages. It spans all classes and occasions. It makes a poor man rich and a rich man richer. It relaxes the soul and comforts the body on both cold, stormy nights and hot summer days.

As you read this history, remember your own. What does a sip of ale conjure up for you? Who does it bring back to your side? Ultimately these memories are what make beer special and significant.

CHAPTER 1

The Ancients and the Gift of the Gods

I have heard him assert, that a tavern choir was the throne of human felicity.

—HAWKIN'S *LIFE OF JOHNSON*

Beer and the Birth of Civilization

From its humble origins, beer has touched cultures throughout the world, become a popular food, and collected a history encompassing the past's most significant events. Where did it all begin?

Six thousand years ago man was a wanderer, and it took something pretty special to make him put down roots. This was a unique area of land. It's easy to picture the Mideast with a dry and hostile landscape, but the image belies the truth. This region, nestled between the Tigris and Euphrates rivers, had abundant water and plant life, and has justifiably been named the "Fertile Crescent." Early man settled here because it was easy to search for and gather food. Even more important, anthropologists suspect man chose the area deliberately because of what would become an indispensable item—beer!

Barley was one of the wild grasses that grew between

5

the rivers, and the ancient ones soon learned these cereals provided nourishment and kept well. It wasn't easy to harvest, it didn't grow in nice neat rows or even all in one spot, but it was available. The people of the region most likely roamed about in crudely made clothing and, in what must have made for a boring and backbreaking lifestyle, slowly gathered the grain by hand. Eventually they found they could plant the grains and a new plant would grow, and if they planted them all in one spot, the gathering went much more quickly. As experience was passed down through the generations, some strains were favored and a process of natural selection resulted. The new domesticated grain became a welcomed addition to their diet as people started to cook everything, but it wasn't the taste of barley, which they made into primitive bread, that motivated them to undertake this arduous work. What made them do so was an event that occurred shortly after they first started gathering grain. At that time they constructed earthen jars to store their food, and these worked well until one night a rain flooded the jars. Imagine waking up and finding this mess, especially after you had walked all over what was then creation to harvest the grain by hand. With this process taking days or weeks to fill the jars, would you just dump them and start over? Most likely the gatherer who suffered this misfortune felt the same way. The logical course was to spread the wet grain out to dry. With relief the owner saw it worked. Later, when the grain was cooked into their crude loaves, the owner found it especially sweet. In this way our ancestors stumbled upon the malting process.

Loaves of malted barley soon became the world's first fad. They were baked with abandon and stored in the same type of jars. Then disaster struck again. Imagine our early brewer as she discovers rain has flooded another jar of loaves. Because she had learned to cover the jars, she didn't check the supply constantly and so she didn't discover the problem for several days. During that time wild wind-borne yeast had found its way into the slop and fermentation had begun. It wasn't long until the jar was filled with a thick, foaming, bubbling mass.

When she looked upon the sodden mess she was probably disgusted and annoyed. Then perhaps she thought

"When the jars flooded last time, it turned out okay, so maybe . . ." She picked up the jar, and what followed was that stunning moment in time when a pair of lips was first wetted by beer. The first sip was surely with some trepidation, but she was of a tough stock who tried to eat almost anything that didn't crawl and even some things that did.

She must have been delighted. She took another sip to be sure, then a gulp followed by a long draft—and found that it was good. Soon she had her family and friends try it, and try it some more. In a little while they were all lying around laughing. "What luck!" they must have thought, then, "Think it could happen again?" No doubt there was a mad dash to fill the loaf jars with water. These innovative people were quickly fermenting the world's second batch of beer.

Barley was soon in great demand, but someone must have worried about the grain running out. No doubt that person decided it would be a good idea to plant a little patch down in the bottomland where it would be convenient to harvest. And as grain went from offering their diet a bit of variety to making life worth living, the peoples of the early world gave up their wandering, settled down in one place, and became farmers. Thus the Fertile Crescent became the cradle of civilization. More and bigger harvests meant more beer, and soon both irrigation and the plow were devised to increase yields. They noticed sowing was dependent upon the return of warm weather, and concern about producing a good crop made them figure out the best time for spring planting. This need for brewing supplies led to inventing the calendar, which in turn brought about the first use of mathematics. If only they also had a TV set to watch baseball with their beer, they would have had it all.

Does all this seem a little unbelievable? Maybe so, but a good number of anthropologists, such as Professor Solomon Katz of the University of Pennsylvania, speculate that the accidental discovery of beer is exactly what caused man to settle, begin crop cultivation, and eventually develop commodity living.

When Anchor Brewing Company of San Francisco first heard of Dr. Katz's theory, they wondered what that early brew was like, and they called Dr. Katz. According to Anchor salesman Bob Brewer, Professor Katz supplied them with an ancient recipe, and soon the Anchor employees were happily mixing honey, dates, and barley, forming grain patties, lightly baking the mixture, and cutting it into strips that had the consistency of dog biscuits.

Dr. Katz also told them how the women of antiquity were the brewers, so the men of the Anchor crew popped open a few beers while the female employees tossed their malt-honey-date strips into their brew kettle. Finding containers that resembled the old earthen amphorae, they set the beer to ferment with ale yeast, which is a modern, cultured cousin of the wind-borne varieties. It wasn't long before they, too, had a bubbling mess with a big foamy top that eventually dried into a hard crust. This led them to resurrect a method of beer drinking seen in hieroglyphics. Poking straws through the pancakelike crust, they sucked the beer out from under the unpleasant top layer. According to Brewer, it looked like a bunch of people sitting around a giant eight-person hookah, and they got similar results. The beer wasn't a commercial success—it was unhopped and rather sweet, and in fact, they offered very little for sale—but it was an event no one at Anchor would ever forget.

Recent archaeological digs have provided additional support for Dr. Katz's theories. A glimpse of this early form of community can be found at Hacinebi Tepe, a site investigated by Dr. Guillermo Algaze, an anthropologist at the University of California–San Diego specializing in the colonialism of ancient civilizations. Located near the Euphrates River in Southern Turkey, Hacinebi Tepe was an early trading outpost of Mesopotamian civilization, and its founding was a direct result of the events happening seven hundred miles downriver.

There in the Fertile Crescent, the people of 3500 B.C. rejoiced in larger and larger harvests of barley from improved methods of farming the bountiful soil. They managed this primarily through a tremendous technological breakthrough: irrigation. They were so successful in achieving the first known grain surpluses, they resorted to keeping accounts of their harvests, and with their wealth they built one of the first modern cities, named "Uruk." But their economy had a flaw. Although the land made them rich in agricultural products, it lacked luxury items. And who could survive long without those? They wanted other natural resources such as metals, semiprecious stones, and timber. The solution would warm the coldest capitalist's heart. They set up trade with less advanced neighboring groups who could be taken advantage of.

This was the function of Hacinebi Tepe and the closer Godin Tepe. These posts were designed as part of a larger master plan that included a central fortress and surrounding village. Among the artifacts recovered are clear remains of articles traded, including some of the earliest evidence of beer. It seems logical for beer to be found there. The government back in Uruk had an excess of grain, and transporting this bulk would have been extremely difficult. Beer, however, was grain condensed, and the alcohol ensured some stability (preservation) over the trip.

The accomplishments of the early Mesopotamians laid a foundation for the later empires and cultures of their descendants, the Sumerians, then the Babylonians. The Sumerians established the first true civilization. They had a sophisticated agricultural system, which included irrigation and selective use of planting. One of their more important contributions was a direct product of Uruk beer making. They expanded the beer accounting system into the first cuneiform alphabet, and from the clay tablets they used for paper forty-five hundred years ago, we know of their brewing methods and beer-drinking habits. We've learned that they developed a marketing strategy that would be used later by the mass-market brewers of the 1980s and 1990s: If you want to establish a larger market base, offer a greater variety of the same basic product. A written record of the Sumerians indicates they brewed at least nineteen different types of beer.

The Sumerians were rightly awed with the magic of fermentation and elevated brewing to a spiritual level. The place for brewing was soon firmly situated in the temple. Professor Katz notes that the Sumerian poem "The Hymn to Ninkasi" has the oldest known beer recipe. The goddess Ninkasi lived on mythical Mount Sabu, which means "the mountain of the tavern keeper." And in the temple the women priests were the first official brewmasters, which set the stage for women to historically fill prominent roles as brewers.

Beer also touched the women of royalty. Queen Shu-Bad

sipped beer through a golden straw, a drinking method found in many cultures and ages. One of Dr. Katz's most prized exhibits in the collection at the University of Pennsylvania is an example of the queen's straw. These straws are usually found with decorated bowls, also made of precious metals. Could this be the origin of the rhyme, "Wasn't this a dainty dish to set before the queen?"

Sumerian culture was then integrated into that of the Babylonians, who conquered the Fertile Crescent and distinguished themselves as the world's first great builders. They constructed many wonders of the ancient world, including the mysterious hanging gardens of Babylon. The trade routes they established were astonishingly far-reaching and even crossed the great deserts. Best of all, when the thirsty travelers returned home, they could always find a beer.

Along with the basics of Sumerian religion, culture, and language, the Babylonians inherited their rich brewing heritage. Their clay tablets contain a vast written record of brewing, and as one might expect, the root of Babylonian beer words was *kassi*, derived from the goddess Ninkasi's name. The translations provide a description of the styles and methods used to make their beer. The word root *kas* in *Lukasninda* signifies "man of the beer loaf" and the writings tell how to soak the beer loaf man's loaves for brewing beer. Don't be deceived by the translation; in general it was once again the women who were brewers.

Their great depth of styles was also taken from the Sumerians. Once again the name of each reflected homage to the patron goddess. Among the varieties (retaining *kas* as the word root) were:

Kassi	Black beer
Kassag	Fine black beer
Kassagasaan	Premium beer
Kassig	Red beer
Kasusasig	Spiced beer
Kurungig	Wheat beer

Interestingly, the Babylonians felt compelled to have a designation for premium beer, another marketing tool Madison Avenue didn't invent.

Within Babylonian society, beer became even more deeply rooted in religious ceremony. It was even offered to the goddess of fertility in the hope of buying off her pleasure and securing a good harvest. Each goddess needed to be enticed with her own special brew, and other styles created for this purpose were the forefathers of stout, holiday ales, and wit, a Belgian wheat beer style. No small debt do we owe these ancient wise ones.

The production of beer and the quality of the supply were of such importance, they resulted in laws governing the recipe and method of brewing. Brewers making lousy beer today get off rather easy. Back then the penalty for deviating from the approved method was death.

Beer had become so important to society, even the price was regulated. To keep the priestess-brewers from gouging customers and controlling the economy, an official exchange rate was established by which the women were compensated with a specified amount of grain. Any brewer found accepting any other type payment was punished by being cast into the water.

Speaking of water, no story of ancient beers would be complete without a trip up the Nile River. At a time predating the Egyptians, while Sumeria and Babylonia were thriving, culture was developing in the area just south of Egypt known as Nubia. The emergence of Nubian beer at approximately the same time as Sumerian and Babylonian brews leads scholars to conclude that beer was accidentally discovered in several areas at once, probably by the same method.

The Nubians affect our beer culture because of a brew they named *bousa*. There is speculation that this word became the basis for both *booze* and *beer*. Like their neighbors, they developed a variety of beer styles, and aside from their standard beer, *hktsty*, they also produced a spiced beer known as either *hes* or *hek*, which seems to be a close relative of the Babylonian spiced beer *kasusasig*.

Egyptian settlements came after the Nubians and developed into one of the greatest civilizations of the ancient world. Their organization and civic structure were the marks of an advanced people. Their knowledge of mathematics and engineering is unquestioned, and to this day the methods used to construct the pyramids remain a theoretical problem for engineers. And one of the most important aspects of their everyday life was beer.

In the same fashion as the Babylonians, Egyptians believed beer was a gift from the gods. They were blessed with it by Ibis, the deity of nature. The effects of beer drinking were also worked into their religion, and the goddess of joy, Hather, was credited as the inventor of brewing. At the temple of Dendra, in the ancient capital of upper Egypt, is a stone carving honoring Hather, and next to her is Menqet, "the goddess who makes beer," holding two large beer jars. This rather large number of gods related to beer was no accident. Beer was considered so important, it was necessary to ensure there was a god to look after each step of the process. From sowing to harvest through malting and brewing, a god was invoked to assure all went well.

We know so much about Egyptian brewing because of the great number of hieroglyphic references to it. They show their brewing technology was much like that of other regions. One of the oldest Egyptian recipes was outlined by the ancient chemist Zosimus of Panopolis, who described in detail the preparations for brewing.

> Take fine clean barley and moisten it for one day and draw it off or also lay it up in a windless place until morning and again wet it in six hours. Cast it into a smaller perforated vessel and wet it and dry it until it shall become shredded and when this is so shake it in the sunlight until it falls apart . . . Next grind it and make it into loaves adding leaven, just like bread, and cook it rather raw and whenever (the loaves) rise, dissolve sweetened water and strain through a strainer or light sieve . . . In baking the loaves cast them into a vat with water and boil it a little in order that it may not froth nor become lukewarm and draw up and strain it having prepared it, heat and examine it.

What Zosimus recounts is easily recognized as the manner in which barley is malted, mashed, and lathered in preparation for brewing. The baking of bread into "rather raw" loaves was their method of kilning and drying the grain after germination had taken place. It released the grain's starch and sugar for fermentation. Keeping the water heated but not boiling completed the conversion of sugars in what was their equivalent to mashing. The *wort* (sweet liquid) made through this process was then ready to ferment. This method of brewing (with the exception of turning the grains into loaves) would remain virtually unchanged for over a thousand years.

That's why the Egyptians contrived a way to carry beer with them when they traveled. Of course, it wasn't a matter of dropping in at the local convenience store. Instead they carried a starter. In a jar they carried some of the moist, fermenting bread crumbs. On arrival at an oasis, they simply added water and waited for the magic to happen. (Yeast, deposited by the wind, wasn't yet known to be the cause of fermentation.)

The beers they made were generally from all barley, and some translations refer to them as "barley wine." The Egyptian word for brewer was *fty*, and brewing was *th*. As in Sumerian, Egyptian had a linguistic root for beer, words that used the letters *H* and *K*. Beer was called *hkt*, *hek*, or *hekt*. This designation lasted well into the twentieth century and was recently revived in an Egyptian beer made for export. The names of these beers are very similar to, and may have originated from, Nubian brewing. Another theory is that both the Nubian and Egyptian words were derived from the Babylonian *hiqu*, which means "mixture" or "to mix"; it implies the crumbling and mixing of loaves into water. Whatever the origin, it meant the same thing: a beverage a fellow could sit down with after a hard day of surviving the desert sun.

Because glasses still hadn't been invented, the Babylonians, Syrians, Hittites, Armenians, Egyptians, and Greeks drank their beer as the Sumerians and later the employees of Anchor brewing did. They sat around large jars and used a straw or tube. Pictograms frequently illustrated this method, as did the writings of Xenophon, the Greek historian and essayist who was one of the most important Greek prose writers. In 434 B.C. he recorded Egyptian customs among his histories in the *Anabasis*.

For drink, there was beer which was very strong when not mingled with water, but was agreeable to those who were

used to it. They drank this with a reed, out of the vessel
that held the beer, upon which they saw the barley swim.

Not the most attractive scene. The straws were probably
used as much to suck up brew from below the floating
mash debris as to avoid looking at the unsightly mess, but
it must have tasted good, because everybody wanted
some.

In drinking, royalty was, of course, waited on, and they
were provided with straws of gold such as those shown by
Professor Katz. But beer wasn't just restricted to the nobility, it was a staple of all classes. Of course, the rulers managed to set aside the best for themselves. Poorer-quality
brew went to the unfortunate lower groups who were assigned tasks like making bricks without straw and building
pyramids. Meanwhile the royals sat around gold inlaid
bowls, drank the premium beer, and probably looked
around for the ancient equivalent to pretzels.

Beer's popularity made it an item that any self-respecting
host or hostess just had to have at any socially correct
soiree. Queen Tiy, wife of Amenhotep II, in 1375 B.C. hosted
one of that season's prime social events. Her menu included all the delicacies of old Egypt: duck, gazelle, and
porcupine. As one of the world's most accomplished host-
esses, she did not leave the selection of an appropriate
beverage to chance. Her choice for an accompanying beverage had to be the best, which, of course, meant beer. There
was even a precedent established for the good Queen Tiy.
During the era of the Egyptian Middle Kingdom (1800 B.C.)
the royal bookkeepers made notations of accepting 130
jars of beer daily at the court, and the queen received 5 of
those jars for her personal use. There is also reference to
special beers (if translations are correct) flavored with
honey, cedar, lavender, and nutmeg. So today's homebrewers aren't doing anything new when they create beers with
unusual combinations of ingredients. Back then there was
even one special style brewed for the ladies which contained flowers.

But beer was not limited to parties or even daily life. It
was adopted for the serious business of curing the ill. The
reference book for Egyptian physicians, the Ebers papyrus,
listed seven hundred different prescriptions. It included

careful descriptions of each medicine's ingredients, and over one hundred of these used beer liberally. True, the cures may not have worked, but given the main ingredient, the patients probably didn't care.

And if the patient didn't survive, beer was still the answer. As early as 3000 B.C. a barley brew was mentioned in the Egyptian Book of the Dead. In the long journey royals took to join the gods, they were eased along the trip by jars of fine beer; sort of spirits for the spirits.

Mr. James Death, who consulted at Egyptian breweries in the 1800s, insisted beer also played an important role in the Exodus of the Jews from Egypt. He considered the leavened bread in the Bible the equivalent to beer loaves— a type of quickie grain mash. He also noted that Judges 6:19–20 mentions boiling bread and drawing off a broth.

Although not widely known for the use of alcohol, the Jewish culture does contain other references to a brewing background. The Hebrews in captivity in Babylon drank *bre* as a magic protection from disease. Some sources reason this may be another origin of the word for beer. A measure of credit for the spread of beer could be attributed to the Jewish people carrying brewing knowledge throughout their travels. By the Middle Ages, when the Christian church controlled brewing, they relied on the Jews who stepped forward as the first distributors and wholesalers. In addition, beer has a place in the Talmud, and at least three of the rabbis who compiled it were brewers.

Further back in biblical history is the story of Noah. An Assyrian tablet of 2000 B.C. describes Noah's antediluvian days. As it catalogs Noah's preparations for a sea cruise, it refers to beer as one of the ship's stores. Perhaps, Noah interpreted his instructions as requiring two "hogsheads" of beer.

By the time the Greeks ruled the world beer had been brewing for thousands of years. It's common to associate the ancient Greeks with wine, but in reality, they were beer aficionados. Herodotus, the Greek father of history, born in 484 B.C., wrote extensively on the customs, geography, and history of the Mediterranean with a particular emphasis on the Egyptians, and in 460 B.C. he supplied posterity with a hefty treatise on beer. Likewise, Sophocles, the famous Greek treasurer now known as the father of theater, touted the many positive aspects of beer drinking. He was always quick to lecture on his successful diet of moderation, which included bread, meat, vegetables, and a daily beer, well before doctors started extolling its benefits.

The extensive Greek writings ensured the continuation of brewing, and their library in Alexandria served as a repository for this knowledge. As the Romans took over, they were able to draw on the brewing experience of a great many previous civilizations. Pliny, the historian and scholar of A.D. 23–79 wrote about how the Greeks learned brewing from the Egyptians. He also detailed the Egyptian use of corn in brewing. Pliny went on to describe how the Roman empire, along with their enemies the Gauls, Germans, Celts, Visigoths, and Vandals, replenished strength expended on the battlefield by consuming mass quantities of beer. He records that the Gauls concentrated their drinking on "barley wine," while the Romans favored wheat beer. Both the Gauls and the Romans, however, called their beer *cerevisia*, a word derived from Ceres, the Roman goddess of agriculture, and *vis*, Latin for "strength," and which survives in Spanish today as *cervesa*.

The early civilizations provided the discovery of beer and brewing, but it would be their introduction to the Roman Empire and infant Europe that transform beer into what we recognize today.

CHAPTER 2

England Through the Middle Ages

Yes, my soul sentimentally craves British beer.

—THOMAS CAMPBELL, 1777–1844

Good ale, the true and proper drink of Englishmen. He is not deserving of the name Englishman who speaketh against ale, that is good ale.

—GEORGE BORROW

The Church and Saints, the Tavern and Guild

The immediate post-Roman era is a fairly big disappointment for historians. Following the fall of the empire, chaos ruled, and it didn't leave much of a written record. The Germanic barbarians who helped topple Rome were too busy looting and pillaging to record their history. Thus, there is a void in the history of beer. Of course, other vestiges of civilization also suffered. Law and order, government and science, civic organization and the economy: The very base of civilization disappeared, as did the well-maintained roads and efficient systems of communication which held it together. So while brewing did continue, to be sure, it was done with nowhere near the organization the Romans provided. It would take a strong, aggressive, determined group bound together under a centralized administration to take brewing under its arm. And it wouldn't hurt if that group also had a strong sense of fiscal responsibility, a profit motive, and the ability to create monopolies. The church was ready to do just that.

As with the ancients, beer was to be entrusted to God. One of the earliest examples of how entrenched brewing was in the church is illustrated in the story of Arnou, the bishop of Metz. This much-beloved bishop had the misfortune of passing from this world in A.D. 640. Worse still, he died far from his flock. But so beloved was he in Metz that the town's grief-stricken people marched off in 641 to retrieve his body.

On the return trip the solemn procession reached the village of Champigneulles. By that time the devoted ones had raised a considerable thirst. Unfortunately, the villagers had only one goblet of beer to offer the weary travelers. But then a miracle happened. As each of the interment party partook of the beer, regardless of how much was drunk or how many containers were filled, the goblet never emptied. This was truly a great miracle. All agreed it was deserving of canonization, for surely the departed bishop had arranged this to demonstrate his love for his flock. Thus, Arnou was elevated to sainthood, the first of many patron saints of brewers. One mystery remains, though: Whatever became of the blessed mug?

Shortly thereafter, Charlemagne was putting together the Holy Roman Empire. A master administrator, he knew how to keep the masses under control. As he laid out criteria by which towns would be managed, he detailed which trades the district administrators needed for smooth operation. Craftily, Charlemagne ensured brewers occupied a prominent position on the list.

Charlemagne can also be credited with the promotion of brewing science. The star he imported to run his brewing think tank was the first modern brewer, Saint Gall. Fresh from his work with pagan, but beer-loving, Celts, Gall brought a fresh approach to brewing for Charlemagne's abbey. As he refined the brewing process, he was soon producing three different styles of beer. The methods he introduced for mashing, fermenting, storing, and caring for beer changed the face of brewing and Gall became yet another of the many Beer Saints.

The precedent established by Charlemagne, combined with the power of the church, positioned monks to control brewing over the next several centuries. The church was, in fact, "the" brewer and wholesaler, and as the church tightened its grip over the individual lives of its members and extended its influence over all of society, they also regulated beer consumption. Thus, proper respect for the church became a prerequisite for drinking. The local abbots learned well how to combine a carrot and a threat. They let their parishes know that if they wanted beer, they had to participate in church rituals such as the commemoration of a parish's patron saint. Small wonder these celebrations and their associated feasts became known as "church ales." Of course, these included the bride-ale, in which a bride would dispense ale in return for wedding gifts. The modern term *bridal* thus is with us because of both the church and beer.

The church's control did have its threats. The development of basic technology brought the introduction of crafts, and workers of similar trades soon gathered in associations called guilds. Along with assuring that only quality products were made and acceptable work was done, guilds provided members an opportunity to use a totally new concept, leisure time. They assisted in this by encouraging members to gather for socializing over beer. To maintain control over their parishioners, the church quickly realized they needed to have a measure of influence on guild meetings. It accomplished this by coordinating a wide range of activities such as rituals, masses, meetings, socializing, processions, and trips to the church on guild day. With each of these the church ensured good attendance by rolling out the beer. An account is left by the guild of St. Elene, who celebrated their feast day by first attending mass and then retiring to the guild hall, where they would "eat bread and cheese and drink as much ale as is good for them."

Beer consumption combined with the fraternal feelings that marked any guild day were an important way for workers to attain solidarity. Even the brewers got in on it. According to legend, the first guild for brewers was formed in Brabant, Belgium, during the reign of Duke Jean I, "Jan Primus," who was honored throughout Europe as the "king of beer." He founded the guild for brewers known as the "knights of the mashing fork." To this day his name is frequently seen, although corrupted to "Gambrinus," as in the Czech Republic's Gambrinus beer.

Despite this growing activity, independent breweries were slow to appear. With the church provisioning the thirsty masses by distributions to travelers, and supplying celebrations for the local faithful, there just wasn't a big demand to buy beer. After all, why buy what the church at least appeared to be giving away? In the same context, there wasn't much demand for gathering at a market when the church yard provided everything needed for the conduct of trade, including the blessing of the holy fathers and the regulation of their watchful eye.

But despite the church's ready supply, a few ale makers did establish themselves. To be sure, their numbers were limited, as was their impact on beer. Their motivation was only to pocket a little extra cash, as none of them were full-time brewers. In general they were alewives operating out in the country, away from the monastery's reach. But in the 1300s, the church would lose its long-established monopoly and these independents would become the vanguards of a whole new profession.

In the year 1347 a traveler from the Crimea would have a tremendous impact on Europe: the Black Death, whose four-year stay resulted in over forty million fatalities. As Europe emerged from the plague years, its customs and economy had undergone an irreversible change. The huge decline in population resulted in less demand for land and fewer people to do work. In addition, the wealth was redistributed over a smaller population, and thus the lucky survivors gained not only higher wages but also a bigger bank account. By 1400 the average worker collected twice the real wages the same craftsmen had received only one hundred years earlier. Naturally there was more discretionary income; and the people spent money like mad. Suddenly it was fashionable to be fashionable. This led to increased imports, trade, and a reason to embrace the latest fad, markets.

Alewives who had previously brewed only occasionally now found large, thirsty gatherings eager for a little refreshment. Even more important, the merchants who traveled between these markets were in need of a place to stay. And who better to spend an evening with than someone with a steady supply of ale?

The houses of these brewers were soon regular meeting places for travelers. As the overnight guests increased in number, the brewers started to develop additional amenities as a means of liberating more cash from their guests. Not that this was hard, the spending frenzy went by the principal of opening the wallet and saying "help yourself." Business people found the inn a good deal more enjoyable than the crowded, confusing open-air markets. It became much more fun to haggle in a comfy seat near the fire while refreshed by a tankard of ale. By the end of the Middle Ages, the inn was firmly established as a trading center and things were never the same afterward.

The inn also enjoyed a boost from jealous spouses. Much like today, the spouse at home was left to take care of the domestic chores and felt left out of the good life on the road. The traveling merchants, remembering the welcoming ale of the tavern, made it up to them by arranging an evening out at their local establishment. When this started to happen, enterprising tavern keepers quickly made their inns the setting for feasts, plays, concerts, balls, dinners, and shows. And where there is money to be made, there is also competition for it. Thus, there was an absolute explosion in the number of drinking establishments, from almost none in the 1300s to more than seventeen thousand by the year 1577, which equates to at least one new tavern per week in lower England alone.

The typical tavern was built on the village main street and was usually the most dominant structure in town. There were four main buildings, each two stories high, which formed a central courtyard. In addition to drink, meals, lodging, and entertainment, the inn provided warehousing space for the merchant's goods and stabling for the horses. The guiding word for tavern owners was *convenience*, followed by service, quality, and profit. And with patrons from the land-owning, professional, and merchant classes, there was such great profit in the business that by the 1500s the innkeeper was commonly one of the ten wealthiest people in town.

The poorer sorts also saw the advantage to establishing inns. A much less lavish version of the inn was opened to satisfy the thirsty needs of the laboring class. Of course, with this version there was seldom need for rooms to rent. When the patrons ran out of money, they were told to walk home.

This stratification resulted in a three-tiered system of taverns. In general, inns catered to the most affluent of clients, taverns were the meeting place for those a bit less prosperous, and alehouses serviced the downtrodden folks who still managed to have a good time while existing on the low end of it all.

As the number of inns, taverns, and alehouses grew, the rise of industrialization forced even more people to the comfort of ale. As early as the mid 1300s the first signs of environmental problems appeared in Britain. Along with towns disposing of garbage, and in some cases sewage, in the rivers and streams, the waterways also became a medieval toxic waste dump for the barbers, leather tanners, and a score of infant industries. The rivers, which had been the main drinking supply for the lower class, became unusable. The alternative was to find a beverage that had been boiled, thus ensuring sanitation. If the drink also had a low level of alcohol for preservation, even better. Of course, ale was ready to fill this void. Before long everyone was drinking it, rich and poor, men and women, grandmothers and infants. It became the most favored drink of the times.

This popularity made the government more than a little uneasy. How do you control all these rowdies, all this new development? Legislate it, of course. Several English laws had already been passed governing beer. One of the first was by Ethelbert, King of Kent, who dictated a set of regulations aimed at ale sellers in 616. The area of Kent would later become better known for hops than anything accomplished by old King Ethelbert, so his rules weren't exactly a stunning success. By the 900s King Edgar decreed there would be only one alehouse in each settlement. This shouldn't have been necessary since the church controlled brewing at that time, and they basically held a monopoly. However, sales and demand grew over time, and the barons, who were starting to get a small piece of the action, were intent on their right to brew. The issue was considered so important to nobility that King John included a clause on standards for ale in the Magna Carta in 1215.

By 1309 London was easily one of the most visible of cities with growing alehouse populations, and its excellent records of beer-drinking activities offer some incredible numbers. There were more than thirty-five thousand residents within the city limits, and these thirsty Englishmen were serviced by at least 354 taverns and another 1,330 brewshops. That comes out to one alehouse or tavern for every twenty-one inhabitants. These numbers outlined a problem all too apparent to the government and were cause for additional measures to limit drinking.

Sin taxes were, even then, one of the favorite methods to deal with all this. In general, the concept seems simple. Tax the people who could still afford to drink, thereby avoiding outright prohibition while raising a bit of coin for the royal coffers. The problem this causes for historians is the difficulty in determining how many inns, taverns, and alehouses there were after the tax was enacted. The taxes were based upon the status of the business, and then, as now, the clever businessman made an attempt to get around higher rates through a little middle tax dodging. As the distinctions blurred, it caused more than one magistrate to complain they could not tell the difference between an inn, tavern, and alehouse, a task that, looking back from today, is no easier. It's easiest to just acknowledge there were a lot.

Though the growth of alehouses and associated laws was certainly a significant development, the biggest impact on beer during this time was the first major alteration to the recipe. Up until the Middle Ages, English ale was a rather ugly product, a rough brew made from barley, but variations also included wheat, oats, and even millet, and on occasion it could be coarse enough to rip your throat raw. No wonder the barons who twisted King John into signing the Magna Carta wanted standards for brewing. Those early ales were not fully attenuated (not completely fermented), and were flavored with spices, commonly long peppers for both taste and preservation. Overall it was a thickish liquid, low in alcohol from the incomplete ferment. One person from the 1200s described it as "for muddy, foddy, fulsome, puddle, stinking; for all of these ale is the only drinking." It was also well described in a rhyme about a notorious Cornish ale cited by Andrew Boorde in 1540.

> *Ich am a Cornishman, ale I can brew*
> *It will make one to cacke, also to spew.*
> *It is thick and smokey and also it is thin*
> *It is like wash as pigs had wrestled there in*

Much of the fault can be attributed to the brewing process. It should be remembered that these were times not noted for their cleanliness. The problems in keeping brew areas neat and tidy in those days are nowhere better described than in the "Tunning of Elinour Rumming."

> *The hens run in the mash vat*
> *For they go to roost*
> *Straight over the ale-joust*
> *And dung, when it comes,*
> *In the ale tuns.*
> *Then Elinour takes*
> *The mash-bowl and shakes*
> *The hens dung away,*
> *and skims it into a tray*
> *whereas the yeast is*
> *With her mangy fists . . .*

Surely this is an extreme example, but the fact that this problem was immortalized in verse is a clear indication it was a common problem.

The Germans were the first to conquer the quality problem. The earliest of their regulations was issued in 1487 by Duke Albert IV, which became the basis for the famous *Reinheitsgebot* of 1516. Established by William VI, elector of Bavaria, it was a purity standard which only allowed four ingredients in beer: water, malted barley, malted wheat, and hops; yeast was still unknown and taken largely for granted.

The Germans also made the most significant modification to brewing when around 768 they began adding hops to their brew kettles. The boiling of this relative of cannabis had two effects. First, it balanced some of the sweetness of the malt. Of even more importance was its quality of stabilizing and preserving the beer. By 1079 Abbess Hildegard of Rupertsberg was writing of the natural preservative power of the bitter hop.

Of course, the conservative English would have none of this newfangled corruption—the hop additions were thought to be a contamination of ale. So strongly did the English feel on this subject that hops were banned from their beer. As late as 1524 the British were still resisting the use of hops as seen in a quote from that year.

> *Hops, Reformation, Bays and Beer*
> *Came to England in one bad year.*

Despite some on-and-off use of hops by monks, the first appearance of note in the British Isles is thought to be shortly after the Hundred Years War between France and England (1337–1453) when they were used by Dutch and Flemish brewers. They were exempted from the law banning hops because, after all, what self-respecting loyal subject would be caught dead drinking such vile foreign brew? As it turned out, most of them.

Despite the sorry state of production, ale was firmly rooted as a major dietary staple. This was recorded in a scene from Shakespeare's *Henry V* when the English king led his troops against the French at the battle of Agincourt on October 25, 1415. The English with 8,000 troops faced a French army of over 30,000. The fighting see-sawed each way. Then Henry played his trump card. Held in the rear was his secret weapon and it was in the hands of 1,000 of his men. It was the Welsh long bow, and when they put it to use the slaughter was simply incredible. Over 10,000 French troops lay dead. But the French commander did not attribute the loss solely to this frightening new weapon. His observation was . . .

> *"Where have they this mettle? Can sodden water . . . their barley broth, decoct their cold blood to such valiant heat?"*

Good thought, with the Bard's love of beer. He was even

said to be a brewer. There is little doubt it was actually the long bow which carried the day, because who could credit the awful ale-goop they were drinking? The ale spoiled quickly and the only advantage to it was ease of production.

As hops slowly were accepted by English brewers, in the southeast sections of the country, its preservative powers made for another change. It was now possible for larger breweries to go into operation and ship their product throughout the kingdom. In transit it underwent additional aging, which resulted in more natural clearing of the finished beer and a more appealing taste.

Thus, brewery output increased dramatically, so much so, the English language was changed. The great compiler of the first great dictionary, Samuel Johnson, included the following definitions:

Ale: "A liquor made by infusing malt in hot water, and then fermenting"
Beer: "Liquor made from malt and hops"

The designation "ale" virtually disappeared from use while *beer* became the new name. Ale would resurface centuries later when there was a new need to differentiate between the lagering with a cold-acting yeast (beer) and the method of a warm ferment (ale). But its use in describing an unhopped malt beverage was gone forever.

Other changes to language can also be attributed to beer. Two of the most prominent inns outside London were situated across the road from each other. When stages traveling in either direction pulled up, the disgorged passengers would mingle together to swap news from the opposite points of origin. As time went by, secondhand news took on the name of these two taverns, and the term "Cock and Bull stories" became firmly rooted in our language.

Another phrase that dates back to this era refers to the method by which beer and ale was served. The tavern keeper would pull drafts into tankards or jacks that held either a quart or a pint and then hand these over to barmaids who delivered them to tables. It was the responsibility of the barmaids to keep track of each table's tab, and the ever vigilant tavern keeper constantly reminded the servers to "mind your p's and q's."

While all this was going on, the brewers, just as any other industry, sought ways to improve their product and give them a competitive edge. The ability of hops to preserve beer awakened the brewers to the possibility of locating their breweries a distance from their customers. It allowed them to find good clean sources of water and build the brewery next to an unfouled supply of beer's largest component. For example, during the reign of Richard I (1189–1199) the abbey at Burton upon Trent was already well known for the quality of its ale. Because of the high gypsum content of the water, it was perfect for brewing, and Burton Ales became famous throughout the world. Thus the growth of larger breweries transformed the early alcohol gruel into smooth pale ales.

A source of clean water was essential for brewing. Despite efforts to protect streams, the incidence of pollution had once again increased. People were literally treating the rivers like toilets, despite the efforts of Parliament. This problem caused even more people to drink beer. By the mid 1400s the bias against drinking water was deeply ingrained. Sir John Fortescue wrote of the English peasants, "They drink no water unless it be . . . for devotion." This attitude would hold for more than four centuries, and it would be taken with colonists as they crossed the ocean.

The final segment of beer development took place in Ralph Harwood's Bell Brewhouse in Shoreditch. His customers began ordering what was called "three threads" or "entire," a drink made of three different beers mixed together. Ralph was pleased with the business but grew weary of mixing the beers one at a time. He reasoned things would be much smoother if he could brew one beer that had the traits of "three threads." When Harwood unveiled his creation, it was an instant hit with the tavern's regulars, the marketplace porters of London. A new style had been born; it would borrow its imbibers' name and be known as English porter-style ale.

By the sixteenth century brewing and beer became such an intrinsic part of English life, it even colored beliefs about beer's origin, and despite its development by Mid-eastern and North African cultures, White Anglos seemed to assume sole dominion over the idea of beer. But for all the English brought to beer, and all that beer brought to them, as 1600 progressed, it would have an even greater role and would change a continent.

CHAPTER 3

Massachusetts— Brewing in the 1600s

Here sleeps in peace a Hampshire grenadier,
Who caught his death by drinking cold small beer;
Soldiers, take heed from his untimely fall,
And when you're hot, drink strong, or not at all.

—UNKNOWN, EPITAPH, IN CHURCHYARD AT WINCHESTER,
ENGLAND, 1764

A New World,
New Challenges, and New Beers

In today's world distance is no longer a major factor when traveling. For example, scores of flights cross the Atlantic, some at supersonic speeds. But in the 1600s this was a voyage of perseverance. Unlike the settlers who crossed the prairie, the first immigrants from Europe did not leave a trail. The sea reclaimed their wakes quickly, and few monuments or milestones remain to declare the immigrants' bravery and heartbreak. Replicas of their ships are more for tourists than transportation. An inspection of the *Mayflower* replica really doesn't tell the story of a crossing in 1620. It looks clean and the lower decks are wide-open.

Try to imagine instead a two-month ordeal over a gray sea beneath an even grayer sky, of cramped, cargo-laden spaces, sickness, bad food, and fouled water.

The Pilgrims set sail from England on September 9, 1620 after delays in procuring a seaworthy ship. They wanted to settle near New York on land secured from the Virginia colony by their leader, William Brewster. Navigation even worse than their supplies caused them to overshoot their target travel far up the New England coast. All the land was an amazement to the weary souls of the Old World. The space was boundless, with none of the small, chopped-up parcels left over from Europe's feudal days. What they saw was an unbelievable expanse of virgin forest. Even the trees were spectacular, for England's trees had long ago been chopped down for firewood. Despite their enthusiasm, wonder, and the apparently endless supply of land, they had bought a specific parcel, and having just secured their escape from religious persecution, they felt no need to get the Crown irritated at them. They wanted to just go quietly about their business.

Unfortunately their error in navigation became apparent before long. As they sailed north they tried to find a suitable harbor, for although they did run away from home, the leaders realized trade with the old country was necessary for economic survival, not to mention a supply of beer. Sailing past present-day Boston, they curtailed their search and returned to the most favorable spot they'd seen, near Plymouth. Indeed it was the thought of beer that caused them to finally make up their minds. As William Bradford recorded in his firsthand "History of Plimouth [sic] Plantation," they decided to put ashore, "for we could not take much time for further search, our victuals being much spent, especially beer."

This may seem very unusual, but on these ships, beer wasn't the diversion it is on today's airliners. The water stored in the hold of ships soon spoiled, and they had no way to replenish the supply. Even if the water could be kept in good shape, there was the unhealthy view of water they carried with them from the old country. Thus, beer was considered a matter of great importance to the infant colony's well-being. Clearly, it would have to be to get these immigrants to leave the ship. That November was especially cold, and legend has it their clothes, drenched in the surf, froze stiff as boards. Fortunately they found a large rock to tie their skiff to and set foot on their new home.

Shortly after their arrival, Native Americans welcomed the Pilgrims and taught them tricks of New World survival. In gratitude the Pilgrims invited their new friends to a communal feast. Those early expressions of thanksgiving had a great deal in common with our modern celebrations because the Pilgrim fathers raised a drumstick and downed a beer, with only parades and football missing. Even the major Native American participant, Samoset, joined in with enthusiasm. Samoset was documented as both a lover of ale and a responsible drinker. This alliance with the tribe would be important to brewing because the Native Americans would introduce the colonists to corn.

The popular version of beer in the 1600s was a dark, somewhat cloudy brew, flavored with hops and with 6 percent alcohol. Except for the hops, it was very much like the beer that had been served up for the past several hundred years. Even if glasses had been available, the modern beer drinker would have opted for the wooden or earthen tankards in which it was commonly sold, the beer was such an unsightly mess.

Despite beer's foul appearance, its role as part of the Pilgrims' daily bread was so secure that it caused their first crisis. When the *Mayflower* was anchored out in the harbor, sailors on board knew their stock of brew was running low. To continue issuing rations to those who transferred ashore would leave an insufficient supply for their return trip to England. Thus the crew had no recourse but to cut off their former passengers. The reaction on land was panic, anger, and increased grumbling followed by desperation. Bradford once again noted how the settlers "were hastened ashore and made to drink water, that the seamen might have the more beer."

Drink water! Most assuredly things were in dire straits. Bradford argued strongly for a ration of brew, but the sailors responded they would give none, "not even if he were their own father." Now the Pilgrims had poor shelter, low food supply, a hard winter—and no beer. Finally, even though the *Mayflower*'s captain thought it put his crew at risk, he was overcome by the settlers' hardship and declared there would be beer for all who needed it, especially the sick.

This brought a sigh of relief, but the Pilgrims had learned a lesson hard, frightening, and effective. Their critical shortage made a brewhouse a priority among the structures erected that first winter at Plymouth.

Even if the Pilgrims' supply weren't scarce, the need for a brewery was immediate. The population of the small colonies expanded faster than ale could be shipped from Europe. And of all the hardships the settlers endured, the lack of beer caused them most displeasure. Bradford, the governor, was known to complain long and bitterly about this deprivation, and with good cause. These pilgrims had experienced the defiled rivers of Europe and were reluctant to consume even the pure waters of New England streams. Roger Clap of the company recounted how it was "not accounted a strange thing in those days to drink water."

In the work "New England Prospects," Wood complained of drinking water. He had neither taste nor patience for it and summed up his feelings with the understandable statement "I dare not prefere it before good beere." In all, the custom of the day held a beer was good for your health while water might be the end of it.

The Pilgrims' situation was not unique. Passengers on those increasingly frequent transports had little more trust for their water, even when it was fresh. When compared to the palatability and longer shelf life of hopped beer, the choice of thirsty travelers was easy. Even the strict Puritans had to agree. The *Arabella*, which carried the Puritans to Boston in 1630, made its voyage with over three times as much beer as water. On arrival people hit the beach and began brewing.

As settlements arose, most kitchens were home breweries, and once again, women were the brewmasters. Unfortunately, the first attempts to grow barley in Massachusetts did not produce results. Thus, malt, along with hops, was imported from England. And when traditional supplies were scarce, the brewers simply turned to other ingredients. Governor of Connecticut John Winthrop Jr. (son of John Winthrop, governor of Massachusetts) produced a reasonable beer from Indian corn. They were so impressed with this feat back home that the brew, and discovery, was considered good enough to merit Winthrop's election to the Royal Society of London. Many of the "Pious Pilgrims" went even further in their search for substitutes, as a poem from the 1630s shows:

> *If barley be wanting to make into malt,*
> *We must be content and think it no fault,*
> *For we can make liquor to sweeten our lips,*
> *Of pumpkins, and parsnips, and walnut-tree chips.*

In the face of shortages, several brewers and their taverns became well known for concoctions and variations of spruce, birch, and sassafras beer. By the mid-1650s these shortcuts, substitutions, and other corruptions reminded the leaders of the problems that had occurred back home. They raised such concern over quality, they drove several colonial governments to enact statutes to regulate the brewing process. The consumer desperate for any beer was thankful for the laws, as long as they didn't interfere with getting a drink. Of course, the laws had no effect at all on homebrew, and the non-tavern-owning brewers, who also sold significant quantities, were exempt, leading to still further corruption of beer. By 1667 the continued problem of quality prompted Massachusetts to dictate that beer had to be made from good-quality malt and not diluted with molasses or coarse sugar. Thus, beer led to some of the country's first consumer laws.

Two factors conspired to inhibit the construction of commercial breweries: the distribution of wealth and the agricultural society. Wealth was concentrated on the coast, where the new merchant and trade classes lived and where they had easy access to British markets and beer imports. Meanwhile, inland areas remained devoted to the production of agricultural goods, and the farmer was usually on the short end of the commodities stick. The fruits of their labor were shipped to the coast, where the merchants reaped the profits.

Taverns, however, thrived, especially as the economy grew. Just as in England in the 1300s, the tavern was a place for meeting and conducting business. After all, even a Puritan could get thirsty. The number of taverns managed to grow at a rate that would have made the old country proud. And as hard currency became available for use, beer was relatively inexpensive. The common price for a quart was just a penny and was regulated. By 1634, sixpence was the legal fixed price for a meal, and an ale-quart of beer cost one cent. As the demand of taverns for a steady beer supply increased, it finally led to the start of commercial brewing. As early as 1635 Captain Robert Sedgwick was licensed as a common brewer in the Massachusetts Bay Colony.

Observing the spread of taverns, the government couldn't resist getting involved and soon began licensing them. There were but a few registered in Boston during the 1630s; however, by the 1680s there were dozens. Taking a lesson from the economic history of England, government leaders recognized the significance of the tavern to trade and marketing. As community centers, taverns were considered so important to the growth of New England, the royal governors enacted laws to encourage their proliferation. The government could, and did, direct local areas to open one in each village. The idea was to make the Puritan businessman's travel and business activity more comfortable and therefore more frequent. The system worked and the small inland towns began to grow.

The miserable state of communications also contributed to the tavern's success. In those days the latest—with an emphasis on *late*—news was circulated by word of mouth or through the rare newspaper shared by all. It's not hard to imagine the end of a day's work spent in a candlelit tavern room. With tankards or jacks of ale, the locals gathered around a newspaper read aloud by one of the inhabitants who could read. Thus, in America, as in England, the tavern filled a much greater void than just a drinking establishment.

The difference between an inn and tavern was even less distinct than it was back in England. They both were names for houses where lodging was available along with stabling, meals, and beverages, including beer, cider, and wine. Sales of these refreshments outdoors were unrestricted, but taverns were subject to regulation. The license of each establishment defined the sales restrictions. Despite the disadvantage of needing a license for the sales conducted indoors, the taverns flourished. After all, who would want to stand outside with a beer on a New England winter evening? Thus, as our Puritan roamed the streets of 1677 Boston, he could have his choice of twenty-seven places to quench his thirst. In only seven of these would he be able to order wine, but beer was available in all. This was, in part, because beer was still considered a victual. Of course, this number represents only legitimate taverns. A great many others quietly conducted business on the unlicensed sly and continued to as long as there was no mischief.

One of the easiest ways to locate colonial taverns is through records courtesy of the courts. In colonial times people didn't go to trial, the trial came to them. Traveling judges "rode the circuit," and one of them, Judge Samuel Sewall (best remembered as writing the first American protest to slavery in "The Selling of Joseph"), kept an extensive diary of his travels on the circuit from 1674 to 1725. Sewall might be thought of as the original responsible drinker; once he checked in to a tavern, his horse stayed for the night. His journal is filled with thousands of entries, but curiously, his mention of taverns when home is usually restricted to the rare event such as a 1697 dinner with a "company of Young Merchants" who entertained the governor and council at a favorite Boston watering hole, Monck's Blue Anchor Tavern. It was one of few times he entered a tavern in the city. In all probability Sewall never made a leisurely visit to a Boston tavern, not even to the Wallis Tavern in his own neighborhood on the south side of Boston. On the road was a different story because he had no choice, and his diary records over three hundred stays at taverns in Lynn, Scituate, and Roxbury.

Judge Sewall aside, the general population welcomed and provided enthusiastic support for their local tavern. The business was profitable and spread relatively rapidly when compared to the growth of other enterprises, and for good reason. The taverns were in the position most businesses dream about; they sold the very thing everybody wanted. The first well-known American writer, Cotton Mather, a teacher, clergyman, and recorder of early New England life, observed that ale and beer had become so commonplace in Massachusetts by 1675 that every other building in Boston was an alehouse. Although this was perhaps an exaggeration, it does make a pleasant thought. So entrenched in daily life did tavern keeping become that Governor Pownall made the same remark one hundred years later, despite the government, much as in earlier England, increasing pressure to slow its spread. A testimony to how good business was is the example of Boston's Green Dragon Tavern on Union Street, which first tapped a keg in 1680 and remained popular till the end of the 1700s, over 120 years of serving drafts!

In Boston, as in most port cities, the taverns were usually situated in the commercial districts, which were along the waterfront. This was most convenient to sailors, who have been known on occasion to tip a few. A typical example was Thomas Bailey's Blue Anchor near Haver's Dock. It promised "Refreshment & Entertainment of Boatmen and others." But the relationship with the docks made it clear there was another competitor with taverns for the precious supply of ale.

As the 1600s continued, so did the belief that the simple act of drinking water was taking your life into your hands, and this was especially true among sailors. There had been little if any progress in the technology of effectively storing water shipboard. It was looked upon with such scorn, there was little hope in convincing a sailor in the concept of water being good for him. This feeling was held so uniformly that from 1638 the ration for each member of a New England sailing ship's crew was one quart of beer per day, a rule sailors in our navy no doubt wish were still in effect. Thus, the stores-loading party for any vessel would have an appropriate amount of attention directed to the procurement of beer.

With this convenient market at hand, it was logical for entrepreneurs to step forward. One of these is seen as a recurring entry in the ledger of John Hull's general store. Hull was a chandler who specialized in the outfitting of ships, and his ledger recorded him making frequent purchases from one Seth Perry. Through the years 1685 to 1689 the accounts credit Perry with filling orders such as for the ketch *Endeavor* with seven barrels and the brigantine *Robert* with six. These were fairly ordinary amounts, but what is noteworthy is that these ships were actually small enough to be properly called boats. Certainly they must have had very happy crews. Mr. Perry, like many brewers of the time, was also a supplier of malt, and the store showed sales to "Mr. Nathaniel Clark—20 bushells" and "Mr. Abell Plats with yet another 20." These two customers were probably among the many citizens who continued to brew their own, and this is precisely what makes it so difficult to determine colonial production and consumption.

Throughout the colonial period there were so many people tied to brewing, it's hard to find someone who wasn't. Not even the clergy abstained from the pleasure of a beer. When Reverend Thomas Shepard of Newtowne, Massachusetts, was ordained head of the church, a special "ordination beer" was on hand for the festivities. The celebration left many of the attendees glad they were on horseback, for the stability of their own legs failed. And such religious celebrations were not uncommon.

Another segment of beer drinkers was found on campus. A good many people may think the idea of college keggers originated when they went to school, but the American roots go back a bit further. Before he left England, John Harvard, founder of the university and namesake of a modern Boston brewpub, allegedly learned the art of brewing from none other than William Shakespeare. On founding his college in 1636, he made securing a beer supply one of his earliest priorities. He ensured there were plans to construct a brewhouse for servicing the needs of the faculty and students. Harvard's first president, Nathaniel Eaton, didn't have the same priorities, however, and served a prematurely shortened term as a result.

President Eaton was responsible for a variety of functions considered essential to the smooth running of Harvard's college, but in a monumental blunder he turned over one of the most important to his wife. Ms. Eaton did not place much importance on maintaining the beer supply, and rations were often extremely limited or nonexistent. By 1639 the students had had enough. Turning more and more bitter, they finally revolted against a situation in which "they often had to go without their beer and bread." And so it was that the first student strike at an American college was over an issue of undisputed worth. Moreover, it was a success.

The Harvard beer situation was greatly eased by 1686 when Increase Mather, son of Cotton Mather, a student of history, and no fool, was appointed to run the college. One of his first jobs was drafting the Code of College Laws, and here he made sure he addressed the concern of beer supply. A shrewd administrator, he even confronted the old problem of just how much a barrel held. "The steward shall deliver in unto the Butler his bread at five shillings per bushell, and his beer at 4 per barrel, each barrel consisting of sixteen gallons of Beer measure."

This wasn't Mather's last involvement with beer and brewing. He recognized it as a concern that could make him a success or failure in office. Therefore, when presented with a threat to the students' beer supply, he acted. Thus he found himself involved in a legal action with Sister Bradish, who supplied many of his students with their ration. In a letter to the court he petitioned jurists to encourage her that she might be "countenanced" in her baking of bread and brewing of beer, "such is her art, way, and skill that shee doth vend such comfortable penniworths for the relief of all that send unto her as elsewhere they can seldom meet with." The students were permitted to purchase a set amount from her, and his quick and decisive action won the admiration of the overjoyed student body. Who says college presidents have never had the interest of their students at heart?

At first, brewing by people such as Sister Bradish was a common means of securing supplemental income. Of course, it didn't take long for the government to see all this activity as a means to raise revenue, and soon a brew permit was required. With this license the brewer was allowed to sell outdoors or to taverns. When William Whyte of the colony was accused of selling ale without a permit, his defense was that he only wanted "to brew a little beere, for ye Collyers and other workmen."

The judgment against Mr. Whyte was only one of the efforts to curb the drinking of the working class, yet another ruling was designed to discourage the practice of drinking at work. During this period the amounts consumed during the workday made the three-martini lunch look like a warm-up. It was a custom brought over from Europe where laborers received drink as part of their wages. It was an almost universal feeling that they could not get through their day without refreshment to "comfortably proceede in their works." It comes as no surprise to find laws were passed to prevent such activity. The "Fitness for Duty" laws of the late twentieth century had their roots here. The first in a series of these statutes was recorded in 1633 but was widely disregarded, and a ration of ale as part of a work contract would continue well into the 1700s.

The authorities were alarmed not by just the drinking in the workplace, but by a general trend of increased consumption. By 1648 the colony had "hoalsome laws provided and published" for the encouragement of temperance, but these were largely ineffective. Overall the feeling of colonial leaders was that drinking was an unfortunate characteristic of a community that otherwise could be considered a model of reform. In 1682 the visiting Edward Ward referred to the general disregard of any statute to curb the public's ale consumption when he remarked, "All their laws look like scarecrows," and the public was the wise and ignoring crow.

As the 1600s came to a close, the preference for small drink (beer) was as prevalent as ever, and in fact, it had steadily expanded throughout the century. Home and farm brewing had spread through the rural areas, and commercial breweries had begun appearing along the more populous coasts. More important, the settlers copied the English method of stimulating commerce through the establishment of taverns and inns. But even this pales in comparison to the impact a neighborhood tavern could have on a village. It was the community's social, information, and business center, and soon would be the center of something much greater. For there people started talking politics.

CHAPTER 4

Boston in the 1700s

While briskly to each patriot lip
Walks eager round the inspiring flip;
Delicious draught, whose pow'rs inherit
the quintessence of public spirit

—JOHN TRUMBULL, 1756–1843

Fermenting a Revolution

Colonists in Massachusetts began the new century with a feeling of optimism. There was an expanding economy, permanent settlements, and the beginnings of unique American customs. Most important, their healthy thirst for beer was being satisfied in one way or another. By this time beer drinking's place in society was so secure that beer was considered an essential item in the colonial pantry, chill house, or cellar. As much as farming, running a store, or any other job was part of life, so was obtaining a supply of beer. Indeed, everyone was in some way touched by brewing, from the lowliest farmhand to the most prosperous merchant.

Newspaper accounts of the day show just how important beer was. Back then, papers were interested in stories that provided readers advice on ways to cope with everyday life in the young country. Beer- and brewing-related articles

were as common as columns with hints on how to keep
bears out of the garden and which moss was best to seal
cabin walls. One example appeared in the *Boston Newsletter* of November 28, 1728, offering the writer's model budget for a typical family of eight. His "Scheme of Expense"
was designed to assist the planning of "Families of Middling Figure who bear the Character of being Genteel." He
rightly devoted the most ink to what was typically a family's greatest daily expense: "4 Small Beer for the Whole
Day Winter and Summer. In this article of the Beer I would
likewise include all the molasses used in the Family, not
only in Brewing but on other occasions."

The article also illustrates how the colonists dealt with
a poor supply of raw materials for brewing, a difficulty
held over from the 1600s. Though inconvenienced, the
colonists refused to muddle along in a life without beer.
Instead they dug deep into the tradition of Yankee ingenuity and came up with certain modifications and other
liberties with the conventional brewing process. In general this consisted of substituting other types of sugars,
like molasses, for the traditional barley malt. This was
neither the first nor the last time shortcuts and substitutes would be made. In fact, tinkering with the basic
formula for beer to get around shortages was a trend that
would surface again later in the century. So the brave
(or was it desperate?) settlers went on making beer out
of almost whatever was available.

For those who didn't produce their own, beer was considered an essential part of any employee benefit package.
The workplace was nearly swimming in beer. Like their
English ancestors, colonial laborers and craftsmen expected beer breaks as part of their compensation. Ben
Franklin, a native of Boston, remembered this part of labor
in his early work in the print shop.

We had an alehouse boy who attended always in the house
to supply the workmen. My companion at the press drank
everyday a pint before breakfast, a pint at breakfast with
his bread and cheese, a pint between breakfast and dinner,
a pint at dinner, a pint in the afternoon about six o'clock,
and another when he had done his day's work.

The distribution of beer at work and as compensation continued despite repeated legislative discouragement. The ineffectiveness of those laws is clearly demonstrated by the number instituted to control the problem. From 1645 to the middle 1700s, one law after another attempted to create that era's equivalent of fitness for duty. And in Boston, cook Richard Briggs firmly believed—beer benefited workers. He warned that brew should be of high quality because beer "that is not good, the drinkers of it will be feeble in summer time, incapable of strong work, and will be subject to distempers."

The restorative effects of beer were respected far outside the workplace as well. As in ancient Egypt, it was the base for many period cures, and would no doubt be favored by the patient over the other common method of healing, bloodletting—although both probably made the recipient lightheaded. Alice Morse Earle's "Customs and Fashions in Old New England" offers one example of a popular beer-based medicine:

> Take four gallons of strong Ale, five ounces of Aniseeds, Liquorice scraped half a pound, Sweet Mints, Angelica, Eccony, Cowslip flowers, sweet marjoram, of each of these handfuls, Palitoy of the Vval one handful. After it fermented two or three dayes, distill it in a Limbech and add Cinnamon, Fennel, Juniper, rose buds, Apple, dates, distil again, add sugar candy.

Ms. Earle goes on to ask why a person would go through all this trouble when the four gallons of strong ale with spices would fully answer the purpose.

In general the populace took beer as we would take vitamins. It was so intertwined with wellness that its use in daily activities became second nature. The consumption of beer or cider was common at both the family dinner table, with even the children partaking, and in community events. A barn raising, harvest, field clearing, or church gathering would be considered odd without a keg present.

The success of crops and its effect on beer making was always on the colonists' minds, including those of such notables as John Adams. Even while thoroughly embroiled in the deliberations of the Continental Congress, he managed to interject thoughts of brewing among the famous letters he and Abigail exchanged. More than once he wrote her because he was "a little anxious" about their barley fields. John did not question her ability to run the farm, he thought her "so valorous and noble" a farmer. Yet, while helping set the framework for a new country, he couldn't help offering advice about how to manure the fields.

The crops could be expected to thrive, however, for barley did well in the maritimes. And although consumption outpaced production, the city dwellers usually had sufficient supplies by augmenting local crops with imports from the motherland. Nonetheless, there were occasional years of trouble. In 1711 Boston experienced a shortage of barley and the town was thrown into near panic. The worry was so great, a large crowd gathered and blocked an attempt by Andrew Belcher to ship barley out of the city.

What is significant about the Belcher event is that by the early part of the century, the economy had grown robust enough to allow people to have these types of concerns. Prior to this time they considered barley a necessity, but one that they had to produce for themselves. As the economy grew it was possible to indulge in the luxury of purchasing beer from someone else. It became one of the items on an expanding list of luxuries that came within reach of the growing populace.

It wasn't long until the shipmasters themselves got in on brewing as a means to make a little money on the side. Captain James Pitt owned a brewhouse, and Captain Nathaniel Oliver operated one on Water Street. If you had to let your crew have a beer ration, why not supplement your income while cutting your expenses a bit?

During this time, taverns continued to be used as an extension of government. Circuit-riding judges, like Samuel Sewall, needed someplace to hold court. With low governmental operating budgets, courts were forced to make do and were encouraged to use whatever space was available in the area of their jurisdiction. More often than not, the only communal building in an area was the local tavern. The example of John Turner was common. His tavern hosted so many sessions of the Boston court, he actually designated one of the rooms as court chambers. In those times a barrister needn't travel far to celebrate a successful case; the convenience was in the next room.

Our friend Judge Sewall (who didn't patronize taverns within Boston) was nonetheless often in the town's ale-houses and presided over many cases heard in the court chamber of George Monck's tavern. This tradition of conducting a trial in the local watering hole continued for more than a century. Years after Sewall's career, the ever proper John Adams was himself riding the circuit and gladly visited many a tavern. He recorded his impressions of them for posterity, but his ratings should be looked upon with skepticism, judging by how many he described as "most genteel."

The first serious threat to the tavern business came as the 1700s began and was caused by a gesture of friendliness. As early as the mid 1650s the government was alarmed by intemperance among its citizens. However, complete abstinence was never one of their goals, they just wanted to keep things under control. But one of the new social drinking rituals gave them no end of grief: the drinking of toasts.

The custom began innocently enough. Raising a glass to someone's health was a means of promoting good spirit and a routine that gathered all together in a tavern's main room. What better way to cement a new friendship than over a mug of foamy ale? And who could refuse such a friendly gesture? Of course, it meant you were obligated to return the compliment. Unfortunately, things quickly got out of hand. People began raising a mug to not only each others' health but to the king, the queen, the royal offspring, the colonial governor, his spouse and offspring, and on down to the royal dog catcher. Clearly something had to be done.

Historically, when faced with such issues, governments tend toward the same type of quick fix—regulation. The first laws in the 1640s were, of course, largely ignored, and it wasn't until 1712 when the "Act Against Intemperance, Immorality and Prophaneness, and for Reformation of Manners" put some teeth into enforcement. In reality it wasn't the act that raised a fuss. It was the conscientious acts of a dedicated lawman that would give February 6, 1714, its historical significance.

That night was typical of any midwinter night on Massachusetts Bay. In Boston the shops had long since closed and shuttered their windows. Even at an early hour the streets were relatively empty, but that didn't mean everyone was asleep. A group had gathered in John Wallis's tavern to commemorate the queen's birthday. As they began their festivities they anticipated the arrival of a distinguished guest, none other than a member of the Governor's Council and esteemed justice of the Superior Court.

Entering the tavern, he was warmly greeted, with the assembly raising their glasses to the queen's health and then to his. But instead of pleasing this guest of honor, they only succeeded in raising his ire; it seems they were violating one of the colony's newest laws and the guest was not amused. Judge Samuel Sewall was angry. It was this "tavern disorder" that prompted the constable to call Sewall away from the warmth of his fire, and he quickly ordered the band of revelers to disperse. Instead of following his directive, the group stood their ground in protest. Then, after more than an hour of heated debate, they left the tavern; however, any hope Sewall had of this being the end of the confrontation immediately evaporated. The merrymakers only moved the fun to one of their nearby homes and, after settling in, called for the colonial equivalent of a six-pack to go.

This defiance was more than Sewall was willing to overlook. Before long he had his associate justice Edward Bromfield threaten them with calling out the militia. They infuriated Sewall further by jokingly spelling their names for his future use in court and compounding this by insisting the colonial government was incapable of passing even "one good law." Sewall would see they had their day in court.

We shouldn't conclude from this that Sewall was against tipping a glass of beer. In fact, he was known to freely partake not only of beer but wine and cider. His journal recounts many evenings of hoisting a tankard and he even owned a malthouse. But the law was the law.

This incident serves to illustrate the paradox created by colonial law. There was no question the establishment of taverns was beneficial to commerce. Statutes encouraged each town to have one, but the powers also saw the problem of people gathering and drinking. As sure as people may have gathered initially for social purposes, their conversation inevitably turned to politics. And it was the political discussions that made the royal governors nervous, for the colonists were questioning both the Crown's wisdom and authority. Thus, they outlawed toasts, but their intention was to inhibit political gatherings. So although the government was encouraging the growth of taverns, they concurrently enacted laws to discourage their use.

Beer was not the issue here; other laws of the period allowed outdoor sales of ale if the price was a penny or less per quart. Growing dissension and political strength was. Before long the government limited towns, with the exception of ports, to only one tavern. As the law was enforced, the existing taverns suffered, from not too little business but from too much. By 1727 the selectmen of Redding, Massachusetts, were petitioning for relief from this restriction. And although the government meant to reduce rebellious talk, they only reminded the citizens of what little voice they had while making it easier to decide where to meet.

The years passed and the situation grew more tense. Increasing political action, a need for more control, and a huge British debt from waging war with rival France led to imposing the Revenue Act. This act established a direct tax on liquor, and among the first to respond were students. At Yale College they announced in the *New York Gazette* of November 22, 1764, "The Gentlemen of the College cannot be too much commended for setting so laudable an Example . . . All Gentlemen of taste who visit the College will think themselves better entertained with a good glass of Beer or Cider." It was a tax revolt and a sign of things to come.

The next British miscue was the Stamp Act. It imposed, on top of local assessments, a fee for taverns in the form of special stamps that had to be purchased and fixed to the license. The colonists responded with their first organized resistance to the Crown. It quickly became fashionable to drink American beer, a real stimulus for local brewing. The Sons of Liberty wrote from their tavern meeting place to the other colonies suggesting the formation of a Stamp Act Congress. One of their ideas was a nonimportation agreement. In addition, the colonials found it easy to destroy the stamps, a vulnerable target. Because of its ineffectiveness, the law was eventually repealed, and the tavern-going colonists enjoyed their first real flexing of political muscle.

But they had little time to savor the accomplishment. The Crown merely replaced the Stamp Act with the even more unpopular Townshend Acts in 1768. These laws issued wide authority for search and seizure (the British had become really nervous by this time), and economically they replaced the Stamp Act's method of taxing goods produced within the colony by a tax on imports, including beer. Of course, this was another boost to American brewers.

These acts prompted Samuel Adams and James Otis to action. It's too bad more people today don't know about Otis. John Adams observed that it was Otis, a great orator, who caused the thought of Liberty to be born. They drafted a letter, adopted by the Massachusetts Assembly, to the other colonies pointing out that the Townshend Acts violated the British Constitution. The royal government demanded the assembly rescind the letter or face an official order to disband. The vote was ninety-two to seventeen in favor of refusing the Crown's order, and thus ninety-two became Massachusetts's patriotic number.

Acting as firebrands and the heat of politics could certainly lead to a powerful thirst, and since alehouses were one of the few places to meet, beer drinking and politics had an early marriage. The Black Horse Tavern in Winchester was one of those, and became a frequent meeting place for Sam Adams and his chief monetary backer, John Hancock. There, over tankards of beer, the seeds of a new nation were planted.

Sam Adams was an austere, simple-dressed man. Contrary to revisionist history and public relations, he was not a brewer. His only connection to brewing was his inheritance. In his will dated July 18, 1694, Joseph Adams, Sam's great-grandfather, left his family's malthouse to his son Peter and started the process that would lead to eventual ownership by Sam. As to the claim of patriotism, there is no debate.

Born in 1722, he attended Harvard in 1740, and it's hard not to imagine him claiming his share of beer. A student of the classics, he was inspired by Ovid's *"Principii obsta"* or "Take a stand from the start." Possessed of shaky hand and a quivering voice, Sam was not destined to be a great speaker; instead he wrote inflammatory articles and worked behind the scenes. He is considered by historians as one of the true masters of revolution. For his part Sam was content to pull the strings while encouraging the speech making of other Sons of Liberty, including Joseph Warren, James Otis, and cousin John. Sam's job was to plan the attack, secure financial backing, and organize the followers. His ability to pull in members and keep them was in part aided by the rituals he devised, and one of the group's favorites was a ceremonial drinking of damnation to the British ministers.

Completely frustrated, England tried to make life difficult for the rabble-rousers through a variety of methods, with most of the actions directed at the ringleaders. One tactic that backfired was an attempt to confiscate John Hancock's sloop *Liberty*. This smallish coastal sailboat was one of Hancock's trading vessels, and the Crown accused Hancock of using it to smuggle wine, although if they knew their opponents better, the accusation should have said beer instead. Rallying behind Hancock, the rebellious citizens of Boston forcefully "rescued" the ship, adding to their glee while further tweaking the king's nose.

The British acts of retribution only served to further unite the colonists. As they met in taverns all over the colonies, mugs of foamy ale inspired and emboldened the partakers to new levels of resistance. The various colonies came to agreements of nonimportation, with the plan to hurt the government where it mattered most, in the pocketbook. These agreements also helped birth the brewing industry in the colonies. As ports experienced a decrease in business of 45 to 50 percent in Boston and up to 83 percent in New York, the beer shortage led to the operation of more breweries and a slackened reliance on imports.

By 1770 the British were starting to feel the pinch, and in a conciliatory gesture they repealed the Townshend Acts, except on tea. The Sons of Liberty recognized this policy for what it was, however: a demonstration showing that the colonials could not dictate terms to London. This led to glasses of beer in the Green Dragon Tavern on Union

Street. It was there, on December 16, 1773, Sam Adams and John Hancock met to implement their latest act of defiance. Thinly disguised in Indian garb, the leaders and a band of Sons of Liberty raised pints of beer to fortify themselves for the evening's activities. Outside it was cool, quiet, and brightly moonlit. They knew they would be recognized as other than a party of Indians, but then again, that was their plan. Heading for the docks, they made directly for the moored cargo ships of tea, and what transpired was a deliberate and overt act of rebellion. Their action may have been over another beverage, but the "Boston Tea Party" was organized over tankards of ale.

The British government saw this act exactly as it was intended, and decided the rebellious children in North America had to be taught a lesson. The Crown felt the message had to both be strong and have an impact on all colonists. It was a royal caning known as the Intolerable Acts. In London, Lord North observed, "The die is now cast. The colonies must either submit or triumph."

The first of these measures was the Boston Port Act. It effectively sealed off the city until the colony made "satisfaction" to the Crown for the tea party damages. Edmund Burke, the greatest backer of colonial rights in Parliament, said, "The rendering that means of subsistence of a whole city dependent upon the king's private pleasure, even after the payment of a fine and satisfaction made, was without precedent, and of a most dangerous Example." Burke was Parliament's most moderate and accurate voice regarding the American colonies. Perhaps Burke knew the inhabitants would be even more testy without their beer.

The closing of the port and boycott of imported goods had two direct results. The first, as the former supply of beer dried up, was to once again encourage the growth of commercial brewing. Second, it united the colonies against the British. In Virginia the assembly, behind Patrick Henry, Richard Lee, George Mason, and Thomas Jefferson, designated June 1, 1774, the date the Port Act was to go into effect, as a day of "fasting, humiliation and prayer." Understandably, the royal governor was outraged by this resolution and dissolved the assembly. No problem; the dissidents simply moved to the nearby Raleigh Tavern in Williamsburg. There, among beers, they declared "an attack on one of our sister colonies, to compel submission to arbitrary taxes, is an attack made on all British America." Shortly after this, the colonial committees of correspondence called for convening of the first Continental Congress.

The Continental Congress was an act of union with the purpose of reaching an understanding and lasting agreements with the government in London. However, the Massachusetts delegation would brook no compromise. They thought the time for remaining Englishmen was long past, and their "Suffolk Resolves" was essentially a mandate for a free and independent state. Finally, the Congress did something that would be unheard-of today; they took action. Adopting a nonconsumption accord, they agreed to bring an end to imports from Great Britain on December 1, 1774. Subsequently the Congress voted to encourage the population to abstain from imported tea, Madeira, and port wine. Local beer, of course, they exempted.

To refresh a phrase, a revolution was brewing. As hostilities approached, beer became a military issue. Throughout the colonies' history, defense of the settlements was generally the responsibility of a volunteer militia. The regular British army was either present in low numbers or chasing around North America fighting the French. Protecting the rural farms and villages was thus left to the inhabitants.

The success of any army depends largely upon the force's ability to act as a unit. For the militia the discipline and coordinated actions required for battlefield maneuvers was gained through the "drill day." Set aside for training the troops, it was an occasion for the outlying areas to gather and socialize.

This method of raising an army had one inherent problem—the socializing. Because the population was usually preoccupied with simply surviving day to day, drill day meant a chance to meet neighbors and quaff a few beers, although members were required to do a bit of marching and fire a few rounds with their flintlock muskets. The volunteers were always anxious to dispense with this part; they were there to dispense beer. The degree of actual training, and sobriety, was always questionable, but everyone agreed it was a first-rate party.

This was certainly not the way to raise an effective army.

Despite the benefit of high training-day attendance and morale, the troops were a far cry from being crack outfits. A day of drill conducted without widespread inebriation was indeed a rarity. On occasion of observing a sober drill at Boston Common, Governor Winthrop was overjoyed. But it didn't last long. Immediately after dismissal from ranks, the volunteers made for the beer. Little wonder that in the upcoming war, British regulars much preferred to go against the militia than the Continental line.

Despite a reputation for ineptness, the Minuteman retains his image of a curious mix of simple farmer, independent thinker, citizen-soldier, and patriot. Our myths surrounding April 18, 1775, are similarly removed from the truth. What they don't show us is how Captain Parker did not have his headquarters on Lexington Green. His command post was actually located nearby, in the comfort of Buckman's Tavern. After a hard day of firing shots heard round the world, it would be good to have a fresh beer close at hand.

During the war for independence, beer stepped directly into Independence Hall as a major concern of the new Congress. Along with raising, clothing, equipping, and arming the troops, the fledgling government addressed that necessity as well. After all, it was positioned firmly as a part of the diet and the nation's culture. And if asking soldiers to leave their family for a war of uncertain length was bad enough, asking them to do it without beer was unthinkable. Under the circumstances it made perfect sense for Congress to include beer among the army's authorized rations.

It seems natural for beer to have been on America's collective mind throughout the war. As the soldiers drank their daily allowance, some, like Thomas Peters, harbored thoughts of making fortunes by brewing to supply the army. Peters served his term and then started his planning to build a large brewery in Baltimore to supply the Continental and French troops. Unfortunately for Peters, others recognized the gains to be made during the conflict. The expansion of commercial breweries and the end of hostilities ended Peters dream before construction could begin. But other brewers unencumbered by such obstacles as a term in the army had stepped forward to fill the gap.

As brewery operations expanded, there was a period of unpredictable supply. In Boston John Hancock was provisioned during the period of December 1778 to April 1783 by Andrew Johonot. Hancock must have done well in his relationship with Johonot, and despite the fighting, the records indicate he was supplied with an average of over thirty gallons of beer per month. George Washington fared equally well, as illustrated by the brew presented him by Speaker of the Massachusetts House Caleb Davis. Needless to say, the general took time out from the busy pace around his Dobbs Ferry, New York, headquarters to write Davis of his delight and gratitude while satisfying his thirst.

After the Paris peace treaty ended the fighting, beer faced what would be its strongest challenge. The English grains had always produced beer well, but they were difficult to grow, and though American varieties were beginning to flourish, New Englanders saw an opportunity for an economical and tasty alternative. The apple wasn't native to America, either, but the trees took well and bore fruit abundantly.

The knowledge of cider making traveled with the settlers from Europe where King Charlemagne first promoted cider as a beverage. The climate of the northern colonies wasn't merely great for the trees, but the cold and crisp weather of New England complemented cider and secured its position as a popular drink. Even without war-related shortages of malt, cider would probably still have gained its share of popularity. With ease of manufacture and plenty of apples, cider was always available and was quickly on an equal footing with beer.

The production of hard cider was such a success that it became the agricultural industry of choice. By 1721 one New England village of forty families had reached an output of three thousand barrels of cider. Charles Francis Adams reported that grandfather John Adams consumed a large tankard of cider every morning as his breakfast draft. John had mentioned it himself in his diary of July and August 1778 when Abigail worried about the summer's scorching heat ruining all her hopes of the orchard turning out even a single barrel of cider, certainly troubling news for even the most devoted of patriots.

The appeal of cider, like beer, was shared by all classes. Ben Franklin and John Hancock were known for drinking wine and beer, but both were partial to cider, Hancock having a pint of it each morning before breakfast like Adams. Consumption wasn't restricted to New England. The Middle Atlantic states were just as taken and nicknamed it "Jersey Lightning." It spread as far south as Maryland and Virginia and out to the frontiers of Ohio and Tennessee.

But no matter where cider traveled, New England was its real home. Long before cooking with beer became fashionable, cider was gracing Yankee tables. A favorite meal was baked ham in cider. They started by soaking the ham overnight in cider, then placing it in a 350-degree oven while basting with cider. Remove the skin and cover with a paste of brown sugar, mustard, and dry bread crumbs; stud with cloves. Return to the oven and bake one half hour more, basting again with cider. Another delicious meal was chicken: salted, peppered, dusted with flour, sauteed in butter till golden brown, followed by stirring in cider, bringing the whole to a boil, adding one whole onion, and simmering for forty minutes. Remove the onion, stir in two thirds cup of heavy cream, and thicken.

Cider consumption was, like beer, spread through the full spectrum of life. Hard cider was served at breakfast, lunch, dinner, at funerals, weddings, meetings, and barn raisings. Even nursing infants on cider was an accepted practice. By the end of the 1700s cider was selling so well that New England breweries had excess beer for shipment to southern states. All this would change in the early 1800s.

Cider did not replace beer, however. Ale was secure enough in its own right. Beer had also become a mixer for the 1700s version of a cocktail. One of the most widespread versions of beer mixing was "flip." John Adams reported a person spending a day in the tavern would find it full of people drinking drams of flip, carousing, and swearing. The earliest mention of flip is thought to be in 1690, but a reliable accounting is from the *New England Almanac* of 1704; an entry for December read:

The days are short, the weather's cold,
By tavern fires tales are told.

> *Some ask for dram when first come in,*
> *Others with flip and bounce begin.*

Fortunately, our forefathers wrote about everything, flip included, so we still know how it was made. The most common recipe called for:

> A great pewter mug or earthen pitcher filled two-thirds full of strong beer; sweetened with sugar, molasses, or dried pumpkin, according to individual taste or capabilities; and flavored with "a dash"—about a gill—of New England rum. Into this mixture a red hot loggerhead, made of iron and heated in the fire, was thrust.

Other recipes could be found as regional variations. Lord May of Canton, Massachusetts, devised his own version, which came into great demand. He started with four pounds of sugar and beat in four eggs. To this he added one pint of cream and let it age for two days. When people ordered a flip, he would fill a quart mug two-thirds full of beer, he then added four large spoonfuls of his aged mixture, stirred it with the glowing loggerhead, and added a gill of rum.

Orders of flip often punctuated the entries in General Washington's expense account, and General Israel Putnam had his own well-regarded recipe. Almost anywhere a revolutionary fire was burning, a loggerhead stood by the ready, although sometimes it is referred to as a hottle or flip-dog. It was such a common and well-thought-of fireplace instrument that James Lowell even penned lines of praise.

> *Where dozed a fire of beechen logs that bred*
> *Strange fancies in its embers golden-red,*
> *And nursed the loggerhead, whose hissing dip,*
> *Timed by wise instinct, creamed the bowl of flip*

As people traveled about, they discovered variations of flip. One had a fresh egg beaten into the mixture. In this case it was considered different enough to earn a new name, "bellowstop." As the loggerhead hit this one, the mixture foamed up and over the top of the mug. What could be more fun than sitting around a fire in the taproom and ordering drinks you knew would cause the bartender a big mess? Flip was so widely ordered and of such a fashion that it was a hit well into the mid-1800s.

But flip was by no means the only beer-based drink. A most curious mix was "whistle-belly-vengeance," all the rage in Salem, Massachusetts. It required the tavern keeper to first find a batch of sour household beer. No doubt, with this base, the drink was a thrifty Yankee's attempt to make a truly awful brew usable. The success of this venture is dubious, for after the sour beer was secured, it was simmered in a kettle and sweetened with molasses, then crumbs of "ryneinjun" bread were added to thicken it, and it was served piping hot. The recipe was common enough for Dean Swift to mention it in his "Polite Conversations."

HOSTESS: (offering ale to Sir John Linger) I never taste malt-liquor, but they say ours is well-hopp'd.

SIR JOHN: Hopp'd why if it had hopp'd a little further, it would have hopp'd into the river.

HOSTESS: I was told ours was very strong.

SIR JOHN: Yes! strong of water. I believe the brewer forgot the malt, or the river was too near him. Faith! it is more whip-belly-vengeance; he that drinks most has the worst share.

With an endorsement such as this, is it any wonder the drink was also known as whip-belly-vengeance? Thankfully this was a fad that faded away.

Other favored drinks included "calibogus" or "bogus," which consisted of rum and unsweetened beer, rather like a colonial boilermaker. The variation of this drink was cider-based, going by the name "stone wall," and its effect was reported to be much like hitting one. Yet another drink was "mumm," which had nothing to do with champagne. In fact, it's hard to imagine a drink further removed. Mumm was a charming flat ale made of oat and wheat malt. Even today's worst beer seems pretty tame next to these.

If the colonists grew bored with beer, they could also

enjoy a flip based on cider instead of beer. Another possibility was an "ebulum," a cider-based punch made of the juices of elder and juniper berries. One New England favorite didn't use beer or cider. "Black strap" was a mix of cold rum and molasses. Casks of this were found in most every general store. Next to the barrels were hung dried, salted codfish which the customers could munch on for free. Of course, there was a charge for a drink to wash it down.

As the century ended, beer was in fairly good shape. The commercial industry was growing, and despite the popularity of cider, beer remained the new country's premiere drink. The new states' shared love of beer held them together much more so than any paper agreement. It was their customs and their beer that led to union, helping them overcome differences by means of a shared taste.

CHAPTER 5

Colonial New York

*Every man that had any respect for himself would
have got drunk, as was the custom of the country
on all occasions of public moment.*

—MARK TWAIN

The Dutch, the English,
the Water, and Wall Street

It was just before sunrise and the wind bore a chill in off
the waters of New York Harbor. Lost in thought, he pulled
the frock around him as he walked the Battery. People
living nearby could, if they were awake, hear his peg leg
thumping along as he tried to think. Pausing, he leaned
against the wooden works and looked north toward the
wall that had been built as a fortification and would be the
name of one of the world's best-known streets.

A problem he faced as administrator caused Peter Stuyvesant to take this sleepless early morning walk. He was
somewhat of a tyrant, and when he made up his mind, he
expected strict adherence to his decisions. But this time
the people of his colony refused to heed him. Mulling over
the causes, he thought back over the short history of
New Amsterdam.

The Dutch claim to its North American colonies was based on the explorations of Henry Hudson, who sailed his ship the *Half Moon* up the river that bears his name in search of the Northwest Passage. Hopes grew as the river widened at the Tappan Zee but evaporated by the time he had worked his way up to present-day Albany. These early trips were looked upon as a calculated risk; the Dutch were a leading trading and banking power of the world, and they intended to stay in that position. If the New World had treasures to yield, the Dutch wanted in on it.

Encouraged by reports of vast rich lands, the Dutch decided to move ahead. But how to settle this area while maintaining their frugal character? Simple: They had someone else put up the money. Back in the Netherlands the government came up with a plan known as the "patroon" system. Tracts of land were chartered to anyone willing to settle a colony at their own expense. Just to keep them honest, a settlement was defined as at least fifty adults over fifteen years of age. To sweeten the pot they made sure each tract had considerable river frontage, no small offer because rivers were the highways of America, and tributaries would supply inexpensive power for mills.

When the settlers began to arrive, they brought beer with them. These were more sophisticated brewers than the English, and among the first to use hops in brewing. Although not as desperate for beer as the Pilgrims, they, too, set about building a brewhouse immediately after arrival. Some accounts tell of brewing as early as 1612, but the most accepted date was in 1613 when Adrian Block erected a brewhouse on the southern tip of Manhattan.

As the Dutch solidified their position, they erected satellite villages to expand control over the region. In 1623 a group settled at Fort Nassau, present-day Camden, New Jersey. That same year another established Fort Orange at Albany. It wasn't long before beer also arrived at these outposts. One early Dutch visitor to Albany wrote, "They all drink their beer here from the time they can hold a spoon."

Around 1626 the colony's other famous Peter, Minuit, closed what must be the all-time real estate deal by purchasing the island of Manhattan from the Manhattan Indians. The Native Americans really had a laugh because Minuit paid a tribe that didn't even live there. It may be hard to imagine today, but back then New York was a pristine wilderness. There were reports of the harbor yielding six-foot lobsters and oysters as much as a foot across. Small wonder they included a brewery among the colony's first structures, with such prizes just begging to be washed down with beer.

Before long the Dutch realized the climate and soil were just right for producing all of beer's ingredients. Vast fields of grain were planted along the Tappan Zee, and the grain grew so well that one of the Dutch settlements came to be called Tarrytown from the Dutch word for wheat. With grain on hand, brewing began in earnest. Nicasius de Sille, a councillor for the West India Company who would eventually become sheriff of New Amsterdam, reported, "This country suits me exceedingly well . . . Beer is brewed here as good as in Holland, of barley and wheat."

As in the other colonies, the Dutch settlers did not trust the water either. Thus, it's not surprising to see so many accounts written about the quantity and quality of beer. One early visitor wrote home about how the settlers "brew as good beer here as in our Fatherland, for good hops grow in the woods."

Others had the same observation. Upriver in Albany things progressed at a similar pace. The patroon of Fort Orange was Kiliaen van Rensselaer. He was determined to make settling on his land attractive, and therefore profitable, so his intentions of brewing were like those of many others, and he planned ahead for it. Writing of the tract, he said that with "a supply of grain on hand, I intend to erect a brewery to provide all New Netherlands with beer, for which purpose there is already a brew kettle there."

The brewery mentioned was probably built sometime before 1637. The regulations of Fort Orange, conveniently developed by none other than Kiliaen van Rensselaer, allowed homebrewing but prohibited commercial breweries. Rensselaer didn't intend to monopolize brewing. As long as he got his cut, he was more than willing to allow competition, provided the price was right. On June 15, 1647, the patroon's carpenter was authorized to build and operate a brewery. The licensing fee for the operation was set at an annual rate of six merchantable beavers.

The beaver payment seems much better than the deal made with a brewery in 1649. Among the partners of this establishment was the first of many brewers from the famous Rutgers family. The rate for this operation was fixed at 450 guilders per year plus one guilder for each tun of beer brewed.

In 1660 the colony witnessed a first in brewing history. In lower Manhattan the Red Lion Brewery departed from the practice of using the owner's name and used a brand name instead. From these simple origins the colony would eventually become a major brewing center, first in Albany as a premier ale center of America and later downstate with renowned lager brewers.

Growing slowly, the colony in Manhattan had just 350 residents in 1629, but by 1632 the company saw fit to construct its own brewery. It was located on what was aptly named Brouwers Street. As was the custom of the day, influenced by guilds, similar businesses were all located in one area. For a couple of decades the arrangement worked well; however, over time a problem developed. Breweries were naturally wet and the waste was thrown in that great preindustrial collection area, the street. Compounding this problem was the constant parade of draft horses straining at the loads of lumbering beer wagons. The more the breweries succeeded, the bigger the quagmire. By the year 1657 the thoroughfare's condition was intolerable. The solution was simple, and as a result of breweries, the first paved street in America was built. Even the name was changed to reflect the technological wonder, which retains that name today—Stone Street.

So many breweries crowded Stone Street, it wasn't long until they were constructed in nearby areas as well. Dutch brewer Jacobus opened his on the corner of Pearl and Old Slip Streets. In 1645 Oloff Stevenson van Courtland established another on Market Street. New Amsterdam residents quickly became preoccupied with brewing; it seemed everyone was giving it a try. The patroon was brewing, so were the tavern keepers, and the rest were brewing at home. The number of homebrewers can be surmised from real estate transactions, which recorded the inclusion of home brewhouses.

Regardless of the amount made, they also continued to import beer from Holland. And with so large a surplus, they were able to ship large quantities to Virginia in the 1640s. This didn't mean the New Amsterdamers were abstaining; anything but. William Kieft, a government official, reported in 1638 that residents were regularly "occasioned by immoderate drinking." It was 1651 when Peter Stuyvesant mused about the city having upwards of one fourth its buildings devoted to brandy, tobacco, or beer shops, which brings us back to his walk along the battery that chilly dawn.

He was worrying about how to pay for civic improvements and defense. At times the problems were almost overwhelming. As he reviewed the obstacles to building the perfect city—and he was a perfectionist—he thought about the recent report about the uninhibited growth of drinking. If the electric light had been invented, the bulb would have lit right then. Why not tax the spirits and ale? Surely it would kill two birds with one stone. Very proud of himself, he walked to breakfast with a spring in his step, despite the peg leg.

Too bad Peter hadn't studied his history; he could have predicted the experiment's failure. Aside from his autocratic philosophy and foul temper, which even offended his patroons, the tax itself was bad news. When combined with the large customs duties he enacted, it was a disaster. Instead of raising cash for civic improvement, the law merely drove away traders, while it completely alienated residents. It wasn't long until most were ignoring the law.

Other efforts at curbing beer drinking fared just as poorly. Laws passed in 1648, 1651, and 1658 were dismal flops. Even a law of 1662 that attempted to dissuade citizens from pawning their possessions in order to buy beer didn't work. In 1665 the English took possession of the colony, and they would learn their laws held no more water, or beer, than those of the Dutch. The British had inherited a community in which there was one brewhouse or tavern for every 160 people, and this didn't account for the multitude who brewed at home, or bought English ale directly from overseas.

The local breweries also thrived as trade with Virginia was solidified. However, a problem soon made itself terribly evident. New York lacked a reliable source of drinking water. Freshwater springs were well to the north in Indian-controlled territory, and they hated the Dutch for constantly cheating them in trades. Making things worse, the Dutch, despite their propensity for digging canals, never dug a well. So for want of water, the breweries and citizens suffered.

Fortunately the English sank seven wells to supply the growing town within eleven years of taking over. Even this only temporarily eased the problem. The next solution was to install pumps to increase capacity, and although these helped, the quality was still less than adequate. At best the water was brackish, and conditions around the wells consisted of stagnant pools containing every variety of fragrant refuse and decaying waste. Consumers were, thankfully, oblivious to the fact that this seeped back into the very wells they drew upon. The most notorious of these festering pools was known as the "collect," and beginning in 1732 brewer Anthony Rutgers, of the famous early New York brewing family, took it upon himself to fill it. Thus, a brewer took one of the first steps to change the health and landscape of the city. Nonetheless, the water problem would haunt inhabitants well into the 1840s. Meanwhile the town became increasingly dependent upon imports.

In most ways, the New York tavern business was very much like Boston's. The city saw taverns concentrated along the port area. These became known as slopshops, tippling houses, and grogshops. A typical evening in one was described by seaman William Fredenburgh as he related a night of drinking and gaming in 1720. "Stayed there playing at cards & Truck till two a Clock in the Morning. That the Depon[t] and the rest of the Company which was with him Drank four tankards of Flipp for which the aforesaid Richard Woodman paid to the Said Jacob Swan three Shillings."

Not surprisingly, a fair number of tavern owners were ex-sailors, but beer wasn't limited to the seafarers. New York society used beer at almost all functions. A standard breakfast of the period included "cold meat with a pint of good ale or cider," the colonial "breakfast of champions." And as in New England, drill day had the same emphasis on socializing and consumption. In 1734, on watching a particularly orderly drill, Governor Cosby "expressed great satisfaction . . . and was pleased to order 12 Barrels of Beer to be distributed among them."

Beer was used as a weapon as well as a military morale builder. The Townshend acts were protested strongly in New York by the legislature. Despite a threat of royal punishment, they voted to oppose the acts with the greatest weapon they had. They refused to furnish the king's garrison with beer.

Although citizens were switching rapidly to locally produced beer, several things hindered the expansion of the brewing industry. One was the availability of hops. The industry's inventory of hops depended on a harvest of wild-growing varieties that were common enough but couldn't stand up to the needs of local production. In 1747 the collector of New York was required to report on commerce to the English Board of Trade. As required, the summary included a tally of all imports, and hops was prominently listed. The report for the year 1749 had the same response. In fact, hops continued on this list up to the administration of Governor William Tryon in 1774. Tryon's report did, however, include barley among the colony's "Natural produce & Staple Commodities." It also placed malting and brewing among the significant "manufactures" of the New York region. Hops shortages would continue to plague the brewers into the 1800s when cultivation of hops began thrusting New York into the lead as a major hop producer of the United States.

The brewers also had to contend with a system of roads that, at the start of the revolutionary war, could be described as poor at best. The most common type was dirt. A slightly improved version was made by felling trees. They lined the trunks side by side along the proposed route and covered the whole with dirt. It's obvious why these were known as "corduroy roads." To make matters worse, roads didn't follow direct paths. A good many were developed from trails blazed by wandering cattle.

New York had one sound form of transportation, though: the Hudson River. It could move goods more economically and with greater payloads than all road shipping combined. Along its course from near Canada down past the isle of Manhattan, and situated near the population center of colonial America, the Hudson River was the "Highway of America." Unfortunately New York could not always take advantage of the Hudson to ship beer. In fact, the river sometimes worked against them. The strategic importance of the Hudson was not lost on either side in the upcoming war. For both armies it was a way to rapidly deploy troops; and for Washington, who is underrated as a general, it was one of the essential parts of his campaign. The general employed tactics that featured careful selection of terrain, allowing him to dictate when and where the battles would be fought. A key aid in instituting this was the use of river hopping, which placed geographical barriers between his army and his British opponents.

In New York during the fighting, the availability of British imports, beer among them, was wholly dependent on which side was in charge. But bigger things were at stake. Washington well knew the Hudson River provided the English with "an easy pass to Canada," and in the process it would effectively divide the country. The threat of cutting off supplies from the army, quick movement of troops, and location near the center of the colonies kept Washington in the area of New York and New Jersey throughout the war. Thus, the area was frequently changing hands, along with a fairly constant supply of imported beer from England. Washington could hardly be blamed if he evacuated each time the beer ran low; why not let the British restock the supply?

The importance of the river allowed the British to know exactly where to find the Continental army, and it provided an opportunity to trap the rebels. It nearly happened at the Battle of Brooklyn Heights. Washington's one mistake was remaining a bit too long in Brooklyn, but through a series of brilliant maneuvers and rearguard actions, he managed to extricate his troops. Perhaps one reason he stayed so long was the relative comfort he enjoyed in the city. By this point in the war, New York breweries, spurred on by either patriotism or profit motive, had increased production to serve the army. The result was a capacity of nearly two to three hundred barrels a day. With an army of ten thousand, this amounts to about a gallon for each soldier per day.

As Washington set encampments, a supply of beer, though sometimes limited, seemed always at hand. If beer wasn't available from the general mess, it could likely be found elsewhere, usually in a tent pitched by an independent supplier. But this was no USO operation, these guys were in it for the money. These "suttlers" operated under the premise of serving as another means to provide for the army, but in fact often proved to be nothing more than portable bars. In New York the general was especially troubled by volunteers from the backcountry towns who tended to purchase a bit too much from the "suttler's store." Things got so bad with whiskey and gin that Washington addressed the suttler problem directly. He barred them from selling spirits anywhere near the camp. The one exception was beer. Perhaps he was influenced by own taste for porter and ale or maybe he was convinced by the views of his personal physician, Dr. Benjamin Rush, who touted beer as one of the more healthful drinks a person could want.

Beer was also there during the time when the revolution came closest to taking Washington's life. Fraunces Tavern in New York was one of the general's favorite spots to unwind both during and after the war. Good thing, because Phoebe Fraunces, daughter of owner Sam (a freed black), was credited with foiling an assassination attempt when she overheard the plotting of conspirators.

Fraunces Tavern was also the host when the New York Legislature invited the army's general staff to one of its closed-door sessions on June 8, 1776. They must have had a great time, because the bill shows expenses, along with other spirits, of: "To Porter 23/—Cyder 37/—Spruce [beer] 4/6." Unfortunately the bill also included a number of broken glasses. It causes wonder about what went on behind those closed doors. According to Captain Caleb Gibbs of Washington's staff, who recorded the event, "Many patriotic toasts were offered and drank with the greatest pleasure and decency . . . All the under officers . . . seemed much animated . . . Our good General Putnam got sick and went to his quarters before dinner was over."

Too bad, Putnam was well regarded for his flip recipe.

Washington never forgot the warm hospitality of Fraunces, and when the war concluded, he and his staff gathered there for the famous farewell to arms. It was a touching, emotion-filled moment as these comrades who fought the Revolution gathered together one last time before going their separate ways in the new nation they helped form. What better way to part than over a beer?

In the period immediately following the war, New York brewing remained on a path of continuous growth. As the young nation was formed, a question of much debate centered on where to locate the new capital. Eventually, in a compromise between the northern and southern states, a site was selected on swampy ground near the geographic center of the nation. Unfortunately, it would take more than ten years to complete any of the new buildings for this planned seat of government. In the interim New York was selected to function as the first capital of the United States. It was there, not far from where Peter Stuyvesant walked, that George Washington and John Adams were sworn in as the first team of top executives.

Assigned to duty once again in New York, and needing to set up dinners of state, Washington recalled the best meals he had in the city—at Fraunces Tavern. In appreciation, his appointment as first official steward of the presidential mansion was none other than Samuel Fraunces. There could have been other motives at work as George probably also wanted a ready supply of his favorite drink, porter.

To this day Fraunces Tavern remains in operation in lower Manhattan at the corner of Pearl and Broad Streets. It is designated a national landmark. But at the bar it's still possible to enjoy a beer in the same room where George Washington once sat near the fire and planned his next move, over a tankard of porter.

By the close of the century, the brewing industry was well established. The viability of New York brewers can be attributed to a large local following not as distracted by cider as their northern neighbors in New England. Shipping beer to southern colonies further bolstered business. The only thing that could hold New York brewers back was the limited supply of fresh water. It did. But while they foundered in their drought, Philadelphia was moving to the forefront of colonial brewing. And their taverns would be a setting for events that would shock the world and reverberate to this day.

CHAPTER 6

Colonial Philadelphia

Whoe'er has travell'd life's dull round,
Where'er his stages may have been,
May sigh to think he still has found
The warmest welcome, at an inn.

—WILLIAM SHENSTONE,
"AT AN INN AT HENLEY," 1714–1763

The Birth of a Nation and Its First Brewing Center

For most Americans, Philadelphia means freedom, Independence Hall, innovation, Benjamin Franklin, the Liberty Bell, cobblestone streets, William Penn, and equality. These images, however, obscure the way it was before any settlers arrived. Native Americans lived here and enjoyed the bounty of the land, and the mighty Delaware provided additional sustenance. The region was a patchwork of open fields, woods, and sparkling waters. But when Penn's colonists arrived, this had already changed.

Ships coming up the river were surprised to find a small village spreading along the shore. Ahead of them, and settled in, were the Swedish and Finnish survivors of the failed outpost of New Sweden. Fortunate indeed were the new arrivals. Thanks to crops already growing by labor of the village, there would be no suffering and hardship as there was in Plymouth.

A common misconception is that the Penns were generous, benevolent, agreeable folks. True, they were decent, but consider the famous walking purchase. In 1686 William Penn struck a deal with the local Indian tribe and paid them for a tract of land equal to "as far as a man could go in a day and a half." It didn't take long for his son William to come up with a plan of no small chicanery. First he arranged to clear a suitable path and then he hired the three best runners in the region. Watching them race off, the Native Americans must have known they were had. Paced by riders on horseback, the runners set a brisk pace and slowed for nothing. At noon on the second day a runner slumped and hung on to a sapling, which would mark the extent of Penn's land. In one quick deal he had gained over a half million acres of some of the richest land on the planet.

Penn had big plans for his venture in the Americas, and he intended on doing it right. Like the patroons, he would use the resources of the settlers to finance his dream of an American empire. But Penn went even further, distributing pamphlets in 1682 that advertised the colony throughout Europe. Written in Dutch, French, and German, they modestly hawked the real estate and even gave instructions on how to arrange passage and what to bring. The most appealing part of it all was the deal he extended. A person could rent a two-hundred-acre tenant farm for the low, low price of a penny an acre. For one hundred British pounds a five-thousand-acre estate was secured. Not surprisingly, houses numbered more than 357 in just two years, and in 1685 the population had already reached nine thousand. What Penn offered was not only a good deal on some land, but complete religious freedom, something not looked on kindly back in Europe. The result was an immediate influx of varied nationalities and a town of cosmopolitan flavor. And what flavor! All these cultures brought their rich brewing heritages with them.

The colony quickly prospered and grew into the largest town on the continent. Returning home to England, Penn could boast, "I have led the greatest colony into America that ever any man did upon a private credit, and the most prosperous beginnings that were ever in it are to be found among us."

Probably the first brewery to go into operation fired up its kettle about the same time Penn arrived. William Frampton has been honored with the credit for producing the first beer there by virtue of his efficient combination of bakehouse and brewery. Writing of it in 1683, Thomas Paschall noted the quality already available. He felt he had tasted "as good bread and drank as good drink as ever I did in England."

Considerable impression it must have made, for his son would forsake the family's pewter trade and become one of Pennsylvania's leading maltsters.

Penn himself began commercial brewing on a large scale. Situated twenty miles upriver from Philadelphia, in what is now Bucks County, Pennsbury Manor was the location he selected for his brewhouse. Outfitting it with copper kettles and a wooden mash tun, he was soon turning out beer. Penn wrote of its workings in 1685. "Our beer was mostly made from molasses which well boyld, with Sassafras or Pine infused into it, makes tolerable drink; but now they make mault."

Others promptly followed in Penn's wake, and by the year 1700, only eighteen years after the colony's founding, Philadelphia enjoyed the fruits of a well-established brewing industry. Its success was due in no small part to the ethnic diversity of the community, which included a large German population. And as people arrived, of course, they wanted to transplant the finer things from the old country, so by the same year the city had surpassed New York and challenged Boston as the cultural center of North America.

One newcomer to Philadelphia arrived not by boat from Europe but traveled south down the long, dusty Old York Road past many a tavern, such as the White Oak in Branchburg, New Jersey. He was a young man who, according to legend, arrived in the city with only three cents in his pocket, a runaway from Boston who had fled an older brother who cast a large shadow and demanded too much. From these inauspicious beginnings arose the most eminent citizen of Philadelphia, America's first internationally distinguished figure, and the inventor of the library, the fire department, bifocals, and the stove that bears his name.

Benjamin Franklin started his life avoiding beer and ale. In fact, during his early days he was amazed at fellow print shop workers who would even sacrifice wages for a beer. But as Franklin matured, he took on a different view. He enjoyed his successful business, and fame, and became a man of comfort. He even started going out to taverns, a pleasant experience of which he became especially fond. There was nothing like sitting around the tavern room with friends engaging in philosophical discussion, his favorite pastime, and lifting a few glasses of ale. Later in the evening all would take to singing a few songs, and Franklin penned some of his own. One included verse that illustrates his acquired love of beer.

> *The antediluvians were all very sober*
> *For they had no wine and brewed no October;*
> *All wicked, bad livers, on mischief still thinking,*
> *For there can't be good living*
> *where there is not good drinking.*

Ben wasn't completely correct. Noah did have beer with him on the ark, but the Octoberfest style hadn't been invented. Perhaps he also revealed what type of beer he favored, because in 1745 he confided in a friend, "I like . . . the concluding sentiment in the old song called 'The Old Man's Wish' where in . . . wishing for a warm house, in a country town, an easy horse, some good authors, ingenious and cheerful companions, a pudding on Sundays, with stout ale." Franklin was yet another member of the ranks that looked upon beer as a healthful tonic, perhaps justifiably. He lived to witness the birth and rearing of a new nation and didn't expire until 1790 at what was then considered an extremely advanced age, eighty-four.

As Franklin's wealth and corresponding leisure time grew, he was able to devote increased attention to politics. Fortunately for the colony, his wisdom, wit, and intelligence helped determine a path through the troubled Revenue, Stamp, and Townshend Acts. Pennsylvania's response was similar to that of the other colonies. They looked for alternatives, and means to advance the local production of beer. The American Philosophical Society, founded by Franklin, offered its assistance in the form of a recipe for a pumpkin ale.

> Let the Pompion be beaten in a Trough an pressed as Apples. The expressed juice is to be boiled in a copper a considerable time and carefully skimmed that there may be no remains of the fibrous part of the pulp. After that intention is answered let the liquor be hopped culled fermented & c as malt beer.

Hardly the work of philosophers, but appreciated by all who partook. Other residents during this time devoted their efforts to the improvement of brewing equipment. One created a perforated board that fit over the mash tun. Water was poured on this and it acted as a sparge to rinse the fermentable sugars off the grains following mashing. Another developed a pump that carried the first sparging runoff from the bottom of the tun and used it to sparge the mash once again. These rather simple inventions weren't much use to large-scale brewers, but the small neighborhood brewpubs and homebrewers were greatly aided.

Through all this, Philadelphia ably answered the call to a greater destiny. The actions of the committees of correspondence following the Boston Port Act, and the growing irritation with suffocating laws dictated by the Crown, led to the call for a Continental Congress. Delegates from all colonies would assemble to discuss ways to organize resistance and persuade England to ease its grip while maintaining the colonists' status as loyal Englishmen. The problem was, they always felt like second-class citizens. Nevertheless, they would make an attempt at reconciliation.

Boston was one of the leading cities of the times, but it had a reputation for firebrands and rabble-rousing. Also, its northern location would make the influential southern colonies seem as though they were following rather than leading. What was needed was a central location that could provide as many amenities as Boston. Philadelphia fit the bill nicely.

Excited about going to Philadelphia after being honored

as a delegate was John Adams. He was a proud man who aspired to a lofty position and looked forward to the benefits of an advanced station. John really did like the English way of life, and possessed a trait that would eventually hold him back from the enduring fame he deserved—he was drawn to the ways of the aristocracy. In reality, however, Adams had roots as a common man. He enjoyed Madeira, but he was a regular beer and cider drinker. He was anxious to arrive in Philadelphia so he could begin deliberations with the brightest and most talented citizens of the colonies and, if his past could be used as a measure, debate in the tavern over a couple of pints.

Adams made haste and entered town well ahead of the date set for the Congress to convene, September 7, 1774, and the arrival of most of the other delegations. Until they all arrived, there was no need to meet formally. Thus, with a parched throat, an eagerness to talk politics, and his cousin Sam, John leapt at an invitation to the famous City Tavern; the Virginia delegates had also arrived early. And as Adams's writings indicate, this meeting wouldn't be the first over a couple of beers. As he was wont, John declared the Tavern "the most genteel one in America." Adams must have loved taverns; they all seemed to be the best.

Adams also chronicled Philadelphia society. Following a dinner at Mr. Miers Fisher's, he noted that they enjoyed "ducks, hams, chickens, beef, pig, tarts, creams, custards, jellies, foods, trifles, floating islands, beer, porter." Adams was not alone. Many of the delegates had similar accounts of the hospitality, food, and drink (beer) of Philadelphia. The residents were determined to make a good showing, and all agreed they did. So when it came time to determine a site for the next Continental Congress, the choice was easy. As with the hosting of any other convention, the availability of places to unwind was a major consideration.

Thus, the Second Continental Congress was convened on May 10, 1775, less than a month after the fighting broke out at Lexington and Concord. While the first was held in Carpenters' Hall, this one met in the Pennsylvania State House, which has since changed its name to Independence Hall. Even at this stage, though, the colonists were not so much interested in breaking from the empire as they were in securing what they perceived as basic rights. This is the reason, even after they fought the battle of Bunker Hill (really Breeds Hill), that they offered the English the "Olive Branch Petition" in hopes of averting all-out war. They must have faced difficult decisions, and nightly beers at the city's tavern were a regular feature of the Congress.

Despite all the demanding issues holding their attention, beer was on their minds even in the chambers of their infant government. In one of the first laws of the new country, they directed each soldier to receive a ration of beer. The Continental army went even further. In a gesture of ultimate humanity, they even provided their prisoners with beer. A regimental paymaster visiting captured Hessian troops in Lancaster, Pennsylvania, left an account of just such behavior in his report dated May 31, 1777. "Of provisions, each prisoner receives daily, one pound of bread and one pound of meat, besides a weekly ration of six glasses of beer."

Actual supply of the troops was, of course, often another story. The British had essentially blockaded the colonies from the time they occupied Boston. Imports were virtually eliminated, and the brewers strained to meet demand. People were almost as occupied with obtaining a source of beer as they were with winning freedom. To ease the trouble of both civilians and army alike, Franklin proposed solving a new problem with an old answer. He provided his recipe for making beer with the essence of spruce.

> For a Cask containing 80 bottles, take one pot of essence and 13 pounds of molasses—or the same amount of unrefined Sugar; mix them well together in 20 Pints of hot water: Stir together until they make a foam, then pour it into the Cask you will then fill with water: add a pint of good yeast, stir it well together and let stand 2 or 3 days it will be ready to be put into bottles, that must be tightly corked. Leave them 10 or 12 days in a cool cellar, after which the beer will be good to drink.

The essence of spruce was not added to give it an appealing aroma, it was actually used to preserve the beer. Just as the ancient cultures used herbs, spices, and tree bark, spruce achieved the same ends. In fact, in some

Nordic countries juniper is still used to these ends. Also, hop harvesting in colonial America was dependent upon wild varieties growing in the woods, and the deficit had been made up by imports from the British. With that supply now cut off, it was up to the local brewers to create new substitutes.

Throughout the war the members of Congress mused, debated, and legislated in the State House during the day, and in the taverns at night. At the end of it all they went home, but not for long. Under the Articles of Confederation, which united the independent states after the end of hostilities, the states soon realized how ineffectively the country was being managed. Their problems brought them back to Philadelphia in May of 1787 for yet another convention.

The great diarist of the Constitutional Convention was James Madison of Virginia. From prior knowledge his choice of quarters was the India Queen Tavern where there was always a friendly group of guests meeting over glasses of Madeira, brandy, beer, and games of backgammon. From May to September he recorded the great debate and dialogue leading to the establishment of one of the most remarkable constitutions ever devised. As hard as the delegates worked through the day, it was at night when the behind-the-scenes deals resolved many of the details in the barrooms of the City Tavern, the George, the Black Horse, and the India Queen. This was also the part of the day when gentlemen would put aside differences and raise glasses of beer in friendship.

Conducting business over food and drink was an accepted custom of the day. During the Constitutional Convention, visiting Frenchman Moreau de Saint-Mery reported on what was typical:

"At about two o'clock . . . their dinner consists of broth, with a main dish of English roast surrounded by potatoes. Following that are boiled green peas, on which they put butter which the heat melts, or a spicy sauce; then baked or fried eggs, boiled or fried fish, salad . . . pastries, sweets . . . For dessert they have a little fruit, some cheese and a pudding. The entire meal is washed down with Cider, weak or strong beer."

One of the most significant meetings in American history would take place "at the India Queen on the evening of June 30 . . . amidst the temptations of pipes and bowls, cards and dice, rum and beer," according to historian Catherine Drinker Bowen in her great work *Miracle at Philadelphia*. For that night the taproom saw the problem of how to structure the United States government solved. At stake was fundamental political power. Smaller states like Rhode Island, Connecticut, and Delaware were wary of the influence wielded by the more populous states of New York and Virginia, especially if representation in the government was based upon population. The larger states conversely didn't want to relinquish power to their much smaller neighbors. On that night Roger Sherman of Connecticut was invited by John Rutledge of Virginia to see if they could work out an agreement in a meeting to find a way to make each side feel comfortable. The India Queen was the place where the idea for a legislative body consisting of both House and Senate was born. The smaller states could feel safe knowing the Senate provided them with equal power, and the larger states had a greater say in the House of Representatives, where the number of representatives was based on population. So it would not be incorrect to say that the concept of "United States" actually came of age in an alehouse.

The framers of the Constitution surely realized they accomplished something of such great note that these events must occur but once a millennium. After the members solemnly signed the document, General Washington, who presided over the affair, noted in his diary, "The business being closed, the members adjourned to the City Tavern." With the job they did, they deserved a beer. But this was not the end of the constitutional story. As part of their agreement, the plan had to be adopted (ratified) by at least three quarters of the states. Ten states would have to approve of the Constitution for the country to be truly united.

Ratification of the Constitution proceeded state by state. As it was voted on and approved, excitement built. New Hampshire was the ninth state to ratify, and when news of this reached Philadelphia, plans to commemorate the vote of the critical tenth state began.

People from every facet of life were members of the organizing committee, and virtually every guild assisted in the planning. Down in Virginia, George Washington, John Madison, Henry Lee, John Marshall, and Edmund Randolph led the Federalists in securing unconditional passage on the twenty-third of June. There was unbounded joy in Philadelphia, and the party kicked off in a mood of patriotic fervor.

The day of the festivities dawned near perfect: clean, bright, and sunny. The organizers looked upon this as a sign of divine approval. Bolstered by the cooperation of the weather, they started the day's first event.

The "Grand Procession" was a parade of length previously unknown in the Americas. There were large floats powered by men and horses, bands played lively tunes, militia and dignitaries marched to the approval of the crowds, followed by the guilds. The magic number in all this was ten, representing the ten states. Floats captured this theme in a variety of ways. One portrayed the facade of a great building with ten finished pillars, and three more unfinished but ready to complete the structure. Other groups used the number in similar fashion, including the guilds.

Marching in position number forty between the barbers and sugar refiners were the city brewers. They maintained the theme, numbering ten. Headed by Reuben Haines, they each carried malting shovels and mashing oars while they probably tried to avoid looking like a military gravedigging unit. In their hats were ten shoots of barley and they wore sashes of hop vines. One of the ten was Luke Morris, who carried a banner decorated with the brewers' arms and which displayed the motto "Homebrew'd is Best."

Dr. Benjamin Rush wrote to a friend about the parade, and he was pleased to report it was a day of no spiritous liquors. They were banned. Only beer and cider were permitted. After the parade had run its course, the celebrants gathered at Bush Hill for a "cold collation" (a picnic), which was washed down with "American porter, American beer, and American cider." All went so well during the celebration, it led to this newspaper report of July 23, 1788:

A correspondent wishes that a monument could be erected in Union Green with the following inscription . . . "In Honour of American Beer and Cyder, it is hereby recorded for the information of strangers and posterity that 17,000 assembled in this Green on the 4th of July 1788 to celebrate the establishment of the Constitution of the United States, and that they departed at an early hour without intoxication or a single quarrel. They drank nothing but Beer and Cyder. Learn Reader to prize these invaluable liquors and to consider them as the companions of these virtues which can alone render our country free and reputable."

In Philadelphia it is possible today to visit a reconstructed "New" City Tavern. In addition, there is an effort to rebuild Tun Tavern, birthplace of the United States Marines, the first military force chartered. A contract beer with that name is sold in Philadelphia and the surrounding area, with proceeds directed to the restoration of this birthplace of the U.S. military. All the other locations mentioned in the City of Brotherly Love are open to the public, and after a hard day of sight-seeing, it's still possible to have "an American porter or beer."

By 1790 the city had breweries clustered around a street aptly named Brewers Alley. Thus the century ended with an established brewing industry ready to fulfill the needs of a thirsty and thankful population, and Philadelphia was ready to take its place as the country's early brewing center. Their talent and capacity would provide relief for their less fortunate neighbors, the brewery-barren South.

CHAPTER 7

Brewing in the Southern Colonies

I can not eat but little meat,
  My stomach is not good:
But sure I think, that I can drink
  With him that wears a hood.
Though I go bare, take ye no care,
  I am nothing acold:
I stuff my skin, so full within,
  Of jolly good ale and old,
Back and side go bare, go bare,
  Both foot and hand go cold:
But belly God send thee good ale enough,
  Whether it be new or old.

—Anonymous

Jamestown, Georgia, and George Washington, "The Father of American Homebrewing"

A large amount of the nation's formative events and brewing went on in the North, but the Middle Atlantic and southern settlements shouldn't be overlooked. In fact, the first true colonies were established down the coast.

Thirteen years before the Pilgrims made their famous landfall, the vanguard of English settlers arrived at Jamestown, Virginia, in 1607, the site of the first permanent English settlement in North America. Unlike the New England colonies, the Jamestown party had not the forethought to include brewers among their number. Shame on them. It wasn't until two years later that, faced with growing frustration, the governor advertised back in England for two brewers to make the crossing. So eagerly was the arrival of brewers anticipated that one of the first crops planted in the settlement was barley.

Just as in New England, the inhabitants of Virginia were not partial to water, and for the same reasons. People didn't trust it and avoided it if they could. So along with the two brewers, they imported beer, closely followed by malt for making a supply of their own. And when no malt was available they resorted to the same methods as their colonial neighbors, so it's no surprise to find a record of 1620 that indicates there was makeshift ale produced from maize.

Up and down the eastern seaboard, the story was the same. In Salem, New Jersey, John Fenwick reported the settlement on the Delaware River had its priorities correct. He noted, "They straight away busied themselves in erecting breweries for manufacturing beer for common drink."

Overall the brewing was, as in New England, concentrated on homesteads and farms. Newspaper accounts, particularly in real estate advertisements, give the best indication of how much homebrewing was taking place. One ad placed in a New Brunswick, New Jersey, paper extolled the virtues of a farm on the market by stating, "There is also a large new Brewhouse . . . containing 22 barrels . . . The water is exceedingly good, soft and washes well." Knowing brewers would be immediately attracted to the claim of soft water, the owner probably included that morsel as additional bait to seal a closing.

In the South too, as the population increased, suppliers eventually established themselves, and taverns soon followed. As in the North, these alehouses became social, religious, and trading centers, so the southern authorities also encouraged tavern growth—especially to promote trade. Maryland passed laws to stimulate tavern keeping for "all

persons as well as strangers and others." Good idea, because no other place was available for travelers to park
their horses and grab a bite to eat.

The colonial governments had other more self-interested
reasons as well. They needed locations for conducting the
court, and if the government could avoid a capital project
like building a courthouse, so much the better. Thus,
methods used so effectively in New England developed simultaneously in the South. The Maryland Assembly had
passed its bill encouraging tavern keeping for these dual
ends. For example, the courts needed a place to convene
because of the "distance of our habitacons [while] being
many tymes Constrayned to appeare for the Administration of Justice for the houlding and attending Courts and
upon other occasions."

Once again there was a rush to build inns, taverns, and
alehouses, and the sudden swell in numbers alarmed the
officials. With no more originality than others, they simply
enacted laws to restrict licensing. Feeling horribly left out,
newer settlements, and those that outgrew the established
taverns, desperately petitioned the authorities for relief
from the constraints. In Londonbritain, Pennsylvania,
Thomas Lunn was granted permission to build because he
pleaded, "There is no Tavern in all the Town and the
Town's business being Entirely Done in Y_r Humb. Pett's
house." Edward Thomas, who lived in Radner, Pennsylvania, next to Saint David's Church, similarly petitioned, and
was awarded relief because he was "obliged to Entertain
many People y^e came to worship." Seems like a logical reason. Another explanation for the popularity of becoming
a tavern keeper was to supplement the owner's primary
occupation or trade. This was the case with William Faris
of Annapolis, Maryland. Although an accomplished silversmith, he found need to augment his regular income, and
in August of 1764 opened a tavern adjacent to his shop.
In an attempt to combine both businesses, he designed a
tankard which remains the only known example of its type
in a 1700s silversmith's pattern book.

By this time it should come as no surprise that the
southern colonies also used taverns as centers of politics.
This circumstance was most likely the actual cause of the
Crown's shift from support to limitation once enough tav-

erns had been opened for trade. The other concern was
one shared with northern counterparts: drunkenness. It
should be noted most accounts of this problem refer to
"rhum" or whiskey as the culprit. Beer, on the other hand,
and other small drink were considered parts of a good diet.
One colonial writer, while commenting on drinking, put it,
"Under this tearme of small-drink do I endow such drinks
as are of comfort, to quench an honest thirst, not to heat
the brain, as one man hath ale, another cider, another
methelgin [mead], and one sack [wine]."

Farther south, Georgia's founding came rather late compared to many of the others. One reason for this was the
way colonies were developed. Original settlement occurred
along the coasts where harbors and shipping meant access
to England, both for exporting the harvest of the new
lands, and to import comforts from home. It wasn't until
these areas became more populated and land prices rose
that the interior sections were settled. Georgia, with most
of its area inland, was one of these.

When Governor James Ogelthorpe established the colony
in 1733 he was very concerned about the possibility of wide
and uncontrolled drunkenness. It was because of this fear
that he, and the London trustees of Georgia, banned hard
liquor in the colony in the year 1735. They believed a colony just getting started didn't need to battle with the temptation and distractions spirits offered. At the same time,
however, Ogelthorpe encouraged the inhabitants to drink
good, healthy "English beer." To further encourage temperance he offered each new settler forty-four gallons of beer
with high hopes this would be an effective message they
never drink any stronger beverage. He also provided them
with other supplies, but unwittingly one of these was sixty-
five gallons of molasses, which was promptly distilled into
the "demon rum." Members of the Georgia colony developed a firm taste for spirits, and the law forbidding hard
liquor was repealed in the acknowledgment of its dismal
failure.

Indeed, drunkenness was a real problem, not just a
whimsical concern of pious teetotalers. Even the people
pushing for laws governing drinking enjoyed a beer. The
facts show this period had some of the highest alcohol consumption rates in American history. The problem with

drink was not confined to the lower classes; some of the highest families in the land proved susceptible. The clergy, too, was not immune; in the mid-1600s Virginia reprimanded several ministers for "drunken and riotous conduct."

Beer sold well in the southern areas, but brewing didn't catch on as it did further north. There were several good reasons for this. First, the climate was much too warm except for a few months a year. Fermentation requires maximum temperatures of less than seventy degrees for ales. Above this temperature, yeast produces "fusel oils," which give the beer an undesirable trait similar to strong solvent. Storage was also a problem. Beer is a foodstuff, and for preservation, it must be kept relatively cool. This was a large handicap, whereas the high alcohol content in rum lent it stability and made it an attractive alternative. The inhabitants really did like beer, but what were they to do?

Finally, there was the question of whether breweries were necessary. The South and its agrarian society enjoyed a lively trade with England. It had access to any imports it needed, and it had abundant supplies of the articles in demand back in England, mainly tobacco and cotton. Tobacco was especially attractive for export, since smoking had become all the rage back in England. Moreover, the barter system made it easy to get barrels of good beer for the stuff. By the late 1600s there was almost an exchange rate for it, forty pounds of tobacco per gallon of brew. So why grow barley instead of tobacco?

As hostilities between Britain and her colonies grew, reaction to the Stamp, Townshend, and Intolerable Acts was the same as in Boston. There was outrage and a sense the laws had to be protested, and from the 1760s on, taverns were the hotbeds for political discussions. George Washington himself spent a good portion of his time in the taverns drinking porter and drafting the views that would help him sire a country.

The southerners, then, were as incensed as the northerners when the British blockaded Boston. It was as if their leaders had collectively heard a call to arms. George Washington, Patrick Henry, Peyton Randolph, Robert Carter Nichols, and Richard Henry Lee all steadfastly agreed to the nonimportation measures that would strike a blow for the colonies. This must have been an especially great sacrifice for Washington, who was a devoted fan of English porter. With their fellows left in the lurch, the brewers were determined to do their part to help their comrades avoid importing English brew, and the legislators made it official. The royal governor was furious and was determined to give these colonial dissidents their comeuppance. Following the ineffective lead of the Massachusetts governor, he threatened the Virginia legislature in Williamsburg. If they insisted upon their course, he intended to disband them. The members refused to comply, and he barred them further entry to the House of Burgess. Without missing a beat, they walked the short distance to the Raleigh Tavern and reconvened. In 1770 the original nonimportation agreement was formally adopted by the Association of Williamsburg. "That we will not hereafter, directly or indirectly import, or cause to be imported, from Great Britain, any of the goods hereafter enumerated, either for sale or for our own use . . . beer, ale, porter, malt."

In New Jersey things proceeded a little differently. The governor was William Franklin, a British-siding Tory whose political beliefs led his famous father, Ben, to effectively disown him. His administration passed an act on December 6, 1769, intended to furnish the "Necessaries for Accommodating the King's Troops." However, with boycotts of English goods and embargoes, colonists were quick to reserve local production of beer for their own use. Even William Franklin, always eager to please the Crown, was reluctant to sacrifice, and where there is hesitation, there is a way. The result was a masterpiece in waffling.

> BE IT ENACTED That . . . In Lieu and Stead of Four Pints of Small Beer hereby allowed each Man per day it shall and may be lawful for the said Commissioners to provide and allow to the said troops a Quantity of Molasses not exceeding One Gallon to a Barrel of Small Beer.

Shortages became a way of life, and the dearth of beer became a near crisis. The early dependence on British imports of beer had retarded the growth of southern breweries, and the ominous signs of war foretold inconsistent shipments from northern colonies. With this in mind, Virginia concerned itself with the "advancement of American arts and manufactures." Among the recommendations was encouragement of hop and barley farming because the production of local beer would "tend to render the consumption of foreign liquors less necessary."

Homebrewing was finally catching on, and the attitudes formed during the war years would prevail for decades. Almost everyone seemed to have a way to make up the shortage. Ben Franklin had his recipe for spruce beer, and to this George Washington added his formula for a beer made with a sizable substitution of molasses. His home-brewed small beer could easily be reproduced; all the brewer need do was to:

> Take a large Siffer full of Bran Hops to your taste—Boil these 3 hours then strain out 30 Gall^{ns} into a cooler put in 3 Gall^{ns} molasses while the beer is scalding hot or rather draw the molasses into the cooler & strain the beer on it while boiling hot. Let this stand till it is little more than Blood warm then put in a quart of yeast if the weather is very cold cover it over with a blanket & let it warm in the cooler 24 hours then put it into the cask—leave the bung open till it is almost done working—bottle it that day week it was brewed.

So although Washington is regarded as the "Father of our Country," perhaps he should also be known as the "Father of America Homebrewers."

Washington used beer in his capacity as a general, too. Throughout the bitter winters at Valley Forge in 1777 and at Morristown, New Jersey, in 1776 and 1778, the army struggled with inadequate shelter and supplies. Washington's biggest military accomplishment may have been holding the army together through all this, sometimes securing provisions with his own money. At night the tired general sat by candlelight and penned an endless series of dispatches to Congress. His requests listed the necessities he needed to maintain the troops, and he literally begged for food, clothes, guns—and beer.

George knew morale was low and spirits would raise the army's spirits. But winter consumption of whiskey was believed to be ruinous to the soldiers' health. Washington once again issued proclamations banning its sale near camps and promoted the taking of beer for its healthful effects and as a guard against drunkenness. As in other wars, the Continental army sometimes took supply into its own hands. When pressed by conditions of short supply, the troops resorted to less than honorable methods of procurement. John Lowry, a Virginia plantation owner, filed a formal complaint against Colonel Dabney because his command had "taken and distroy'd a great deal of my barley w'ch . . . they have deprived me of the opp'ty of Brewing any Beer w'ch is the only way I had to get a little money to enable me to discharge my taxes. They took my Brewhouse and Break my locks whenever they are opposed." The saying is "An army travels on its stomach," and with beer considered a major source of nutrition, the colonial army demanded constant replenishment. This and the lack of imported beer during the hostilities contributed to a secure position for the fledgling American brewing industry.

The disdain for things from England, including beer, continued after the fighting. James Madison, during his congressional term in 1789, introduced legislation to impose a tax on all foreign-made beers. Of course, his proposal was more important as a means to promote brewing than it was to raise revenue or punish Great Britain. Habits of the past were hard to break, but they tried. With beer it wasn't so much a matter of ending consumption as it was altering the means of supply. George Washington echoed this sentiment in correspondence to his wartime friend Lafayette. "We have already been too long subject to British Prejudices. I use no porter or cheese in my family, but such as is made in America: both these articles may now be purchased of an excellent quality." He held to this policy through his presidency. Letters from 1790 and on frequently refer to his favorite libation, and a good source of porter was one of George's priorities. One such example was a letter from secretary Tobias Lear.

Will you be so good as to desire Mr. Hare to have if he continues to make the best Porter in Philadelphia 3 gross of his best put up for Mount Vernon? As the President means to visit that place in the recess of Congress and it is probable there will be a large demand for Porter at that time.

The end of the colonial period was by no means an end to America's troubles. The people had yet to face the development of an economy, establishment of foreign alliances, and even the decision about whether to operate as loosely bound states or to adopt a central government. Many of these questions were answered by the Constitutional Convention in Philadelphia, but through all this, beer—as a food, a dietary supplement, and a substitute for water—was one thing they did agree on.

CHAPTER 8

The 1800s

*There are two reasons for drinking: one is, when
you are thirsty, to cure it; the other, when you are
not thirsty, to prevent it . . . Prevention is better
than cure.*

—T. L. Peacock, 1785–1866

The Nation and Beer
Both Come of Age

The 1800s were an era of remarkable change in the United
States. In his exhaustive history of the country, Page Smith
used the phrase "The Nation Comes of Age." From a loosely
formed confederation of former colonies, the new country
survived internal forces of self-destruction and other growing pains to become a world power and leader in commerce. The development of the government, influx of
European immigrants, Civil War, and industrialization of
the workplace all helped shape the beer drinking of its citizens and overall consumption of the beverage.

During his presidency Thomas Jefferson, who was concerned about American drinking habits, and who was also
fond of German brews, set upon a course of action to address both these issues. Writing about beer to a friend, he

explained, "I wish to see this beverage become common instead of Whiskey which kills one third of our citizens and ruins their families."

In the belief beer was a temperate drink, Jefferson invited a number of brewers from Bohemia, now Czechoslovakia, to come train brewers in the United States. But his wife, Martha, was the real brewmaster at Monticello. As house and property manager, certainly she was involved in designing the brewroom in the kitchen under the south parlor, which included a large circular masonry fireplace. And the first batch at Monticello was recorded as September 17, 1813, shortly after her arrival. Beer was important enough to Martha for her to disrupt her settling-in chores and brew fifteen gallons of what was probably one of the better beers of its day. For Martha embraced the use of hops in brewing. Her accounting of kitchen expenses includes frequent purchase of hops and notes bargains such as "Bought 7 lbs of hops with an old shirt."

In fact, that deal would still be a bargain. Martha's were most likely "small beers" with low levels of alcohol brewed with wheat, and aged less than a week, only long enough to ferment. Her talents must have been widely appreciated, for in her first year she made over 170 gallons, enough for more than eighteen hundred glasses of beer. Although Tom was known as the ultimate student and master of near everything he touched, he came in second place to his wife as a brewer.

Indeed, Martha became so proficient, her husband had a hard time keeping up, especially when it came to bottling. By January of 1814 Thomas Jefferson had a problem that still troubles homebrewers to this day. In writing to friends, he mentioned brewing a year's supply of strong malt beer but having too small an inventory of bottles.

Much like his contemporaries Adams, Franklin, Washington, and others, Jefferson took pride in his library. His collection spanned a broad range of subjects and he frequently worked on expanding his section on malting and brewing. As with many colonial readers, he relied upon word of mouth to learn of new titles and where to acquire them. Such was the case with a book that almost led to the establishment of a national brewery. *American Brewer & Maltster*, which included notes on how to use Indian corn in beer, was of particular interest, and Jefferson's letters are full of references to his attempts to locate and purchase a copy. The author was Joseph Coppinger, and Jefferson's trials in attempting to obtain the book could have been eased with the knowledge that he and Coppinger were destined to cross paths.

It was 1802 when Coppinger, "a porter brewer from Europe," first set foot on mainland America. Traveling first to Pittsburgh, he went to work at the confluence of the three rivers. With Peter Shiras he helped establish Pittsburgh's famous Point Brewery. Business went well, but Coppinger had lofty ambitions and the small Allegheny city couldn't hold him.

Relocating back to New York, Coppinger began pursuing his real dream. On December 16, 1810, he contacted President Madison and launched his campaign, writing of

> . . . hopes of ultimate success in calling your attention to what I have long had earnestly at heart, that is, the establishment of a Brewing Company at Washington as a national object. It has in my view the greatest importance as it would unquestionably tend to improve the quality of our Malt Liquors in every part of the Union and serve to counteract the baneful influence of ardent spirits on the health and morals of our fellow citizens.

Of note in this passage is Coppinger's inevitable pitch on the healthful character of beer. He expounded on this theme in his follow-up letter of December 21.

> Those families who are in the custom of using malt liquor freely as their common drink all summer, keep and preserve their health while less fortunate neighbors who are deprived of it are the victims of fever and disease.

There was no need to convince Madison, who remembered his days at the India Queen Tavern during the Constitutional Convention in Philadelphia. Unfortunately, Madison was embroiled in a dispute over shipping and fishing rights with Great Britain, but, though distracted, he believed the idea had merit and turned to a person he trusted as both a leader and brewer, Thomas Jefferson.

The next several years were a low point in American history, and Coppinger's plans foundered. With the exception of brilliant victories at sea, the war of 1812 was nearly the young country's swan song. Devastating defeats on land were no better demonstrated than by England's burning of Washington. One bright spot shone in Baltimore where Francis Scott Key, on a mission to exchange prisoners, found inspiration in the battle of Fort McHenry and wrote "The Star-Spangled Banner" amongst glasses of beer in Baltimore's Fountain Tavern. But overall the war rendered the nation's economy helpless and distracted citizens from any thoughts of improving industry. They were literally fighting to keep the country afloat. Thankfully, the continued European antics of Napoleon helped thin the British resolve.

Following the war, Coppinger once again took up his campaign. His plan was to sell brewery bonds to raise the $20,000 start-up costs. The financial plan projected a 200 percent return on sales of porter and ale. Although Jefferson gave the proposal serious consideration, he was compelled to decline the offer, writing on April 25, 1815:

> I have no doubt, either in a moral or economical view, of the desirableness to introduce a taste for malt liquors instead of that for ardent spirits. The business of brewing is now so much introduced in every state, that it appears to me to need no other encouragement than to increase the number of customers. I do not think it is a case where a company need form itself merely on patriotic principles, because there is a sufficiency of private capital which would embark itself in the business if there were a demand.

The time for Coppinger's dream of a national brewery had passed. If not for the unfortunate timing of the war, perhaps the national brewery would have been as beloved as, or a part of, the Smithsonian.

As the country settled back into peace, one of the more unusual developments in brewing did occur. Beer finally surmounted its nearest competitor, because of, ironically, a temperance movement.

Social conscience over the effects of immoderate drinking was not new. Europe had gone through such a phase hundreds of years earlier. What was different in America was the way it coincided with an explosion of religious sects. Everyone seemed to be either starting his or her own religion or jumping on the religious bandwagon. These things always seem to happen in poor economic times. Nowhere was this more evident than in New England, where Vermont alone was the home of more than two hundred different religions. When these groups got hold of the temperance idea, the results were dramatic.

The birthing of this first American temperance crusade took place in Baltimore, Maryland. There six friends whose lives had been ravaged by habitual overindulgence banded together and in jest, at first, took the pledge. Naming themselves the Washingtonians, they developed the enthusiasm of zealots and carried their message to the people through meetings, lectures, preaching, and testimonials. As things progressed, their center of strength became deeply rooted, as it would be in later movements, in rural areas.

Farmers converted to the cause were caught up in the rapture of religious fervor, and by the hundreds swore to have no part in the production of alcoholic beverage. With this intent they took to their orchards with sharpened axes and leveled acre upon acre of productive apple trees. Cider production was such a large part of the apple industry, no one could think of another use for the crop. Sadly, New England lost not only its apple growing but also many of its noteworthy local varieties.

A story that takes place years later best illustrates the extent of the devastation. A city dweller taking a trip through New England had hired a local with a small coach to transport him through the more rural areas. This young man was a fan of Arthur Conan Doyle and the powers of reasoning possessed by his character Sherlock Holmes. Imitating his hero, this gent practiced making his own deductions. As the pair traveled the countryside, he correctly identified which farms were the homes of teetotalers. Asked if he had been to this region before, the traveler answered no but noted his observations were elementary. Pastures of the nondrinkers remained dotted with the regular pattern of stumps from long-felled orchards.

Although the movement did achieve a certain degree of success and notoriety, not all people rushed to be converted. True, several prohibition laws were passed, but these were generally of short duration. And even at the height of the movement, Americans were still putting it away. In his famous essays Emerson wrote, "God made yeast, as well as dough, and loves fermentation just as dearly as he loves vegetation." Also, during an 1837 tour of America, visiting British naval officer Captain Fredrick Marryat penned his finding:

> Americans can fix nothing without a drink. If you meet, you drink; if you part, you drink; if you make acquaintance, you drink; if you close a bargain, you drink; they quarrel in their drink, and they make it up with a drink. They drink because it is hot; they drink because it is cold. If successful in elections, they drink and rejoice; if not, they drink and swear; they begin to drink early in the morning, they leave off late at night; they commence it early in life, and they continue it, until they soon drop into the grave. To use their expression, the way they drink is "quite a caution." As for water . . . the general opinion: It's very good for navigation.

Although amusing, this passage shouldn't be taken too lightly. Beer was an essential part of early American life. During the temperance movement, beer's cause was aided by its traditional acceptance as a tonic, and following the movement, barley fields were much quicker to replant than orchards, which took years to reestablish. The rising popularity of beer, and the demise of cider, was a smile of lady luck toward brewers.

One of the breweries whose fortunes rose despite the growing force of temperance was the Hudson Valley Brewery of Matthew Vassar. Born in England in 1792, Vassar made the crossing to the United States at the age of four. Young Matthew liked life on the farm but was always excited on market day. It meant taking a wagon trip with his father, and though the road was rough, a journey to town was worth any discomfort. These excursions weren't for entertainment. The Vassar family loaded the wagon with produce they sold, and increasingly they would bring a "spare" barrel of beer. Before long they were so successful, they required a larger and more reliable supply of malt, and out of this need they introduced barley growing to the Dutchess County region of New York.

Sales of beer increased faster than the family could brew, and so it became inevitable to move out of the farmhouse and into a proper brewery. On November 15, 1810, at the tender age of eighteen, Matthew Vassar took over management of his father's business. An accounting of the time listed assets of:

Ale & Beer	$1,200.00
Barley, Malt, Hops, etc.	$1,800.00
The books accts	$1,500.00
Works & Mtrl's including brewery	$8,000.00
	$12,500.00

Business continued to grow and all seemed well until a fire destroyed the brewery on May 10, 1811. A lesser person would have been devastated—imagine losing your father's business within six months of assuming control. But Matthew Vassar was made of sterner stuff. Setting up temporary quarters in a relative's dye-house business, he began rebuilding with a modest output of only three barrels at a time.

As cash flow increased, the brewing operation slowly built enough capital to move into its own quarters. The selection seemed easy enough; where there was a crowd, there was a market. Thus a brewpub was constructed with a twist on the old colonial method. In the past the court went to a tavern, but in this case the tavern traveled to the court. There, in the basement of the local courthouse, Vassar established a new home. Advertisements declared a full return to brewing and promoted a product line of "London Brown Stout, Philadelphia Porter, and Poughkeepsie Do and Ale."

By watching expenses and plowing profits back into the business, Matthew had, by 1813, positioned the brewpub well enough to warrant construction of a new brewery. Vassar gained a reputation as an honest businessman with a dedication to service and quality. With the availability of locally abundant resources, the brewery acquired a large following, and by conservative expansion the company attained financial comfort and a size unprecedented in American brewing history. The year 1836 saw demand for Vassar's beer once again surpassing capacity and a new brewery was built in Poughkeepsie. As his tremendous success continued, Vassar established agencies to handle his sales, and he became known throughout the country. This important milestone marked the first time a brewing company would achieve national status, and it happened more than fifty years before the names of today's national breweries would arrive on the scene.

Most remarkable about the size of Vassar's operation were the technological limits that restricted brewers in those days. It was an era before refrigeration, and so Vassar, like his peers, concentrated on producing beer between mid-August and April. Despite the handicap of an abbreviated brewing year, production hit an annual capacity of thirty thousand barrels by 1860. But this was long after Matthew had lost interest in brewing.

As early as 1850 he had relinquished day-to-day operations and set his sights on a new goal. His dream was to establish a women's institute of higher learning. Using part of his enviable wealth, he succeeded in opening Vassar Female College in 1861. This was one of the nation's first colleges for women and was the first to benefit from a significant endowment. Modern beer ads can be criticized for their portrayal of women, but it was a brewer who took up the early standard for women's rights. Although the brewery folded in the late 1800s, because it stubbornly continued making ales long after the public's taste had shifted to the lighter styles of lager, his legacy remained. In 1867 the school changed its name to the current Vassar College.

The most significant changes to brewing arrived in the 1820s concurrent with a new wave of German immigrants. As they landed in their adopted land it was quite natural, as it was for most ethnic groups, to settle in "German" communities, towns, and neighborhoods. Of course, this meant those willing to take advantage of their fellows' retention of customs and habits would find success in this instant market. And in spite of the temperance movement, German brewers did very well. As historian Samuel Elliot Morison wrote, "The German didn't give up his beer, instead he made Milwaukee famous."

Wisconsin and Missouri in particular were destinations for immigrants who hoped to make them into little German states. Milwaukee along with Philadelphia, New York, Cincinnati, Chicago, and St. Louis all became centers for both German populations and brewing. The beers brewed by these Germans were not just the ales and porters popular in America. They also brought from home the alt and weiss beer styles popular there. Perhaps it was these beers that enabled them to assimilate themselves very quickly into their new culture. As traveler Louis Phillipe recorded in his *Diary of My Travels in America* for April 12, 1797, his party looked forward to visiting German settlements because "beer is available in these German homes,and theirs are the only inns where we have been able to buy it." And so America began its love affair with German styles.

The other great impact on brewing was the arrival of clipper ships. Yankee ingenuity and shipbuilding skills led to the development of the fastest vessels ever built. When these ships began shattering the records for transatlantic crossings, it made the trip short enough for brewers to import a new strain of yeast and an entirely different style of beer—lager. Soon its popularity would sweep the country. But not everyone took to it. Mark Twain related one conversation with an Irishman who said of his fellows and lager, "They don't drink it, sir, they can't drink it, sir. Give an Irishman lager for a month, and he's a dead man."

The Irish notwithstanding, this light, crisp beer was ideally suited to the climate of America, and was a hit from its introduction. At the same time innovations in glassmaking had brought inexpensive barware, which replaced the old pewter, wood, clay, or leather tankards. The new bright and sparkling clear beer in an equally attractive glass was a sensation. Lager even fit the American profile of lots is good, more is better, and too much is not enough. It was so light, a person could almost drink enough to swim in.

The American widely acknowledged to have been the first to produce lager beer was Philadelphia brewer John Wagner in 1840. His brewery on St. John Street, near Poplar, soon had more orders than the brewery had capacity. There is strong evidence, though, that Adam Lemp of St. Louis made a lager as early as 1838. No matter, the Lemp family would gain their own well-deserved fame as the first coast-to-coast brewers. Even New York City, which had lagged behind the rest of the country in establishing breweries, because of its inadequate water supply, benefited.

The completion of the city's first reservoir system fortuitously coincided with the introduction of lager, and the Big Apple was soon making up for lost time.

Up until that time New York wasn't much of a beer town, at least for brewing; that title went to Philadelphia. Part of the problem dated back to the early Dutch settlers and their water shortage even when the city had a population of under five hundred. In those days lower Manhattan looked much like their homeland, with low-lying marshes. Promptly they set about planting crops and digging canals. They even set to building a sturdy lock at the entrance of the biggest canal, which ran along what is today Broad Street, to trap water during low tide to both limit offensive odor and ensure a supply for fighting the town's frequent fires.

The first large-scale attempt to find relief from the water shortage was organized by Aaron Burr in 1799 by means of a state-chartered water company. Built amidst controversy over possible misuse of funds, an improved pump from a deeper well brought 691,000 gallons a day to a reservoir built above ground on Chambers Street, just behind what is now City Hall. A distribution system constructed out of twenty-five miles of wooden pipes eventually brought water to more than two thousand houses. Once again, despite the poor quality, the inhabitants were happy; it didn't last.

By the 1830s the situation became impossible because of the city's continued growth. Finally, in 1837, the city and state were forced to seek more substantial and permanent means to end the drought. A request for proposals was issued inviting bids on twenty-three sections of an aqueduct to provide the city water from upstate. One of the most ambitious construction projects of its time, the schedule called for completion of the system within three years. Today that would prove insufficient time to fill out the required permits. Meanwhile planners selected the Croton River as an adequate site for the reservoir. Even this part of the project went forward in typical New York fashion—land appraised at $65,400 resulted in a final bill of $257,198—but within a few years this would look like a bargain.

Under the watchful eye of chief engineer John B. Jervis, the aqueduct took shape. Constructed of stone and buried except where carried over twenty-five streams by stone bridges, it was an elliptical pipe 7.5 feet wide and 8 feet high with a downward grade of 13 inches per mile. It traversed thirty-three miles from Croton down to the Harlem River where it crossed over to Manhattan by means of the 1,450-foot-high stone arched "High Bridge," which still stands today.

The pipeline continued on in a wide, sweeping arc to the Yorkville Receiving Reservoir located at what is now the Great Lawn in Central Park. From there it traveled a final two and one fourth miles to its terminal reservoir at Murray Hill. In those days the city's population was confined to the area below Fourteenth Street, and the reservoir's location between Fortieth and Forty-second Streets was considered "out in the boonies." Today it's the site of the New York Public Library, but then it was built upon a potter's field and constructed as an aboveground stone fortresslike enclosure. The upper perimeter was built as a promenade, which, despite its northerly location, became quite popular as that era's version of a hot date. The early reservoirs were built above ground, and on these heights, to take advantage of gravity as it flowed out and down through the system.

Finally, at 5:00 A.M. on June 22, 1842, Croton water was directed into the aqueduct, and as it rose it floated and then propelled a tiny boat christened *Croton Maid*. Carrying four of the commissioners, it sailed along the waters of this new river, and when it emerged at Yorkville it visibly demonstrated the water problems were over. On July 4th the waters were admitted to the Murray Hill facilities to the salute of a hundred cannon and the thrill of thousands of spectators. This was followed by a parade more than five miles long and a large cold collation. Philip Hone, the famous diarist of New York, proudly observed, "Not a drunken person was to be seen," but this didn't mean beer was absent, nor did it mean only water was on people's minds.

How much of an impact did the completion of the aqueduct have on the brewing industry? It was just in time. The new style of lager was just arriving from Germany, along with thousands of new Germans. Proof of the effect is in the list of brewers who began making beer immediately after construction was finished. It reads like a who's who of New York beer, including Ruppert, Schaefer, Ehret, and Doelger.

The only problem with the new style was its dependency on cold temperatures, which drove brewers to search for caverns, tunnels, and supplies of ice. Generally the temperature restrictions of the yeast resulted in American brewers following the Bavarian season of brewing, which ran from Michaelmas—the twenty-ninth of September—until St. George's Day—the twenty-third of April.

The explosion in beer's popularity led to another innovation, hops growing. The growth of breweries in the first half of the nineteenth century far exceeded the amount of hops that could be harvested from the wild. Imports weren't a viable alternative either; apart from a young and shaky economy, the Americans just didn't trust foreigners. For almost a century the colonists had cultivated small amounts of hops, usually just enough for household use. The plant seemed perfect for frontier practicality. Tender springtime shoots were used in salads, the flowers were added to farm-brewed beer, the stalks could be woven into baskets, the fibers became a substitute for flax, and wax from the vine was used as a natural dye. A good portion of woodcuts and etchings from that period show hop vines growing up the sides of cabins and houses. But the introduction of large-scale commercial brewing went well beyond this level of production. It was time to get serious about the first wave of growing your own.

The Madison County town of Monroe, New York, had the first real success in commercial hop growing, and across the Hudson Matthew Vassar must have welcomed the opportunity to give up wild hop hunting. The first harvests of American hops made up only a small part of the market, but English crop failures of 1822 drove the last of the importers toward the use of native hops. New York was the direct beneficiary. By 1859 the state was growing almost 90 percent of the country's harvest. Soon the eastern success with hop growing was imitated by the introduction of hop farming in California during 1857, Wisconsin in 1860, Washington in 1866, and Oregon in 1880. Although hop growing is now centered in Oregon, Washington, and Idaho, New York remained the king until a blight in the 1940s ended production there.

With easy access to malt, water, barley, and then yeast and hops, beer became a drink everyone was trying. Oliver Holmes Sr., at school in Cambridge, spoke of its popularity on campus. As Catherine Drinker Bowen described it in her work *Yankee from Olympus,* "Oliver looked forward to that day when he . . . could tell his brother John, grandly, that he and his cronies had been to Porter's last night, for beer and oysters." His son Oliver Wendell Holmes Jr., future Supreme Court justice, had a similar collegiate experience. Just before admittance to Harvard in 1856, he enjoyed school life in Boston, where "he saw along Tremont Street Mall . . . you could buy . . . ginger beer, spruce beer in jugs. Lobsters and oysters too."

The year 1860 brought an occasion of particular note as U.S. commercial brewers first achieved a national production of one million barrels. Though the citizens were enjoying no end to great beer, something else was brewing, what would undoubtedly be the biggest upheaval and internal challenge America had ever faced—the Civil War.

The annals of military history are filled with references to drinking and the reverence for beer among professional soldiers. Indeed it was thought of so highly in military Prussia that Frederick the Great issued orders to encourage his troops to take beer. For "many battles have been fought and won by soldiers nourished on beer." He certainly believed it was more prudent than the debilitating effects of coffee.

As noted earlier, the Continental Congress approved ale as part of each American soldier's daily ration. Although, sadly, the official portions were discontinued in the mid-1800s, it continued to be held in high regard throughout the ranks, and for good reason during the Civil War, as many diaries from that period reveal. Despite some commonly held beliefs, the war was not a series of cavalry dashes, brilliant maneuvers, and continuous fighting. In fact, this first war of modern weapons was encumbered with old tactics of laying siege; thus, a majority of time was spent in encampments. Earlier leaders like George McClellan were so fond of the drill and training of camp, it nearly drove poor Abe Lincoln nuts. This, too, was the reaction of most of the camps' inhabitants. The daily life of a bivouacked soldier was less than exciting, causing Lt. Oliver

Wendell Holmes to write, "War is an organized bore," and a private to complain that camp was just "drill, drill, drill." It's no wonder that in the hours not filled with the military's "make work," these men looked for other diversions. Soldiers distracted themselves by playing cards and baseball, forming clubs, and, of course, drinking beer. Not surprisingly, drinking was readily seen in units made up of ethnic groups strongly tied to the beverage. The journal of one Union soldier revealed, "Among the German troops, especially beer . . . is consumed in great quantities." And the great frequency of people writing about beer is an indication of just how prevalent the beverage was in camp.

The most common source for this beer was the suttlers, a name for entrepreneurs who reaped profits by following the armies and providing services to the troops. Edward K. Wrightman, of the Ninth New York (the Hawkins Zouaves unit), wrote home:

> You see I am well clad and lodged . . . and the Regimental sutler gives us credit for such little extras as we may desire . . . and have every reason to be satisfied with our condition. Bye the bye, I have just been (9 P.M.), by pressing invitation, eating clams and drinking lager . . . smooth the anxious minds of the good ladies who trouble themselves so much about my welfare. My health is very good indeed.

Another testimony to the supply provided by suttlers was the experience of John W. Jacques of the Ninth New York State Militia, who described how "on the road outside of camp was a wagon with lager bier . . . As long as the money lasted, comfort was taken." No doubt the wagon or tent of a sutler was always a welcome sight.

Officers had a much easier time securing beer, and even hard-eyed General Sherman was known to take a smile. Those with a commission could, when supplies were available, draw and pay for allotments from the commissary. The common foot soldiers were not as fortunate, but were able to obtain supplies when signed for by an officer. While in Camp Smith, John Jacques noted his pleasure about "Captain Greene's tent, from which the 'Lager' flowed freely."

Another official source of beer was the military hospitals.

One of the best known was Chimarazo, located in Richmond. It not only boasted a large bakery, but it also helped recuperation of the wounded by means of its four-hundred keg brewery.

Still another means of obtaining beer was through foraging, a method the Civil War soldier elevated to an art form. Tales abound of inventive troops who secured a supply. Units in transit were particularly apt to engage in various techniques of general misappropriation. Indeed, one unit paused while marching through a small town and noticed barrels stacked in front of a store. Some proceeded to divert the merchant's attention by a bit of a circus act. The troops were long gone when the proprietor discovered an empty keg had been substituted for a full one. On another occasion a Pennsylvania regiment heading for Baltimore stole a keg of beer and with subterfuge brought it aboard their troop train. Once under way, they faced a dilemma of how to open the barrel. Finally one brusque soldier beat in the head with a musket butt. "The beer shot up into the air 15 feet like a fountain & fell foaming on everything & person . . . Very little of the beer was left."

For every disappointment the universe maintains a balance through serendipity. The life of a Civil War soldier had many instances when "organizations distinguished for sobriety might under unusual temptation, go on a roaring spree." The Forty-eighth New York was one of these. Stationed on Tybee Island in June 1862, the regiment was blessed when a storm sank a ship and a large number of kegs washed ashore. The commander of the Forty-eighth was a well-known minister, and it was much to his chagrin and disgust when his troops "proceeded to get gloriously drunk." But beer was not restricted to kegs; there are references such as "Company B was having a game of ten pins with cannon balls and beer bottles in the company street." Obviously this was well before the time of nickel deposits.

Finally, if the encampment was long enough, the soldiers would take to the production of homebrew and other liquors. The slang for these included "oh be joyful," "how come you so," "bust head," and "oil of gladness." Most of the references to these come from northern troops, not necessarily because southern chivalry eliminated partaking, but from the northern army's greater access to raw materials, transportation, and the number of brewers who naturally settled in the cooler regions of the North.

The efforts of the people involved should be neither diminished nor forgotten. Their struggle made an imprint that still affects us. However, it's good to remind ourselves that all these noble causes were carried out by average American beer drinkers.

Back home behind the Union lines, beer remained in the news. Struggling to deal with war debt, Lincoln petitioned Congress and received authorization to start the Internal Revenue Tax. Paying for the war became much easier as a tax of one dollar was levied on each barrel of beer.

And when the soldiers returned from the war, beer was there to greet them. In August 1864 Lt. Colonel Oliver Wendell Holmes Jr. was mustered out of the army along with the other three-year volunteers of the Massachusetts Twentieth. The ceremonies included a parade, a brass band, marching around old Faneuil Hall, and a conclusion at the Apollo Beer Gardens, where the troops were treated to beer. Other units experienced similar homecomings, as beer entrenched itself ever more firmly into American life.

The end of the Civil War brought both a new commercial production record of six million barrels in 1867 and a full return to westward expansion. Of course, as the pioneers moved to open the west, they brought beer with them. But what about the Native Americans? Did they have a beer culture? Some sources cite North America as one of the few regions in the world in which indigenous peoples did not produce an alcohol-based drink. This is not entirely true.

On arrival Columbus found the Native Americans drinking a fermented beverage. A common method of making such a drink was to use a clay pot and add Indian corn (maize) along with the sap of a tree such as birch or maple. As in other places, it was wild, wind-borne yeast that magically turned it into a wondrous elixir. Indeed, throughout the Americas, native cultures had alcoholic beverages. The Canadian Indians produced a maple-syrup-based drink. In Mexico there was pulque derived from the agave plant. In South America Indians made a type of beer from manioc, a starchy plant with a root used to make bread and tapioca. In the Amazon the Jivaro Indians drank great quantities of beer. And the story of Amazon Xingu beer, made from chewing plant leaves and spitting the mixture into a pot, is famous. In this manner the natural amylase enzymes in saliva break down the leaf's starches into fermentable sugars. (Commercially available Xingu beer is produced by more traditional brewing methods.) Perhaps the cultures that did not have beer were the nomadic Plains Indians and the tribes in the Southwest where dry conditions prevented accidental wetting of grain. But of course, wherever there was honey, there must have been occasions in which it naturally fermented into mead.

Western myths and Hollywood may claim the most responsibility for the images of Indians and firewater. But this clashes with the factual record of friendly, and controlled, sharing of beer at Plymouth plantation. For the next century and a half, Plymouth settlers would commonly have a barrel of their lesser-quality beer set aside for poorer travelers and Indians.

Also, although genetic research continues, there have been no solid links established between the tribal people of North America and alcoholism. Abuse may be more correctly attributed to the manner in which they learned to drink. Often it was explorers, traders, hunters, and trappers, the type of people who drank hard and often, who introduced the natives, incorrectly, to drink. The stereotype of the drunken Indian is unfortunate, and it may be the result of ne'er-do-wells and other miscreants who caused the situation.

The period immediately following the Civil War brought with it a change in Americans' use of leisure time. One of those newfound pleasures was camping. Many town- and city-dwelling veterans had their first taste of outdoor life while serving in the war's various campaigns. Even the well-to-do enjoyed this experience. Such was the case with Charles Francis Adams, whose letters were full of praise for the army life of sleeping under the stars. Indeed, for many residents of the city, where industrial haze was already obscuring their view of the stars, camping out provided their first glimpse of the Milky Way. And beer was an important tool for any camper, thereby helping stimulate total production to over nine million barrels per year by 1873.

The change in drinking habits along with the broader appeal of lager occurred at precisely the right time. The technological advances in brewing science along with establishment of an industrial economy threw open the door for brewers willing to risk expansion. Americans were ready for a cold beer, and the German immigrants were ready to indulge them. Breweries expanded capacity as quickly as possible and then marketed this inventory through a network of "tied houses." What the brewers had done was to build and operate local beer halls that were "tied" to the brewery. By this method they cashed in on the popularity of beer, dispensing their product directly to the public without a middleman, while also providing an outlet for consumption in more acceptable surroundings than dreadful saloons.

The most famous of the beer halls was New York's Atlantic Garden, located in the Bowery. While it wasn't really a garden, the illusion of a garden was provided by a mural, which temperance folks loved because it was actually a depiction of a graveyard. This hall was reportedly capable of seating more than a thousand happy quaffers at a time, and a new generation of beer drinkers kept the seats full. A writer for *The New York Times* described a typical evening:

> The object is to drink just as much beer as you can hold, smoke just as many cigars as you can bite the ends off of, and see who can sit in his chair the longest. It is an institution worthy of the gods. And, bless us, how the beer pours down! "It's up we all stand, and down she all goes"; and "Here, waiter, fill 'em up again." The man who can drink the most . . . is the best man. There is nothing to eat—and who would eat when he can blow off the foam and have her filled up again? . . . The bill of fare was varied and extensive. Following is a translation: Beer, Cigars, Beer, More Beer, Cigars, Beer, Beer, Beer, Beer, Beer, Beer, Beer, Beer, Beer, Beer, Beer, Beer, Beer, Beer, Beer.

The managers of these beer halls were aggressive marketers. As new legions of immigrants settled into the country, they found a welcome mat in the form of social associations based on nationalities. It didn't take the beer halls much more than a heartbeat to realize there was an opportunity. Beer gardens launched an all-out marketing blitz on this new audience. In what appeared to be a friendly gesture, the halls would offer associations free catering if an event would be scheduled in their establishment, knowing full well they would make back every cent and more on beer sales. The competition for hosting these events grew so fierce that the Atlantic Garden was soon offering association organizers catered food along with five-hundred-dollar rebates for the privilege of catering a party.

Later the beer halls would continue this technique when they actively courted the new movement of organized labor. Workers sought to hold their meetings in private rooms that were supplied without a fee provided the host's beer was purchased. The beer tab was picked up by the union's treasury, and the members were very pleased with this method of managing their dues. Eventually the union leaders attempted to point out a hall could be rented cheaply with less impact on the finances (read that "no beer tab"), but the members dismissed such a notion. They were comfortable with their arrangements. Have a few beers with the fellas and not have to explain a bar bill to the spouse; what could be better?

Beer halls proliferated in the wake of these successes, spreading through cities and across the country. Another of these ventures was started in 1882, when August G. Luchow opened his famous beer hall. With backing from William Steinway, the famous piano maker, Luchow introduced his famous forty-five cent lunch and at age twenty-six was well on his way to a fortune.

Luchow's beer was Würzburger lager, and in recognition of his sales he became its American agent in 1885. At Luchow's the Würzburger flowed like a river and became the subject of an early version of an advertising jingle with:

> Rhine wine is fine,
> But a big stein for mine,
> Down where the Würzburger flows!

Happy crowds belted out the tune while they belted down the inexpensive lunch along with gallons of golden beer. The good people of the town of Würzburg, Germany, were so pleased with Luchow's sales, they presented him with a six-liter decorative stein, and legend has it Luchow was enough a beer drinker himself that this extra large mug fit him just fine. Sales remained brisk for decades and the original beer hall was expanded to over eight times its original size.

Beer halls were a sure moneymaker, and as new establishments opened, they attempted to maximize profits by drawing crowds to larger and more magnificent temples of beer drinking. The largest of them was built by Pabst on 125th Street in Harlem, New York. The grand opening awed patrons, with a seating capacity of more than fourteen hundred, it was simply the largest restaurant in existence. Years later, the *Milwaukee Sentinel* would print a review that praised the hall, describing it as:

> . . . eminently successful . . . Costly and splendid in architecture and illumination, possessing an orchestra that is only excelled in the best theaters, its 1,400 seats are crowded from year's end to year's end . . . Its exterior is on a par with other public buildings . . . Its interior is resplendent with frescoes, paintings, marble columns, colored lights, and exquisite table appointments.

The beer halls owed their prosperity to lager beer. As described by Michael and Ariane Batterberry in their book *On the Town in Old New York,* "Lager beer was the German immigrants' gift to America, and its mass production irrevocably changed the nation's drinking habits. Lager was light, delicious, and, happily, it could be consumed in quantity." The brewers of lager reaped huge rewards for their efforts. They reinvested, expanded capacity, and sold even more beer. But none of this would have been possible if not for the technological advances of the second half century.

One of the first applied technologies was the steam engine. Used to power pumps, run hoists, and power mechanical agitators in mash tuns, it allowed a scale of equipment that had been too big for manpower alone. Combined with advances in metallurgy, it enabled the breweries to build in previously unimaginable capacities.

What really opened the door for unprecedented brewing can be traced to a Florida incident totally unrelated to beer. In 1850 physician John Gorrie was out to make people's lives a little healthier. Gorrie noticed that malaria and a host of other maladies were curiously prevalent in the southern United States. Reckoning it had something to do with the warm, humid, swampy air of those parts, Gorrie thought all he needed to do to achieve a cure was alter the condition of the air. Doing this outside wasn't feasible, but he could certainly change things indoors. What Gorrie proposed was to force a stream of air over ice and thereby cool the room. The catch in this cure was a lack of ice in the deep South. Importing and storing ice from the North was not only cumbersome, but those Yankees would charge an arm and a leg for what amounted to frozen water. The path seemed clear; Gorrie would just have to invent a means of making ice. The doctor failed in his cure, but what he invented was a whopping success, for he is the true father of refrigeration.

With improvements made to Gorrie's machine by inventors all over the world, there was, by 1869, a mad scramble to build ice-making machines, and, of course, secure patents. Soon everyone was making ice. One of those, Samuel David Launt, even made good on a boast by producing ice in, of all places, Phoenix by 1890.

As the craze of ice-making caught hold, the usefulness of the new invention struck several brewers at once. Franz Windhausen of Germany was one of those who realized if you could make ice, it was just as easy to cool a room. No longer would brewers be limited to cool northern states, or locations with caves and tunnels, or even the winter months. Brewing could go year-round, and the brewers took full advantage of the new ice rooms. In 1869 George Merz became the first lager brewer to use refrigeration. He was closely followed by Samuel Liebman of New York in 1870, and Robert Parker of Alexandria, Virginia, in 1878. The first large-scale success with the process was that of Best of Milwaukee in 1880 along with Bemis & McAvoy in Chicago, Anheuser-Busch in St.Louis, and American Brewing in Houston. Soon brewers were happily engaged in a year-round activity of pumping out beer and raking in profits.

With the growing popularity of lager beer aided by refrigeration for year-round brewing, brewers were breaking one production record after another. But all this was not achieved without some casualties. Breweries that stuck to their guns and refused to give up traditional ale brewing saw their markets evaporate like alcohol on a hot day. Lager may have won the country over to beer drinking, but it also killed several venerable old breweries. Poughkeepsie's Vassar was driven out of business in 1896, living on only in civic pride and the name of the college. Albany, New York, with its tradition of ale at Taylor Brewing, which once laid claim to operating the largest brewery in the world, suffered a similar fate as it was forced out by the might of lager. It closed its doors as the century ended.

How sad it was that these once proud breweries and more like them were forced to close even as beer's popularity was reaching unheard-of heights. But as these early success stories came to an end, there were new dynasties being born, and these new giants of the industry would completely alter America's beer business. The 1800s proved to be the country's first golden age of brewing. The completion of New York's reservoir system, the introduction of lager beer, technological innovations like refrigeration, establishment of nationwide transportation systems, and America's thirst for beer were about to make the brewing industry explode in an unprecedented fashion. The results would last more than a hundred years and change America's thoughts and taste for beer. Moreover, they would bring these brewers willing to take a risk market dominance and wealth beyond imagination.

CHAPTER 9

The Rise of National Brewers

We were to do more business after dinner;
but after dinner is after dinner—
an old saying and a true,
"much drinking, little thinking."

—JONATHAN SWIFT, 1712

One Brewer's Story

Any mention of the rise of national breweries would be remiss without including the story of Anheuser-Busch. Few would argue that any of the other large brewers that came to prominence during this era did things better from an overall business standpoint. The name Budweiser rose from as humble a beginning as any of the other fifteen hundred beers and brewers serving America in the mid 1800s. But a combination of seized opportunities, sheer determination, and a little good fortune made success unstoppable. Though it was transplanted from foreign roots, there are few other companies today that are thought of as more all-American than Anheuser-Busch.

The story of the company's rise goes back to Germany in 1839 and the birth of Ulrich Busch's second son, Adolphus. Four years after his father's death in 1852, Adolphus embarked upon a career in business. Moving to

Cologne, he secured a position as shipping clerk in a mercantile warehouse. It was there his real love of beer was most likely born, probably in one of the city's many house breweries which served up the local beer style of Kölsch.

This was the period of large-scale German immigration to America. Social unrest in Germany was forcing its poor huddled masses and brewers into making the Atlantic crossing. Among those who were swept along with the fleeing tide were three of Adolphus's brothers: Ulrich, John, and George. Missouri was drawing large numbers of resettled Germans, and it was there the Busch boys decided to settle. History credits brother John with getting Adolphus to jump across the pond. John had first settled in with George, who worked as a hop dealer but by 1854 struck out on his own, to Washington, Missouri, where he started the John B. Busch brewing company. It was his letters from America's heartland that encouraged and persuaded Adolphus to join them.

Adolphus arrived in St. Louis at age eighteen and even then possessed the traits for which he would become well known. He had unbounded energy balanced by a heavy dose of shrewdness. But as he wandered the city streets, taking his time in deciding on where to concentrate his talents, his fresh-faced looks projected an aura of inexperience. Standing five foot five, he had long, wavy hair and a fair complexion, that combined with youthful enthusiasm, made him seem even younger. Aware of this image and anxious to dispel it, he immediately grew a mustache and offset the rest through his deep, resonant voice.

His sociable nature would also serve him well, helping him make friends with the most influential members of the community. But what he enjoyed most was making money. To launch his business life he stuck with what he knew, and first worked in a wholesale supply house. Not long afterward he started working for himself by entering a partnership with Ernst Wattenberg. Their business was selling brewing supplies, and business was good, for the city was quickly becoming an enclave of expatriate Germans whose thirst for beer resulted in the number of breweries nearly doubling between 1854 and 1858. It was through this business and the contacts it afforded him that Adolphus

Busch would meet not only his future partner but also his wife.

Eberhard Anheuser was born on September 24, 1805, and like his younger partner-to-be, was from Germany. Well educated and trained as a businessman, he, like so many others, left for the United States in 1843 to settle in the predominantly German section of Cincinnati. Already his hair was thinning and his bushy mustache added to his solemn appearance, but he had kindly eyes and loved a good joke, especially with his friend Tony Faust, who ran a bar in St. Louis. One day Eberhard decided a bit of a trick was in order, so he started a rumor that Tony was buying a brewery. So successful was he in spreading the story that Tony started being hounded by the press. Finally Tony decided to answer their questions; he announced that yes indeed he was buying a brewery—one glass at a time. It was just the type of ending Anheuser loved. Little did he know it would be he in the brewery business.

Following the Prussian uprising of 1848, he renounced his German motherland and became an American citizen. As for his business plans, he never intended to become a brewer. He was a soap manufacturer, and his introduction to brewing was by chance. With a well-established business selling soap, Eberhard Anheuser had a secure fortune. As was the custom, he invested in the ventures of more newly arrived Germans in hopes of not just their success but success for the entire German community. When the St. Louis Bavarian Brewery went bankrupt in 1859, Anheuser, as a major investor, found himself in the beer business. It was probably at that time when Eberhard Anheuser made acquaintance with a young, up-and-coming brewery supply salesman named Adolphus Busch. Fortunately for Busch, Anheuser's soap business was located just around the corner from his own shop, which made the courtship a bit easier.

Busch was one to seize opportunity, and knowing Anheuser had little knowledge of the beer business, he worked his way into the brewery's operations. In 1860 the reorganized company resumed production under the name E. Anheuser & Company.

As he found a home in the brewery, Busch continued to work hard courting Anheuser, but no sooner had he succeeded than he started another courtship. Anheuser had a daughter named Lilly. Born in Braunschweig, Germany, in 1844, she was only sixteen years old when Adolphus met her, but her curly blond hair and blue eyes made her nothing short of sensational. Busch was taken with her from the start. If Eberhard Anheuser didn't feel surrounded, he soon would be, for Adolphus's brother Ulrich was courting Lilly's older sister Anna. Though partnership in the brewery didn't occur until much later, the deed was essentially done on March 7, 1861, when Eberhard Anheuser gave away the hands of both daughters in a double wedding ceremony with the Busch boys at the St. Louis Holy Ghost German Evangelical Lutheran Church.

As the second half of the 1800s progressed, Adolphus Busch gained further control of the brewery as Eberhard Anheuser remained more interested in his soap business. When Anheuser retired in 1877, E. Anheuser & Company was producing 44,961 barrels per year, ranking thirty-second in the nation. Adolphus took the ball and ran with it, and in 1879 the company was renamed the Anheuser-Busch Brewing Association.

With full control Adolphus could now pursue his two dreams, which went hand in hand. His goal was to win over Americans to the idea of beer as a national beverage and in the process build Anheuser-Busch into a national powerhouse of beer. Adolphus was of that old school of business that would look with disdain on today's methods of corporate raiding and quick profit. Busch was in it for the long haul. On more than one occasion he would cut his profits to the bone and sometimes even sell below cost to gain market share. His philosophy is best summed up in his own words.

> It is my aim to win the American people over to our side, to make them all lovers of beer . . . It may cost us a million dollars and even more, but what of it if thereby we elevate our position? I stand ready to sacrifice my annual profits for years to come if I can gain my point and make people look upon beer in the right light.

As Busch started his quest he realized he needed to do several things at once, and in the process he would indeed have to make some concessions with profit if he was to succeed. First, he learned a lesson from a neighbor. The Lemp Brewing Company of St. Louis was an early leader in shipping beer across the nation. It wasn't lost on Adolphus that Lemp achieved this success by establishing a network of local agencies to handle sales, and Adolphus liked using what worked. Thus, Busch began his expansion by setting up a similar system.

The next move was to get the beer to the customer as fresh as possible. But the railroads of that era would insist on kickbacks and complained about the heavy weight of the refrigerated beer cars. Often they would deliberately tie up cars and keep them away from the desperate brewers. The solution seemed fairly simple and typified the Busch approach: Build your own refrigerated railcar company. He did just that by forming a subsidiary named the Manufacturers Railway Company in February of 1887.

Adolphus was also highly regarded as a marketer of beer. He is credited with the first truly successful beer advertising promotion, and he owed it all to the misfortune of a man from Monroe, Michigan. It was both a warm and fateful day in Montana on the twenty-fifth of June, 1876. In a few days the country would be celebrating its centennial, but as a yellow-haired colonel of cavalry prepared to attack an Indian village, his penchant for dashing heroics caused his demise. George Armstrong Custer had grossly underestimated the size of the opposing force. Despite warnings, he divided his 600-man force and advanced with his column of 112, including his brother Tom, who had twice won the Medal of Honor. Encountering over two thousand Sioux and Cheyenne warriors, he and his troops were all wiped out with the exception of one scout and horse. Despite this gigantic blunder, General (his Civil War rank) Custer was elevated to a position of folk hero.

A painting of the failed attack titled *Custer's Last Fight,* by Cassily Adams, was such a favorite of the public, including Adolphus, that in 1885 it became the subject of an Anheuser-Busch promotion. Lithograph copies were supplied to taverns and saloons featuring Anheuser-Busch beer, the first real successful beer marketing ploy.

Expansion of territory and brewing capacity along with aggressive marketing catapulted the brewery up with the leaders. By 1895 Adolphus's brewery was ranked second in the United States with production at eight hundred thousand barrels per year. By 1901 the annual sales had grown again, with Anheuser-Busch reaching the magic number of more than one million barrels of beer sold.

Of all the stories and myths about Anheuser-Busch, none is so widespread, and has so many variations, as the tale about the origins of their flagship beer. Some of the alleged beginnings have included a secret recipe brought over with a sample of yeast hidden in an ice cream container. Another is about formulating the beer after tasting the handiwork of a group of obscure European monks. Indeed, on occasion the people at Anheuser-Busch seemed to unofficially encourage these stories. What is considered to be the actual birth of "Bud" stems from the relationship Adolphus had with a friend in the wine business.

Carl Conrad was an importer of wine, liquors, and champagne who made frequent trips back to Germany with his friend Adolphus Busch. On one of these trips they sampled a beer from a brewery located about sixty-five miles south of Pilsen, Czechoslovakia. Adolphus kept copious notes of his travels and noted both the smooth taste of the beer and the name of the town, Česke Budějovice. This name was later pronounced Budweis. On return to the United States, it was Carl Conrad who registered the name, but years later when asked about the inspiration for Budweiser, Adolphus would explain he picked the name because it was "easily pronounced by English-speaking people, and in the second place the brewery bearing that name enjoyed a good reputation."

This story seems to make the most sense. For decades Adolphus Busch made regular trips back to his old homeland, observing progress made in brewing. On his return to St. Louis these advances were incorporated into the Anheuser-Busch production facilities. His brother Anton, in the wine business, was most likely the person who related Pasteur's work on techniques now called pasteurization, and Adolphus was pasteurizing his beers a full four years before Pasteur printed a book on his work and discoveries. Later, as changes in bottling made it practical, Anheuser-Busch was one of the first breweries to market bottled beer on a large scale.

Meanwhile the A-B brewery had entered a contract with Carl Conrad to produce beer under the name he registered, Budweiser. Carl ran his business with a true international flavor. With offices in both Mainz and Geisenheim, Germany, as well as in St. Louis, Conrad had a stable of products to which was added "World Renown Conrad's Budweiser Beer." The beer was sold across nearly the entire United States, and its high quality made it a popular choice at many of the country's finer restaurants. Drawing on his marketing experience, Carl even gave the bottle an upscale look with a wire fastener and foil wrapping resembling a champagne bottle. Unfortunately, Carl Conrad was much better on the idea end of things than with the nuts and bolts of business. In 1882, despite a popular line of beverages, C. Conrad and Company went bankrupt.

Adolphus Busch was concerned and sympathetic to his friend. Conrad was burdened by a debt of more than $300,000—real money in those days. Surprisingly, the largest creditor was none other than Anheuser-Busch, with an unsecured loan of more than $94,000. Adolphus never seemed concerned. Seeing an opportunity to help a friend and close an advantageous business deal, Busch arranged to assume control of Conrad's company and provided a lifetime job for Carl at the brewery. This was very typical of the manner in which Adolphus ran his company, and he passed down to his sons the belief that the best way to conduct business was to be in it for the long run. Busch knew Carl had built a strong reputation of quality for the Budweiser name, and the company would eventually reap large rewards for taking over the brand.

At that time Budweiser was a high-quality brew made by the most traditional brewing methods, including floating beechwood slats in the beer vessels to help settle and clarify the fermenting beer. Budweiser would prove to be the brand by which the company would be known. But it wouldn't be without some obstacles along the way. In the early 1900s the United States had several smaller breweries cashing in on the Budweiser name. One was located in New York and another in Pennsylvania. Even tiny Pocatello, Idaho, in the middle of Mormon country, had a Budweiser beer. Faced with this situation, Adolphus moved to register the name and filed U.S. trademark papers in 1907.

Then a problem surfaced from one of those decades-earlier trips to Germany. From across the Atlantic came a formal complaint objecting to the filing for trademark status. The dispute was based on Budweiser being named after a region. Also, there were at least two other breweries with the same name, and these had been using Budweiser far longer than Adolphus. In order to secure a trademark, Busch would first have to deal with these companies.

Not one to back down from a challenge, Adolphus became, if anything, more determined to secure a trademark for his main brand. Busch was successful in buying off the German brewery for what, in retrospect, was actually a fairly low sum. In 1911, for the price of 82,500 kronen, the German brewery withdrew its objections. This left the small brewery in České Budějovice, but they were not as willing to roll over. Instead they ignored and stalled him. Later in 1911 Adolphus agreed to make a large payment to the Czechoslovakian brewery and in return was granted permission to use the name Budweiser on beer sold within the United States. But the deal went beyond this. The crafty Czechs had retained the right to sell their beer in the United States under the name of "Imported Budweiser." Additionally, Anheuser-Busch was restricted from using the Budweiser name within Europe.

It wouldn't be until 1939 that A-B finally convinced the Czechs to let them use the Budweiser name exclusively in the United States, North America, and all United States possessions. Still the company was restricted from using the name in Europe, and this would later prove a hindrance to A-B's worldwide marketing plans.

If death could be thought of as fortunate, then it may have been for Adolphus Busch. Passing away in 1913, he turned the reigns of the company over to his son August Busch Sr. and was spared from what was about to happen. The gray clouds of trouble had started gathering much earlier, and as 1919 approached, Anheuser-Busch found itself squeezed by the groundswell of a social movement called Prohibition. The question faced by all brewers was how to survive and wait this thing out. The problem was, it would last far longer than anyone had expected.

This was the unfortunate situation that welcomed August "Gussie" Busch as the new head of the brewery. Prohibition caught Gussie's attention early, and from the start he sought any means possible to keep the company afloat. Brewing in and of itself was not illegal, but rather the manufacture, transportation, and sale of alcohol. If the spirits could be removed after fermentation (and sold as industrial alcohol), the low-alcohol beer remaining could be bottled and retailed. This was the birth of "near beer," and though Busch was as unenthusiastic about it as the rest of the general public, it was one of the products, under the name of "Bevo," that kept Anheuser-Busch running. Another marketing effort intended to make use of the A-B malting facilities, and in 1921 the company began distribution of "Budweiser Barley Malt Syrup." As a foodstuff for cooking and baking, it even came with recipes for making malt cookies. But what the malt was really being used for was revitalizing the American institution of homebrewing. Years later August Busch Jr. would remember, "We ended up the biggest bootlegging supply house in the United States . . . Oh, the malt syrup cookies! You could no more eat the malt syrup cookies, they were so bitter . . . It damn near broke Daddy's heart."

In 1927 Anheuser-Busch would bring out yet another product to assist the burgeoning ranks of homebreweries, Budweiser Yeast. This was only the beginning of the vast lineup of products A-B would market during the fourteen years of Prohibition. The company tried selling corn sugar, corn oil, gluten livestock feed, glucose, a malt supplement for nursing mothers called Malt-Nutrine, and even a chocolate-coated ice cream bar named, of all things, "Smack." Gussie went even further, he converted the railroad car subsidiary to building truck bodies and ice cream cabinets. Furthermore, he established a special committee tasked with selling off the company's impractical or obsolete holdings. Gussie may have thought the malt and yeast business saved the company—after all, he was a dedicated beer man—but it was the selling of the assets that kept A-B in the black.

Before Prohibition, Anheuser-Busch was like many of the other breweries; it owned a system of "tied houses" that handled their products exclusively. As Prohibition wore on,

A-B divested itself of these and sold them off to an industry that was supplying the nation with a new infatuation. Thus, the corner saloon was transformed into the corner gas station.

The most important thing for Anheuser-Busch during Prohibition was the way it planned to come out of this black era for beer. There was never any doubt in the family's mind that this, too, would pass. Unlike some of the other large brewers, which complacently trudged through the 1920s, Anheuser-Busch embarked upon a fairly aggressive campaign to ensure their plants and equipment would remain as up-to-date as possible. Thus the company was well positioned for repeal. All this was possible because Anheuser-Busch was run by real beer men. A great example that illustrates their knowledge of their product was provided by Gussie himself.

On a business trip to New York City Gussie found himself thirsting for a Michelob and wandered into the famous 21 club. The restaurant's co-owner and staff practically fell all over themselves in attending to the beer baron, and a waiter promptly served up the requested Michelob. Taking a sip, Gussie immediately knew something was wrong. Turning to the owner, he asked what was going on; he knew it couldn't be his beer. The owner stood his ground and insisted it was. After an escalating argument, a confident Busch challenged the rather indignant owner with a wager—with the restaurant as the stakes. After a moment's hesitation, the owner accepted the terms and suggested they ask the bartender. No way Gussie was about to go with somebody's word. The now-growing party headed down to the chill box to check the kegs and taps. With one look in the cellar, the owner's face turned ashen. It wasn't Michelob that had been served, it was Rheingold.

As Gussie returned to his table, the owner followed offering apologies such as he'd never before heard. Busch rebuffed him and instructed him to remove himself from Gussie's new restaurant. After working the man into a totally distraught state, Gussie relented, cautioning the owner to never again question his knowledge of beer.

With a sound business philosophy, a modernization plan, and a group of leaders dedicated to the beer business, Anheuser-Busch positioned itself not only to recover from the years of Prohibition but to assume the role of brewing giant. Breweries not willing to make these commitments suffered the consequences.

CHAPTER 10

Prohibition

Whoever called it near beer was a poor judge of distance!

—ANONYMOUS

*Mother's in the kitchen
Washing out the jugs;
Sister's in the pantry
Bottling all the suds;
Father's in the cellar
Mixing up the hops;
Johnny's on the front porch
Watching for the cops.*

—ANONYMOUS

The Battle Over Beer

Prohibition did not occur overnight. There had always been those who preached against the evils of drink, and the modern temperance movement can be traced back to the 1840s. At that time, the Washingtonians, a group of six friends in Baltimore who took the oath together, began to influence the views of a growing segment of the populace. As with most temperance movements, it coincided with a period of religious fervor, but the Washingtonians' offspring, the American Temperance Union, didn't gain enough momentum to be effective because it was overshadowed by other issues then tearing at the very fabric of the nation. Also, the members were stalled over policy considerations at the very core of their fight. These were decisions such as:

Should the membership pursue total abstinence?
Would moral persuasion be effective or was intervention on a governmental level necessary?
Were the abolitionist views of northern members at such odds with the views of southern temperance advocates that a unified national effort was impossible?

In the end a lack of consensus over these three critical areas so divided the membership as to render their crusade ineffective. But not before they made a few significant, if short-lived, gains. The first legal maneuvers between the temperance movement and beer were actually initiated by a brewer. In the mid-1800s Albany, New York, was famous as a center for brewing top-notch ale, and the most famous of these ale brewers was John Taylor, owner of the Taylor Brewing Company. In 1840 Edward C. Delavan, a retired wine merchant who had forsaken his old trade to become a prominent prohibitionist, accused Taylor's company of using filthy water for malting. Incensed by the accusation, Taylor demanded satisfaction and filed a $300,000 libel suit. The trial turned into a near circus with a parade of witnesses representing each side's interests. In the end conflicting testimony and each litigant's vigorous campaigning so muddied the trial that despite his best efforts, Taylor lost.

The results of the Taylor case bolstered the army of temperance. Working within the legislative process, they realized their next objective through the hand of Neal Dow, mayor of Portland, Maine. Through the tireless efforts of Dow, the Maine legislature passed the country's first Prohibition law, authored by Dow himself, on June 2, 1851. This bill called "for the suppression of Drinking houses and Tippling shops," and in recognition of his success, Dow is commonly referred to as the "Father of Prohibition."

Other states followed the Maine lead. Minnesota enacted

antidrinking statutes in 1852 along with copycat laws in Rhode Island, Massachusetts, and Vermont. Additional laws hit the books in the states of Michigan in 1853 and Connecticut in 1854. New York, New Hampshire, Nebraska, Delaware, Indiana, and Iowa all passed laws in 1855.

Failure of these laws can be attributed to the inexperience and inability of the temperance advocates to wield political influence. Laws were not strenuously enforced, and in some cases inventive means allowed outright avoidance. In the case of Maine, it was the forerunner of the 1900s speakeasy and birth of the term "blind pig." This referred to a provision of the law that forbade selling beer or spirits but allowed it to be given away. The proprietors of taverns advertised the special viewing of a blind pig for the price of a small admission. Fortunately for patrons, the fee included free beer, resulting in very happy evenings, for the tipplers, the owners, and, of course, the pig.

Other factors that led to the demise of these early laws included the growing popularity of lager beer and the swelling numbers of immigrants from Germany. The country was soon distracted by the more immediate and far reaching issues of the War Between the States. But the temperance forces must have been students of history, and although the movement went dormant during the war and Reconstruction, it was never dead. It lurked around the door of every tavern and brewery in the country, waiting for the right moment to strike.

Modern temperance laid its foundation once again on the back of various religious movements of the late 1800s and was formalized in Ohio with formation of the Women's Christian Temperance Union in 1874. The birth of this organization in Ohio was not by chance; just as with the religious movements, Prohibitionists found strongholds in the rural sections of the country.

Not surprisingly, when the rallying point for the movement appeared in 1890, it came from small-town America. It was in Medicine Lodge, Kansas, on a warm, still evening that characterizes summer on the plains, that a spark struck. Outside a saloon a woman had been reading a Bible for several days. This was a bit unusual because Kansas was a dry state, but like the earlier laws, the Prohibition wasn't enforced. The woman praying for divine intervention to close the den of evil was a recent widow who was convinced her young husband had fallen by the hand of alcohol. After days of praying, she decided the lack of an answer was a sign to take matters into her own hands, and she did.

Grabbing the nearest implement of destruction, an ax, Carrie Nation drew herself up to her full height of six feet and stormed the bar like a soldier engaged in trench warfare. Garbed in a black mourning dress that billowed and flew behind her, she must have looked every bit the foreboding spirit. Customers ducked for cover and ran out the door as Ms. Nation literally hacked the place to pieces. When she finally stopped, the devastation was complete. Bottles of booze lay about in glistening slivers, with the bar resembling the tinder-littered floor of a woodshed, and amongst it Carrie stood alone catching her breath.

Despite the primitive state of communications, the news of this incident swept through the country. How? Why? Today it might be a regional story about the ravings of an extremist, but then it was the time of reform, and progressives were on the political offensive throughout the country. A new group of leaders were stepping forward, and names like McKinley and Roosevelt rode the popular tide of reform into office. It wasn't just an issue of beer, or even alcohol. The bigger picture was fighting all corruption whether it came in the form of unhealthy meat-packing plants or the stifling monopolies of the robber barons. America had had enough and it wanted big change. With growing sophistication the temperance movement hitched its wagon to the stars of progressive politics, and this time they organized with a vengeance.

The first big political test was planned for the very state where the Women's Christian Temperance Union was born. The governor of Ohio, M. T. Herrick, managed to invoke the wrath of Prohibition leader Wayne Wheeler when he vetoed a bill that would have allowed self-determination on a local level. (It would allow towns and counties to declare themselves dry.) Despite Herrick's advantage of being both an incumbent and a Republican in a heavily Republican state, the thorough campaigning of the temperance movement swept his Democratic challenger into office. A gubernatorial election is serious stuff. With this victory, the temperance forces, now known as the "dries," had political power, and leaders from the president down through the most junior congressman were paying attention. Office-holders were casting a nervous eye at the dry forces and the influence they could exercise. Most, like McKinley, privately thought the dries a bit extreme, but not wanting to risk suicide at the polls, publicly they remained silent.

During all this, the action, or inaction, of the brewers may be hard to understand. In retrospect the growing power of the temperance forces seems so obvious. But beer producers had been enjoying year after year of growth, and as with most financial successes, they didn't think it would end. They had been most effectively lulled to sleep by their achievements. When they finally did put up a defense, it was one they thought so logical, it couldn't possibly be refuted.

Brewers only had to look back to convince themselves everything was going to be fine. From earliest times beer had been associated with positive effects. The Egyptians and other ancient cultures founded many early healing beliefs based on beer for the cure. The Egyptian Book of Medicine contained no fewer than one hundred medicines derived from a base of beer. During the late 1700s America's premiere medical authority, and George Washington's personal physician, was Dr. Benjamin Rush. A firm believer in moderation and temperance, Rush published his beliefs along with his famous temperance chart titled "A Moral and Physical Thermometer." This chart was the forerunner of countless diagrams and graphs produced by U.S. medicine, a profession that to this day causes constant shifts in the country's diet. The amazing thing about Rush's chart, though, is its placement of small beer with milk and water as a means to a long and healthy life. Also, as suppliers of the nation's beer, the newly arrived Germans held on to many of the old-world beliefs they grew up with. For centuries the Germans had lived by a philosophy that held that beer enriched a patient's blood. And nearly the entire population of the old country practiced a manner of living summed up by the saying "The brewery is the best pharmacy."

The founder of the present-day Washington, D.C., Olde

Heurich Marzen–style beer tells the story of his brewing grandfather's passage to America. According to Heurich, there was an outbreak of cholera during the crossing. Gary Heurich's grandfather begged people to spare themselves by avoiding the ship's water supply and sticking to beer. Those who did lived. This recurring story of the evils of water and healthful nature of beer was so widely held, the brewers simply couldn't believe anyone would think their product harmful. The result was a weak counterattack against Prohibitionists based on low-key advertising of beer's healthy nature.

Print advertisements of beer's healthful and restorative powers were used by Enterprise Brewing of San Francisco, Milwaukee-Waukesha of Wisconsin, and Consumers of Philadelphia. The original Budweiser printed statements from several doctors attesting, "While it exhilarates, the beer does not intoxicate and may be used with advantage by young and old. We consider this beer a healthful and invigorating stimulant." This theme would be repeated time and again. Peter Doelger, one of New York's famous brewers, located at 407-33 East 55th Street, proclaimed his beer "a natural food product, every drop laden with body building healthful food substances . . . Pure beer for the Whole Family."

Though the German immigrants were assimilated quickly into American life, they retained a number of values from the old country. One of these holdovers was beer's position as not just for adults but as a family beverage. Ads of this era just before Prohibition continuously echoed this theme. Chicago's Wacker & Birk Brewing Company promised "rosy cheeks" and explained how this was the sign of a healthy family. Greenway's of Syracuse, New York, touted their beer "for family or club use" and backed their claims with statements from several doctors. The beer of C. Evans and Sons was "a Natural Product Better than Drugs. A health-giving, nourishing, brawn and sinew making beverage."

In New York the Beadleston & Woerz Empire Brewery was pleased to offer a product that they insisted "Promotes digestion and Benefits the health." But the campaign that made the biggest attempt to focus directly on old fears was the attack launched by the German Brewing Company of

Cumberland, Maryland, which declared a "City Health Officer, who is fighting disease, says, after making several analyses, that much of the City water is not fit to drink! Why not avoid risk and use German Beer! It is pleasing to the taste and Good for your system."

Unfortunately, and unknown to brewers, this campaign was to prove ineffective and inadequate for combatting the growing strength of the dries. After all, they thought, the real problem was with whiskey and the saloons that pushed such products. Certainly they wouldn't target beer. They were wrong, and both national and world events were working against them.

Throughout the late 1890s and early 1900s the subject of Prohibition gained more and more attention. It was during this same period that individual states were slowly providing rights to a large and previously disenfranchised group of citizens. As women gained the right to vote, they were drawn to the progressive movement, and with it the cause of Prohibitionists.

In 1893 a "Committee of Fifty" was formed to study the problem of alcohol. This group determined and attempted to prove that many of the country's problems of crime and poverty were directly linked to the consumption of alcoholic beverages. Citing prior efforts to ease the problem, they explained why these former temperance campaigns failed. They reckoned the previous laws didn't work because they were instituted on only local and state levels. It was fairly easy for those citizens who desired to cross borders to neighboring communities that provided an uninterrupted source of alcohol. They were convinced the only solution was national Prohibition—complete abstinence. Still the brewers were unconcerned. Surely this would be limited to the distillers. How could any group possibly be against beer?

As the horrors of World War I unfolded, the Prohibitionists found a ready tool placed at their disposal, ethnic bias. Most brewers were of German descent, and the temperance army would prove effective in using this weapon as war approached and nationalistic feelings rose. By the convening of Congress in 1917, the stage was set for an escalated battle with beer producers. Drawing on hatred of Germany and all things German, the dries had secured full attention of the national legislature.

On September 8, 1917, Wilson was granted war powers under a Food Control Act, which enabled him to limit or prohibit the manufacture of beer and wine as he saw fit. Proposed under the thin guise of conserving agricultural resources, it was actually the work of Prohibitionists. Not willing to offend either faction, Wilson did not eliminate beer, but did reduce production by thirty percent and limited the alcohol content to 2.75 percent by weight. Finally the brewers grew concerned, but it would prove too late.

The more significant legislative action was a motion that called for a resolution for a constitutional amendment prohibiting intoxicating beverages. In an effort to defeat the amendment, Senator Harding suggested a five-year limit for ratification in the hope it would never gain the necessary three-fourths approval. He found himself in an ugly battle with none other than Ohio's behind-the-scenes string puller Wayne Wheeler, who held out for six years, figuring it could easily pass in that time. Both were wrong. As it turned out, all the arguing and bad blood could have been avoided. When put to a vote, Prohibition was ratified in a bit more than one year as the required thirty-sixth state passed the provision in January 1919. Eventually only Connecticut and Rhode Island would refuse to ratify the amendment, but under the law of the land, they would have to obey it.

Prohibition was a certainty, but legislation was needed to provide enforcement. The brewers mounted a frantic effort by introducing clinical data that supported the theory that no one could become intoxicated on 2.75 percent beer. Once again Wheeler proved a crafty opponent. Using Representative Andrew Volstead of Minnesota as his outlet, he orchestrated the provisions of the bill. Introduced as the National Prohibition Act, and thereafter known as the Volstead Act, it defined intoxicating beverages as anything containing more than 0.5 percent alcohol. President Wilson finally took a stand and vetoed the bill but was overridden by a nervous Congress eyeing reelection in October of 1919. Brewers led by Jacob Ruppert of New York made one last attempt to combat these provisions through the Supreme Court. Bringing forward studies that claimed alcohol levels as high as 2.75 percent were not intoxicating, they hoped to hold off the worst of the law. It was too little too late. The court upheld the law, and on January 17, 1920, the country officially went dry. The noble experiment, a term borrowed from Herbert Hoover, wasn't.

Brewers who had known nothing but unlimited success were now shocked into reality. Looking for any means to keep their businesses alive, they resorted to making near beer, which was universally scorned. The public reaction to near beer was best summed up in the remark "Whoever called it near beer was a poor judge of distance!" Without an alternative, the once proud breweries had resorted to the unthinkable. Various attempts to improve near beer resulted in strange names rolling out of the plants.

Pabst	Pablo
Schlitz	Famo
Miller	Vivo
Stroh	Lux-o
Wiedemann	Quizz
Anheuser-Busch	Pivo

Eventually the brewers turned to other products. Schlitz tried candy and chocolate, Coors made malted products including malted milk, Blatz went to industrial alcohol, Yuengling made an elixir called Juvetonic, F. X. Matts brought out a line of soda pop, Miller introduced cereal beverages, and Pabst tried the unlikely combination of tonic and cheese products. It was during this baptism by fire that the brewers who would emerge from the bad times really learned what being in business was about.

The biggest misconception about this period is that the country actually went dry. In reality it never did. Most of the population never supported Prohibition, and a poll taken in 1926 indicated only 19 percent of Americans favored the Eighteenth Amendment. What the dissidents did was to make their drinking private. With this new practice at least one business made out well—the speakeasies. At the onset of Prohibition the country had an estimated 177,000 saloons in operation, which were replaced by private clubs operating on the fringe of the underworld. In New York alone more than 32,000 speakeasies enjoyed a lively trade right through Prohibition's darkest nights.

The other great change was a turn to the past. With no alcohol produced in the United States, and with much more money to be made with an equal volume of hard liquor in place of beer, smugglers concentrated on the high return of bringing in whiskey, gin, or rum. Beer drinkers suffered and the consumption of beer hit an all-time low. Of course, the real hard core beer lovers weren't to be denied; they were merely forced to turn to the only recourse available, the ancient and patriotic custom of homebrewing. Breweries that turned to production of malt extract inadvertently made the brewing of beer at home easier than ever. Writer H. L. Mencken reported:

> Every second household has become a homebrewer . . . In one American city of 750,000 inhabitants there are now 100 shops devoted exclusively to the sale of beer-making supplies, and lately the proprietor of one of them, by no means the largest, told me that he sold 2,000 pounds of malt-syrup a day.

So Americans separated from their favorite beverage took to brewing their homemade beer while they waited for salvation.

The first true fight for repeal came in 1928 with presidential candidate Al Smith of New York. Al made repeal a major part of his campaign. Unfortunately, he lost. His defeat can be blamed on the public's opposition to electing a Catholic into the White House, and as a result the temperance crowd was given a reprieve. But what Al Smith did accomplish was to get the country thinking and talking. By the next election, allies to the "wets" were stepping forward. Some of the notables who bucked the political influence of the dries included General "Black Jack" Pershing of World War I fame, Mr. Walter Chrysler, Dr. John Mott, Mr. Sloan of General Motors, and Mr. Harvey Firestone, the tire giant. But the most improbable was Mr. John D. Rockefeller. A teetotaler, Rockefeller was above all a busi-

nessman, and of course, the country was deep within the
Great Depression. Rockefeller wrote,

> Failure of the Eighteenth Amendment has demonstrated
> that the majority of this country are not yet ready for total
> abstinence, at least when it is attempted through legal coer-
> cion. The next best thing—many people think it a better
> thing—is temperance. Therefore, as I sought to support total
> abstinence when its achievement seemed possible, so now,
> and with equal vigor, I would support temperance.

The business community recognized beer as a piece of
the economic recovery. Even people who made fortunes
during Prohibition looked forward to its end. Al Capone
said, "Prohibition has made nothing but trouble—for all of
us." This was a major turning point, and the brewers and
beer-loving public cast hopeful eyes on the election of
1932.

Several of the candidates were prepared to make Prohibition a campaign issue, and the Democratic nominee made
it a pledge. Nine days after being sworn in, FDR asked
Congress to amend the Volstead Act and raise the alcohol
limit of beer to 3.2 percent. It was a very thirsty Congress
that immediately complied. The higher limit went into effect on April 7, 1933, and essentially spelled the end to
Prohibition, which, though still in effect, would shortly be
repealed by the Twenty-first Amendment.

At midnight of April 7 the beer began to flow. On a nationwide radio hookup, Gussie Busch stepped up to a mi-
crophone and, using FDR's campaign song, observed,
"Happy days are here again." Then, striding over to a bar,
he beamed as he pronounced, "Gentlemen, beer is served!"
In Washington, D.C., the president received shipments of
beer from nearly every grateful brewer in the country, and
to the delight of the Washington press corps, he turned it
over to a jubilant group of newspapermen. Meanwhile in
New York, Anheuser-Busch had not forgotten the courage
of former candidate Smith. As Al walked out of the Empire
State Building, one of his other accomplishments, he was
met at midnight by a team of Clydesdales pulling a wagon
full of Budweiser beer. By the time the party wound down,

a satiated American public had consumed over one million gallons of beer.

In retrospect it didn't matter whether or not FDR liked beer, or even if he thought Prohibition was wrong. He knew he had to get the nation back to work, and at the same time generate some tax income for the government. His stand on repeal was simply a matter of doing what made sense. But the cost had been high. Of sixteen hundred pre-Prohibition breweries, only about seven hundred reopened. Underfinanced and burdened with obsolete equipment, five hundred of these would soon be out of business, which had a tremendous and long-lasting impact on American beer.

CHAPTER 11

The Westward Expansion

*I drink when I have occasion, and sometimes
when I have no occasion.*

—CERVANTES

Miners, Pioneers, Farmers, and the New Brewing Centers

Prior to takeovers, market squeezing, Prohibition, mass marketing, and homogenization of style, the United States enjoyed a golden age of beer. The brewing centers provided their regional customers with full-bodied and lively-tasting beers, and their story of success paralleled the growth of the nation as the brewers followed closely in the footsteps of the pioneers making their way west.

Beer was always a popular drink in New York, but after the Croton Reservoir system eased the city's water problems, things really took off. New York was the home for many of the German settlers who would land ashore and immediately settle, and wherever there were Germans, beer was always in great demand. The first of the growing number of New York brewers was George Gillig, but others soon followed to create a resurgence in New York brewing. Within three decades of completing the reservoir system, the city would be a leading producer of beer, and in 1877 George Ehret led the country with output of more than 139,000 barrels. Two years later New York had seventy-eight breweries, and Brooklyn, which was then a separate city, had forty-three more.

One of the famous names to emerge from this frantic pace of brewery expansion came from a grocery store. Arriving in America with the first wave of his German countrymen in 1835, Franz Ruppert started his business life peddling produce. Franz did well but by 1850 was ready for a change, and so he purchased the Aktien Brauerei. Borrowing the name of his section of the city, Ruppert renamed the young enterprise Turtle Bay Brewing, and after enlisting the help of his son, Jacob Ruppert Sr., he began making beer.

As Jacob Sr. learned the ins and outs of brewing, he greatly furthered his position by marrying the daughter of George Gillig. As the son of one brewer and son-in-law of another, it was only a matter of time until he set out on his own. That time came in 1867 as Jacob turned twenty-five, just two years before his father would sell out his interest in Turtle Bay. Jacob started small, and legend has it he cut timber and cleared the land for the brewhouse with his own hands and then started making beer in a facility that measured only fifty square feet.

Ruppert's beer enjoyed great popularity, and before long he was constructing a real brewery on what is now Ninety-second Street and Third Avenue. Fortune smiled on his efforts and Ruppert's new plant produced five thousand barrels in its first year. As lager's popularity grew in the last half of the 1800s, so did Ruppert's fortunes, and in 1874 he constructed a new plant. Taking full advantage of the advances in refrigeration, he built icehouses in 1877 and 1880 and set on a path that would make him one of the biggest brewers in the country. Surprisingly, Ruppert never expanded beyond the metropolitan market. There was no need to, though, because New Yorkers loved his beer and apparently couldn't get enough of it. As time passed, Jacob Sr.'s wealth expanded. Of particular satisfaction was when, following family tradition, Jacob Jr., born in 1867, also joined the business. By 1916 Jacob Jr.

hit the magic figure of one million barrels, the first non-national brewer to achieve this milestone.

Rupert achieved real fame, however, the year before brewing a million barrels. In 1915 he and a partner, Cap Huston, purchased the New York Yankees Baseball team for $460,000. By 1919 he was building the team into a powerhouse that would dominate four decades of baseball, and he started it by making a deal, with the cash-poor Red Sox, for a pitcher-outfielder named George Herman Ruth.

Only one other diversion followed Ruppert's purchase of the Yankees. When World War I broke out, the Rupperts responded in the same manner as other German-American brewing families. In addition to providing financial backing through war bonds, Jacob Jr., a colonel in the New York National Guard, served in the conflict with distinction during combat in France. On returning home, and even after serving three terms in the U.S. Congress, he would always be best known for his military service and was respectfully referred to as "the colonel."

Ruppert's heroic return to New York was dulled by the waiting embrace of Prohibition. This wasn't exactly the type of welcome home any GI expected. Disturbed and uncertain of their future, the Ruppert family nevertheless was lucky; business had been good and with a fortune secured, they remained well off.

Jacob Jr., in a respite from the business demands of running a brewery, resumed a sporting life and could be seen regularly on Long Island Sound in his magnificent yacht the *Albatross*. He was an active member of the Atlantic, Larchmont, and New York yacht clubs, the latter of which was the regular defender of the America's Cup. But his ties to sailing stretched even further. He was such a large contributor to Admiral Byrd's second expedition to the Antarctic that the expedition's flagship was christened the *Jacob Ruppert*. Ruppert was overjoyed, and to ensure the fifty-six-man crew had enough to drink, he packed along twelve hundred cases of beer, which works out to more than twenty-one cases for each crew member.

Through all this, Ruppert's first love remained baseball. The Yankees started to roll at this point, and the baseball Giants were growing more than testy about sharing the Polo Grounds with the new juggernaut. Thus it was no surprise when they asked the Yankees to find another home. So Ruppert decided to build a proper showcase for his team. What a palace it turned out to be. Yankee Stadium became the largest private construction project then known to the world, opening on April 18, 1923, to a sell-out crowd of nearly sixty thousand fans. For decades after, when New Yorkers thought of baseball, they thought of Ruppert Beer.

Two problems with Ruppert Brewing were magnified after repeal. Although among the leaders in selling a million barrels, Ruppert never moved beyond the regional New York market, and during Prohibition there were no plans made to modernize equipment. By the end of World War II the company made hurried attempts to expand, but time had passed Ruppert by, leaving one more brewery tombstone. Still, thousands of New Yorkers fondly recall the colonel's brewery up on Third Avenue.

The Ruppert success story is all the more remarkable for its context. Remember, New York was also the home of other famous breweries. One of those was founded by a young immigrant who arrived in 1838. As a twenty-one-year-old from Wetzlar, Prussia, Frederick Schaefer had arrived in the city and soon gained employment in Sebastian Sommers's Manhattan Brewery; he had his plan for success. The next year he sent for his brother Maximilian. Working as a team, the two saved their earnings like misers, but in three short years they amassed enough to buy out their employer, and in 1842 they were New York's first lager brewers. Their original brewery was located near what is now Grand Central Station. Soon enough they were moving operations uptown to Park Avenue (then called Fourth Avenue) and Fifty-first. By 1915 the beer was successful enough to open a large plant across the East River, joining the legacy of Brooklyn breweries.

Schaefer also remained solvent throughout Prohibition through the guidance of Rudy Schaefer, who assumed control at age twenty-seven in 1927. The youngest brewery president in the United States, he led the company by the production of ice and near beer. Then, after repeal, Schaefer's enjoyed a second stretch of golden years. The company reopened the Brooklyn plant but managed to acquire the facilities of Beverwyck Brewery in Albany, New York; Baltimore's Gunther plant from Theodore Hamm; and the Standard Brewing Company of Cleveland, Ohio. These made Schaefer a power in the nation's population centers. All the older plants terminated operations in the late 1960s, but in a move unlike Ruppert's, the company was able to stay in business by constructing a modern brewery outside New York in the Lehigh Valley near Allentown, Pennsylvania. The plan worked and in the 1970s Schaefer enjoyed eighth place among U.S. brewers. In 1981 Schaefer was acquired by Stroh, which maintained the brand in its stable of beers.

Another immigrant to make good in New York was Samuel Liebman. Born in 1799 in Württemberg, Germany, Liebman was an old, experienced beer man when he finally made the crossing in 1854. Building a brewery in Brooklyn, he created another of those handful of beers to become a New York favorite.

Liebman's flagship brand, Rheingold, borrowed its name from a Wagner opera, but Liebman wasn't the only one with that idea. There were at least two other successful Rheingold beers. One was by Weibrod & Hess of Philadelphia, and the other was produced by a conglomeration named United States Brewing of Chicago. It was actually the United States Brewing Company that introduced the marketing concept that would become Liebman's trademark, a "Rheingold Girl." The first Miss Rheingold appeared in their ads as early as 1911.

When Sam died in 1872, his sons assumed control and changed the name to S. Liebman's Sons. Up until the early 1900s they expanded the company holdings through a plan that had them absorbing other local breweries. Riding out Prohibition, the company remained comfortably profitable until aging plants caught up with the company in the 1970s.

It began to seem as though a brother partnership like the Schaefers' and Liebman's sons was the ticket to New York beer success, and Gottfried Piels's sons, Michael and Wilhelm, weren't about to change what worked. They entered the New York beer world from Düsseldorf, Germany, in 1882, and by the next year they had purchased a brewhouse in Brooklyn's East New York. The company was noted for several innovations, which included bottling in colored glass, a technique that would protect the beer from breaking down in sunlight. They were also noted along with Anheuser-Busch as the first to introduce an automatic pasteurizer.

Yet one more noteworthy New York name was located in Brooklyn. The famous Bushwick neighborhood was the gathering place for a "row" of brewers including Trommer's. In 1896 John Trommer purchased the Stehlin and Britkopf brewery, changed the name to "Evergreen," and prospered, as did many brewers through the late 1800s. Unlike others, Trommer found a rather unique way to ride out Prohibition. He made a shrewdly calculated move by lending money to people interested in starting hot dog stands. But as with a lot of loans, there was a catch. Part of the loan agreement stipulated the vendors were required to feature Trommer's White Label Near Beer. Between the interest on the loans and distribution of his near beer, Trommer's was one of the few brewers to actually expand during the noble experiment. Unfortunately Trommer's also succumbed to the price of doing business in New York. It met its end when the company's two plants were eventually sold off, the Newark plant going to Rheingold and the Brooklyn facility to the Piels brothers.

The major brewers in New York City eventually came to the same fateful end. High real estate prices, taxes, and labor costs led to impossible financial conditions. When union truck drivers called a strike against city breweries, it was done with some compassion for local beer drinkers—out-of-town beer was still delivered. This is when the St. Louis and Milwaukee beers first got a foot in the door. Following years of dreaming about cracking the fierce Gotham beer market, they finally realized what a prize was to be had. An aggressive sales force did the rest, and the New York brewing scene was slowly flattened.

High times weren't just limited to New York. As mentioned earlier, Pennsylvania was the early brewing capital of the nation, with its large percentage of citizens of German extraction. (One village was even named Germantown.) Philadelphia alone had more than ninety-four breweries by 1879. And of all the breweries still operating in the United States, the oldest is located in Pottsville, Pennsylvania. In 1806 David Yeungling was born in Germany, and at the age of twenty-two, crossed the Atlantic. His search for clean brewing water led him to his new home west of Philadelphia. Just a year after his arrival, he was already running his own brewery. Like Matthew Vassar, Yeungling endured destruction of his brewery by fire, which struck in 1831, and just like Vassar, he rebuilt the operation and continued on. Yeungling became highly regarded for its beers, and guided by David, who ran the company until his death in 1876, Yeungling achieved a ranking of eighteenth among the country's brewers. This at a time when Pennsylvania had more than 360 breweries, each carving out its own market.

Fredrick G. Yeungling and his brothers had entered the company in 1873 and the name was changed to D. G. Yeungling and Sons. Fredrick rose among his siblings to assume control after his father's passing and guided the company well despite the attempts to expand with two New York City breweries in the late 1800s. Both facilities were located on 128th street, one at Fifth Avenue and the other at Tenth. Unfortunately both operated at a loss from the time they were established until their closing in 1884 and 1897 respectively. Despite this, the Pottsville brewery remained strong, and during Prohibition the company survived by producing near beer and other cereal-based beverages.

The importance and size of Philadelphia brewing is borne out by its claim as site of the first lager brewing in America. And it certainly turned this to its advantage, gaining a reputation as a major brewing center. One of the most famous Philadelphia concerns was the firm of Bergner & Engel.

The company started brewing in the 1840s as a partnership of Charles Wolf and Charles Engel. Interestingly, it was Wolf who credited Wagner of Philadelphia as the first lager brewer in the country through an article he published in 1903. But it was the retirement of Wolf that resulted in Engel entering a new partnership with Gustavus Bergner. Situated in the nation's third largest city, the company thrived, and by 1877 it ranked third in U.S. production. Brewing was suspended throughout Prohibition and resumed briefly after repeal. Sadly, the problem was the same that brought an end to many other brewers. The outmoded facilities and equipment could no longer be operated efficiently, and thus Bergner & Engel shut their doors forever.

The other significant brewer of this time was William Massey, who, with a number of partners, had founded an ale brewery in 1849. By 1870 Massey gained full control, and under his guidance the brewery rose to eleventh in the country by 1877. Unfortunately, the importance of Massey's leadership became painfully evident with his passing. Following Massey's death in 1891, the brewery survived its namesake by only a few years.

Philadelphia brewing names that lived into the late 1900s included a small brewery started in 1860 by August Kuehl, who sold it to Henry Ortlieb in 1893. The Ortlieb family remained in control and was as widely respected as the brewery founded by Christian Schmidt, C. Schmidt & Sons, which was founded by Christian on his arrival in the United States from Württemberg, Germany (also the home of New York brewer S. Liebman). Schmidt headed operations until his death in 1895 when his son Edward A. Schmidt took control and guided the company through several acquisitions and Prohibition. By the late 1970s the company had grown to tenth largest in the country and the name Schmidt's was nearly synonymous with Philadelphia. By 1987 this was reduced to a memory as the Schmidt's brew kettle emptied for the last time.

As the country moved westward, brewers followed to satisfy the thirst of a growing population, sometimes even before there was much of a population. On the western end of the state, Pittsburgh was just such a town, poised to build a brewing heritage as it built itself into a city.

As early as 1795, following the Whiskey Rebellion, a Scotsman named Peter Shiras decided the town needed a brewery. His plan was to satisfy the seemingly unquenchable demand for ale and porter beer by both the city's residents and the passing tide of settlers heading west. This brewery was located at the confluence of the Allegheny and Monongahela Rivers, and the point of land was both the location of the brewery and its eventual name, "Point," which came to life in 1802. By 1815 the town had four breweries, and a street on the point had been renamed "Brewhouse Alley." Sadly, the people attending Three Rivers Stadium are largely unaware of the significance of their location.

By 1890 there were in excess of thirty breweries in the Pittsburgh area. As was the trend of those times, consolidation took place and twenty-one breweries joined together to form the Pittsburgh Brewing Company. Pittsburgh is also noted as the home of "Miss Frothingslosh," a marketing invention that claimed to be both "the beer with the foam on the bottom" and "the stale pale ale for the stale pale male." But in the modern era it would become more known as the home of contract brewing.

The customers of the early brewers of Pittsburgh were settlers about to make the trip down the Ohio River to westward lands. Of course, a person could get mighty thirsty on a flatboat, and this came to be a boon for a river town. Like other new cities in the young nation, Cincinnati was founded on the banks of a navigable river and located in a position that was a focus for both the overland emigrants from southerly directions and those waterborne travelers from Pittsburgh. It was a natural stop before heading on to the Mississippi and westward up the Missouri.

First settled in 1788, Cincinnati was built upon land purchased by New Jersey Congressman John Cleves Symmes, who, like nearly all politicians and people of money in those days, was inclined to speculate on western lands. In the case of Congressman Cleves, his intuition proved correct and the city grew in rapid fashion. As with other brewing centers, Cincinnati can give thanks for its beer to the many Germans who came to call the Ohio River town their home. So many, in fact, that one neighborhood was nicknamed the "Over the Rhine" section of town.

With such a naturally large supply of customers, no time at all was lost on constructing the first brewery. Credited to Davis Embree, it was built at 75 Water Street sometime before 1810. Later, in 1816, David Thomas wrote about the operation, "The works now in a progressive state, are now sufficiently extensive to produce annually five thousand barrels of beer and porter, and the quality is excellent." Embree wouldn't be without local competition for long. Even at the time of Thomas's visit, there were other breweries springing up. An 1815 report by Daniel Drake outlined the extent of the city's brewing. "Their products are beer, porter and ale, of a quality at least equal to that of the Atlantic States. Large quantities have been exported to the Mississippi, even as far as New Orleans, the climate of which they are found to bear very well."

By 1844 the first of the lager brewers appeared, courtesy of Fortmann & Company. As elsewhere, the success of lager was immediate, and for good reason. Over ten thousand Germans were among the city's forty-three thousand residents by 1840. The effect of the German population shouldn't be underestimated; the city had one of the largest consumptions of beer per capita in the United States. Some speculate that had it not been the era before refrigeration, when Milwaukee had easier access to natural ice, then Cincinnati might have become the beer capital of the country.

One of the famous names in Cincinnati brewing was Christian Moerlein. Born in Truppach, Bavaria, in 1818, he emigrated to the United States in 1841. To make ends meet he took up blacksmithing. It could have been his heritage or destiny that led him to brewing, or perhaps it was the heat of the bellows-fanned furnace that made him dream of beer. The motivation is secondary to the results, which began taking shape in 1853. It was then he opened a brewery in partnership with Adam Dillman. Only one year later Dillman passed away and Moerlein found a new associate in Conrad Windisch. The new relationship would last twelve years until Windisch struck off on his own to found yet another famous brewery, Lion.

In 1872 Christian's son George took control and expanded operations throughout the 1870s and 1880s. By 1875 the brewery ranked thirteenth in the nation, and in 1895 still held the fourteenth spot. Unfortunately George passed away in 1891 just as the company was positioning itself as a national brewer. Lacking aggressive drive and leadership, the company started its decline. Without an efficient rail system, the brewery made a short go at surviving Prohibition by producing a near beer called Chrismo, but 1919 brought the end of brewing.

Another of the Cincinnati pre-Prohibition breweries was established by John Hauck. Arriving from Germany in 1852, he started beer making in 1863. Named the Dayton

Street Brewery, it changed hands when Louis Hauck, the son of John, assumed control in the mid-1890s. The company attempted to limp through the dry years by marketing near beer but was forced to shut down in 1927.

As bad as it sometimes looks, Prohibition didn't shut down all breweries; sometimes there were surprises. But just as surprising as the survival of Hudelpohl Brewing was the birthplace of its founder. Going against the near prerequisite of birth in Germany was Louis Hudelpohl, who was as homegrown as you get. Born in Cincinnati, he was a late entry on the city's brewing scene in 1885, but through determination he built a well-regarded, and well-sampled, business. When Louis died in 1902 his widow, Mary Elizabeth, also bucked trends by taking over as president. Through expert management she survived Prohibition with the production of near beer and soda pop. On repeal Mary Hudelpohl had rightfully earned her retirement, and through it all she never doubted a woman could run a major brewery. It's no wonder her choice as successor was her daughter, Celia Hesselbrock, who went on to run the brewery an additional thirty-six years.

As late a start as Hudelpohl made, it still wasn't the last out of the blocks; in fact, the other famous Cincinnati brewing concern didn't even get a start until 1933. Schoenling Brewing Company was established to take advantage of Prohibition's demise, and in another nonconformist move, the company built a strong following carried on the appeal of its ales. In 1986 Schoenling merged with the last of its local rivals, Hudelpohl, and continued on Cincinnati's brewing past by resorting back to the town's original brew in the form of "Little Kings Cream Ale" and "Sir Edward Stout," proving after all that you can go home again.

Cincinnati never was a terminus. It was a byway through which traders, pioneers, and businessmen moving west traveled on their way to the area around southern Lake Michigan. A most inviting place, the flat, fertile land beckoned many farmers and settlers. Even more valued was its access to the interconnecting Great Lakes, a vast network of rivers that made transportation to a large area of the interior frontier easy. The people simply found it irresistible and began building one of America's great cities. Chicago would become known as the hog slayer of the world, the city of broad shoulders, the home of the first American saint, and the site of the first nuclear reactor and chain reaction. It was also a home to beer.

Recognition as the city's first brewer goes to either Adolph Mueller or William Lill in 1833. Of these two, Lill is more widely credited, mostly because of his success. Lill's first partner was William Haas, and together they built the company's first facility on the city's west side. In 1840 Michael Diversey bought out Haas, and with a new partner the Lill & Diversey brewery grew with the region. By 1860 the company was producing nearly forty-five thousand barrels per annum for a market that stretched the length of the Great Lakes and down the nearby Mississippi. The ale, stout, and porter from Lill & Diversey was enjoyed from Buffalo to St. Paul, and as far as St. Joseph, Missouri, to New Orleans.

Other early brewers included J. J. Sands, who opened the Columbian Brewery on the corner of Pearson and Pine Streets in 1855. After establishing a reputation for ales, he expanded into the tough Milwaukee market through a buyout of the Spring Brewery. A Milwaukee newspaper welcomed the newcomer and provided sales assistance through a review that read:

SANDS of Chicago have been eminently successful in manufacturing . . . the wholesome qualities of English Porter, without any of its deleterious characteristics. They have produced an article of ale, which has become a staple of commerce all over the Union, and is universally acknowledged by good judges to be a healthier and better drink than the imported bottles.

Unfortunately, Chicago's soil and subsurface strata were soft, porous, and spongy, making it almost impossible to dig the basements and caves necessary to ferment lager beer. This feature, despite an inexhaustible supply of ice, made lager brewing slow to arrive. But as elsewhere, when introduced, lager rapidly won the hearts and taste buds of the population. The first of these breweries was built by John Huck in 1847. Many more quickly followed, most building on the North Side where the ground was slightly higher.

The other part of the Huck story involves Frederick Leh-mann, who arrived from Germany in 1848 and formed a partnership with Conrad Seipp. The two began brewing in 1854 by renting the M. Best Brewery until it was destroyed by fire in 1855. Fires were common in old breweries be-cause of the combination of grain dust and open flames. Slowed only temporarily by this setback, the two soon built their own brewhouse and resumed production of their in-creasingly popular beer.

Eventually Conrad Seipp bought out his partner. Then in 1872 he began merging with other brewers, as was being done in Pittsburgh and elsewhere. Among those absorbed was Huck, along with the G. Biellen Malt House, forming the Chicago Consolidated Brewery and Malting Company. Seipp was so successful that by 1877 production had reached 95,167 barrels, ranking the brewery fifth in the country. By 1895 it still held the number nine spot.

Other breweries were also consolidated during the great British buying spree of the late 1800s. The Downer and Bemis Brewing Company, which became Bemis and Mc-Avoy and finally McAvoy, joined the Wacker and Birk Brewing and Malting company, among others, as a consoli-dation that produced the Chicago Breweries, Limited.

During this period America was becoming entranced with industry and science. Thus it was inevitable that a marriage of these and beer should take place with Chicago as the setting. As early as 1868 scholars gathered to ana-lyze, poke, prod, and otherwise dissect beer, the year when a German immigrant and doctor founded the Zymotechnic Institute for the purpose of studying beer making and fer-mentation. The school is to this day known by the name of its founder, Dr. John Ewald Siebel. Schools such as Sie-bel's conducted research in brewing science and served as the training ground for brewers. Discoveries were also a part of the business, and success could mean instant re-ward. Such was the case with the research team at Chica-go's Takamine Ferment Company, where they identified a method of using corn as a base grain in beer, a throwback to the early methods used by the Pilgrims. But it made the company millions and set the stage for the later dilution of American beer.

One of the most amazing stories about Chicago beer had

far-reaching political overtones. Through the middle to late 1800s the discontented of Ireland were aligning themselves with Germans against the English. This alliance was so strong, it even extended as far as Chicago, where a group who hated anything to do with foreign culture was about to come to power.

The Know-Nothings, an ultraconservative, xenophobic group, managed to elect their candidate, Dr. Levi Boone, to the mayor's seat. Mayor Boone had a bone to pick with the Germans who had formed their own neighborhoods, churches, trade unions, and even theater. This was all just too foreign for the mayor to bear, and he looked upon beer drinking as one of those evils uniquely German and definitely un-American. When combined with the Irish, a group looked down upon throughout the country, it was plain unacceptable. Taking it as a personal challenge, he set out to right this alien wrong and harm both groups as much as possible. The weapon he chose was beer.

In a move aimed directly at both the Germans and their Irish buddies, he increased liquor license fees by 600 percent and coupled this with a three-month moratorium on issuing licenses. Next he ordered enforcement of an old law prohibiting alcohol and beer sales on Sunday. There was no doubt who Boone was targeting; it was all those small taverns located on the North Side of town where the Germans lived near their beloved breweries.

On the first Sunday the law was implemented, over two hundred German beer drinkers were arrested and a trial date was set for April 21, 1855. As the morning's court was about to open, a crowd of three hundred barkeepers approached Courthouse Square complete with fife and drum and threats for the judge. Proceeding to Randolph and Clark Streets, the column was headed off by the police and forced back toward the North Side. Later, about three o'clock in the afternoon, the protestors returned. This time the police were ready, and after about half the crowd had crossed the river, they opened the drawbridge to split the opposition forces. This only further ignited the group, and it was then the police learned the North Siders had armed themselves. Shooting broke out and both sides suffered casualties. As night fell, things quieted, but the beer lovers had made their point and Boone eased his hate campaign.

The long-range effect of the "Chicago Lager Beer Riots" was to discredit the Know-Nothing party, which faded from the Windy City's political scene.

Yet this wasn't the city's most famous incident regarding beer; that would be reserved for an event that would virtually destroy it. Ask anyone to name one thing they know about Chicago and the most frequent response would be the Great Chicago Fire. It had a big impact on beer. Nearly one third of the city was made homeless on that night of October 8, 1871, and as the fire swept north, the breweries were among the casualties. Many rebuilt, but not before the beer companies from Milwaukee had taken advantage of the misfortune of Chicago's brewers by grabbing a huge share of the beer market.

There were some periods of resurgence such as during the Chicago World's fair of 1892 when over a million barrels were sold in the city. But the real blow came during Prohibition. As law-abiding breweries tried to limp along, the mob gangs of Bugsy Malone and Al Capone became rich by running as many as twenty breweries right through Prohibition and making more than $100 million in the process. More than any other city in the country, Chicago enjoyed its speakeasy-supplied beer with barely a ripple to disturb its flow. In the wake of such unfair competition, the real breweries went belly-up. Those gangland-controlled breweries that managed to survive the crusade of Elliot Ness soon joined the closures as the repeal of Prohibition brought an end to their massive, and illegal, beer profits. Although a few small breweries hung on, the business all but vanished as the neighboring cities of St. Louis and Milwaukee quenched the thirst of those along the lake.

Today Milwaukee is only a couple hours drive away, but in the 1800s it might have been another world. Despite ready access by water, the local brewers of Chicago had business pretty well wrapped up. But if ever there was a city where brewers could succeed, it was Milwaukee. A good harbor and access to a wide area of distribution, plentiful ice, subterranean rock that lent itself to lagering caves, and the settlement of German immigrants; it had everything in place for the first brewers to open up shop and make their fortune. How unusual it was that the first brewery was owned and run not by Germans, but by three Welshmen. Richard Owens, William Pallet, and John Davis opened an English-style brewhouse producing ales in 1840, and called their enterprise the Milwaukee Brewery.

Starting with a copper-lined wooden box as a brew kettle, they began making five barrels at a time. A year later Owens secured a true kettle from Chicago and more than doubled production. By 1845 the name had changed to the Lake Brewery and Owens had bought out his partners. Tired of brewing, Owens rented out the facility to a Powell and Pritchard from Chicago, who continued to run it until going out of business in 1880. The cause of death was the same as elsewhere. The only ale brewery in Milwaukee, it succumbed to lager's popularity.

Two of Milwaukee's big three breweries can trace their origin not only to the same year, but to the same man. In 1844, when Wisconsin was still a territory, Jacob Best started what would turn into one of brewing's most recognized names. Best was yet another of the many German immigrants who shaped the country's brewing history, and he began in the same fashion as his peers, opening a brewery with his four sons. Phillip, Charles, Lorenz, and Jacob Jr. made a significant contribution to the operation while absorbing the details of brewery start-up and operation. The name they selected to represent their venture was Best Brewing Co.

A high concentration of German settlers and a midwestern climate perfectly matched to the light, crisp taste of lager helped propel the business toward success. Following eleven years of growth, Jacob Sr. made the decision to retire in 1853. His desire to have the business continue on with people he could trust resulted in his selling the company to his sons Phillip and Jacob Jr. Within a few years Phillip bought out brother Jacob's half interest. Now with one owner calling the shots, nearly everything was in place to vault the brewery to national attention. But fate added one last element needed to fulfill destiny.

Off the shores of Milwaukee a steamboat captain plied the often chilly waters of Lake Michigan. On stops to the port of Milwaukee the captain engaged in the activities expected of sailors "on the beach" and started courting a young woman who would lure him from life upon the water.

There are several classic ways to become partners in a brewery. One, of course, is through hard work as a loyal apprentice. Another is to acquire enough capital in other business to "buy in" to the brewery. Finally, the most popular method of the 1800s was strategic wedlock. Before the days of stockholders, and until the 1980s tactics of hostile takeovers, the path to quick riches was an 1800s version of corporate raiding. It worked for Adolphus Busch and Jacob Ruppert, and what was good enough for them was good enough for Captain Frederick Pabst, who in 1862 married Phillip Best's daughter Maria. Actually this judgment may be a little harsh. The captain worked another two years before taking a position at the brewery.

In 1864 Captain Pabst became Phillip Best's partner. A quick study, Pabst soon worked toward an understanding of the business, and it was a good thing, for Best had retirement on his mind and was anxious to see a replacement. In two short years Pabst went from grasping concepts to grasping the reins. When Best retired in 1866 it was Frederick, along with Emil Schandein, another son-in-law, who bought control of the company from Phillip.

In 1873 the business was incorporated as the Phillip Best Brewing Company. Things rolled along in a smooth fashion with strong sales and quiet expansion for the next nine years. Then in 1882 the company made a move that would eventually alter its name.

During this period of the late 1800s brewers used awards they captured as a major marketing tool. It almost seemed they felt success was keyed to obtaining a testimonial. Even more than a hundred years ago, the idea of image was popular and Pabst came up with a great one. Somebody in the company suggested the company's "Select" brand could be more marketable with the adornment of a little piece of blue ribbon around the neck. All this seemed rather simple, cheap, and harmless, so they gave it a try. The results were nothing short of amazing. Sales rocketed and Select was catapulted into a position of outstanding popularity. It was all Frederick Pabst needed as he steered an ambitious course emphasizing bottling, establishment of agencies to distribute the beer, and development of a rail system for shipment. As a result, Best Brewing surged toward the nation's number one brewing spot.

Shortly after starting the "Blue Ribbon," the company was using more than three hundred thousand yards of the blue silk every year. At Schandein's passing in 1888, Pabst assumed complete control of the company, and a year later it was renamed Pabst Brewing. But the most significant milestone would come a year later in 1892 when the business would be the first to break the million-barrel-a-year mark as the nation's number one brewer. Frederick passed away in 1904 and left the company to his sons Fred Jr. and Gustav. During Prohibition the brewery put out malt syrup, tonic, cheese, and near beer.

From the brewery originally built by Jacob Best Sr., Pabst grew into one of the national brewing leaders. But Pabst wasn't the end of old Jacob Best's legacy. Two of his other sons, Charles and Lorenz, were also to benefit from experience gained in the family brewery. While Phillip was off building Pabst, Charles and Lorenz entered into a partnership called Best Brothers and began making beer at Plank Road Brewery, also known as Menomonee Valley.

While they slowly established business in the early 1850s, a brewer to the royal court in Hohenzollern, Germany, migrated across the Atlantic. Working for a time in Rochester, New York, he subsequently roamed the United States for almost a year until he settled on Milwaukee as a location for a brewery. It was at some point in 1855 when he first met the Best Brothers and, surveying their operation, entered negotiations to purchase the entire Plank Road operation. The sale was completed that same year and Frederick Miller began building yet another of Milwaukee's brewing giants. Thus two of Milwaukee's great breweries would share common backgrounds of Jacob Best's brewhouse, two owners named Frederick, and national prominence.

During the next thirty years Miller guided the company along a course of aggressive expansion while developing a practice of modernization. By 1888 the brewery was incorporated as the Frederick Miller Brewing Company, and upon his death that year his sons Ernest, Fred A., Emil, and son-in-law Carl Miller took over management.

Frederick's commitment and savvy guidance resulted in

expansion from the original total of three hundred barrels to an 1888 figure of eighty thousand. Following the philosophy laid down by the founder, the brewery continued to expand and modernize. The result was continuous production increases leading to a total of five hundred thousand barrels by 1919. During Prohibition the company stayed afloat in the manner of other brewers. They produced cereal beverages, soda, and various malt-based products. Following repeal, Miller embarked upon modernization and expansion by obtaining plants around the country.

By far the biggest change occurred after Miller Brewing had comfortably settled into ninth place in 1969. That was the year Phillip Morris purchased 53 percent of the company's stock. The following year the remaining 47 percent was obtained. The new management followed the company's long-standing philosophy of modernization and acquisition. In addition Miller Brewing continued to purchase other brands, including Meister Brau, Buckeye, and Lite from Meister Brau, the legacy of the Peter Hand Brewing Company.

Another innovation was an agreement to produce Löwenbräu in the United States. But overall it was the test marketing and subsequent wide distribution of Lite that caused a stellar leap in Miller's production and sales. From five million barrels in 1970, the aggressive posture of the company and new brewery construction resulted in an increase to more than twenty-five million barrels in 1977, thrusting the company into the number two spot and close on the tail of front-running Anheuser-Busch.

The third of the Milwaukee big three traces its origin through a restaurant and on to Germany. From the country of brewers, August Krug set sail for America. Settling in Milwaukee, he opened a successful restaurant on Chestnut Street. With an eye toward more efficient and reliable operation, he constructed a small brewhouse in 1849. In 1850 Krug made two moves that, though appearing insignificant at the time, would have a dramatic impact on his company. One was the hiring of a twenty-year-old bookkeeper and the other was sending for an eight-year-old nephew in Germany named August Uihlein. In 1856 Krug died and the bookkeeper, Joseph Schlitz, assumed management. Schlitz was an ambitious young man and he made his way toward ownership by means of variation on a familiar theme. He married Krug's widow, Anna, and in 1858 the company was renamed Jos. Schlitz.

Joseph Schlitz was born in Mayence, Germany, in 1831. His father was in the beer and wine business, and the younger Schlitz had early training in both the beer and business fields. Expanding the brewing operation and market, he made his mark by quick action following the great Chicago fire of 1871. With tainted water supplies, Chicago was thirsty, and Schlitz was determined to ship the parched city a flood of beer. His quick response netted the company a sales jump of over 50 percent. Within a year the brewery would be using the slogan "The Beer that Made Milwaukee Famous" and its future was secured.

By 1874 the brewery was one of the largest in the country; unfortunately, Joseph Schlitz wasn't destined to enjoy this success for long. In 1875 he scheduled a long-awaited vacation back home to Mayence. He booked passage on the steamer *Schiller,* and the choice proved fatal when the ship went down, claiming his life.

Control of the company reverted to the closest relatives, the now thirty-three-year-old August Uihlein along with his brothers Henry and Edward. August completed the company's destiny by establishing agencies across the United States and developing a far-reaching rail distribution system. August's direction led the brewery from number ten in 1877 to an 1895 ranking of third. Surviving Prohibition by making near beer, yeast, sodas, malt syrup, chocolate, and a candy named "Eline," Schlitz emerged after repeal with a plan of acquisition and new facility construction that eventually resulted in a position of number one or two in the country for over forty years. After reaching this lofty height, Schlitz fell victim to the belief of image over substance. The company pumped loads of money into advertising but cut corners on brewing. The result was a dramatic drop in sales from which the company never recovered. Eventually Schlitz was purchased by Stroh, which relegated this once proud beer to a secondary status.

As the 1800s progressed, the farmers and settlers gradually pushed west to take advantage of the free or cheap fertile land that could produce exceptional harvests. But events out on the far west of the continent, not even within

U.S. territory, would accelerate the westward plodding to an all-out sprint.

Too often California is thought of as beginning life with the gold rush. In reality, exploration and settlement had begun centuries earlier. Moving north from Mexico, the Spanish worked their way up the coast, building a series of missions, each of which acted something like a regional government. Mission Delores, the Bay area's example, has been preserved and can be visited to this day. Sir Francis Drake, who sailed up the coast in his ship the *Golden Hind*, claimed virtually everything he saw, and even more he didn't see, for God and queen. Not to be left out, the Russians built outposts in the north coast areas and achieved a moderate degree of success in trading. Thus there were a significant number of settlers in California long before gold was discovered at Sutter's Mill. The very fact that a mill was being built indicates a fairly sizable population had already gathered. And where there was a population, there was sure to be potential customers longing for the comfort of a beer.

The earliest known supplier of beer in San Francisco was William McGlove, a sailor nicknamed Billy the Brewer. On occasion Billy must have run out of beer at sea, and being deprived was enough to set him to brewing. Sharing the spotlight was Adam Schuppert, who is also credited as the first. Whoever truly deserves to be applauded as the groundbreaking brewer may never be known, but what is certain is that these two beer lovers were rolling out the barrels by 1837, a good twelve years before the country would look toward the West Coast in a speculative frenzy.

None of this preceding history is mentioned to downplay the significance of the gold rush. It is merely presented to demonstrate beer was patiently waiting for a population to arrive. Regardless, it was with the first gold strikes that the area saw a sudden boom in population. Tens of thousands were caught up in the excitement and braved the cross-country trip or the equally challenging ocean voyage. When they finally arrived it was to encounter even more trials. They faced hard work, conducted under adverse conditions, and exposure not just to the elements, but also through the refining process, which was conducted with hazardous materials such as arsenic and mercury. God knows these tough miners would require long drafts to wash away miserable memories of life back on their claims. All this amounted to a loud message for brewers to expand westward themselves.

The first brewer of some permanence was William Bull, who located his Empire Brewery at Second Street near present-day Mission in 1850. More breweries soon followed, such as John Neep, who opened the California Brewery on Vallejo between Powell and Mason. Also on the scene was Ambrose Carter, who built his brewhouse on Sacramento between Stockton and Powell. By 1852 the sleepy little town had rocketed to a population of thirty-six thousand, with one saloon for every one hundred inhabitants.

Although there was a ready market, the brewers did face several obstacles. The biggest of these was the San Francisco climate. Unlike other brewing centers, which usually developed where there was a convenient supply of ice, San Francisco had no access to frozen rivers and lakes. This was especially important in the era of lager. How were they to brew and condition beer without the benefit of ice? The solution involved a little improvising. The city of San Francisco does benefit from the Pacific's current of cool water coming down from the Arctic, which results in a relatively cool (not cold) climate year-round.

What the brewers did was to construct large, shallow cooling pans. This exposed a greater surface area of the beer to the cool air, thus accelerating the cooling process. After cooling as much as possible by air, they pitched lager yeast. The fermentation that then took place was warmer than normal for lager; in fact, it was almost in the temperature range of ale. This would develop a soft fruitiness in the beer, higher than that found in lagers but not nearly as dominant as in ales. After fermentation ended, the nearly flat beer was placed in kegs where it would be carbonated. To add the required fizz, they resorted to an old method that involved adding to each keg a measured amount of new, lively fermenting beer. Then the kegs were sealed and left to carbonate. This carbonation method relied upon two basic principles. The new fermenting beer would also ferment any leftover malt in the original beer, and the sealed kegs would hold the leftover carbonation expelled by the fermenting yeast. As pressure built in the keg, the carbon dioxide would go into solution.

The end result of this process was a beer that had plenty of pop. When the kegs were opened they often would release a hiss and an escaping cloud of vapor; hence the name "steam beer." This unusual method of making do resulted in a uniquely American beer that soon became not just a local favorite but the preferred method of producing beer throughout California, the Northwest, Idaho, Colorado, and even the supposedly "socially dry" state of Utah. Wherever there were miners to be found, a steam beer plant was usually nearby.

The acceptance of this alternate style was a blessing to the infant Bay brewers. Breweries started popping up all over town, including the support businesses of malting. Francis Tilgner opened the Pioneer Malt house on Stockton Street, and business remained good past the turn of the century. Self-pride has always been a part of San Francisco, and though still relatively young, it held its own industrial exhibition in 1857. Brewers showing off their wares and competing for prizes included Lyon & Co., John Mason, L. Delafond, Adam Meyer, Philadelphia Brewery, E. Anderson, and L. S. Ford. The 1870s arrived with the introduction of lager beer, most notably the beer shipped in by William Lemp Brewing of St. Louis. There were as many as twenty-seven breweries operating in the city by 1860, although some of them were very small, and despite the competition from lager, a large part of the population remained loyal to the local style of steam.

Local production improved year after year and seemed as though it would continue in that fashion. John Wieland, yet another brewer from Württemberg, Germany, opened his own brewhouse in 1856. By 1879 he was the largest in the city with sales of more than forty-four thousand barrels. In that same year he was joined by fellow brewers H. Aherns of the Chicago Brewery with twenty thousand barrels, and F. Hagerman's Albany Brewery with another thirteen thousand barrels. Strange as it was, the city's breweries adopted names from all over the United States, without a single one calling itself San Francisco.

The North Beach section was once home to ten breweries near Telegraph Hill, and because of the challenging terrain, deliverymen adopted a method of minimum effort. Rather than exhausting their horses by climbing all over the hills, drivers employed a much simpler method of taking their beer wagons right to the top. From the summit they enlisted teams of young men who would roll barrels down to the accounts in exchange for a few glasses of beer. This same group would then roll the empty pickups to the bottom of the hill, where the driver would collect them for return to the brewery.

Brewing on the Bay hit an all-time high in the decade of the 1880s. San Francisco supported not only a growing number of imported beers but at least forty breweries including the famous Anchor Steam, which opened in 1851. The 1890s was a period of considerable activity. Also, as in other parts of the nation, English investors were busy putting together syndicates. Ten of the local brewhouses were thus banded together to become San Francisco Breweries Limited, which eventually went under at the repeal of Prohibition.

Opening San Francisco was a boon to the entire far West, and one of those cities that benefited from the gold prospectors flooding the Rockies was Portland, Oregon. Founded in 1845, the city grew because of its location at the junction of the Columbia and Willamette Rivers. Serving the needs of farmers, miners, and the lumber trade, the steamboats that plied the interior rivers used Portland as a terminus and the city grew. Brewing arrived in 1852 when a young German immigrant named Henry Saxer constructed a brewhouse at what would become First and Davis Streets. Calling his business the Liberty Brewery, he was not only the town's first brewer but also the first commercial brewer north of San Francisco.

Across the river in Vancouver, Washington, another brewery was opened in 1856 by John Muench. Named the Vancouver Brewery, it became a rival of Saxer's and established a reputation for high-quality lager. Before long both of these breweries were joined into what would become one of the Northwest's big three in brewers. Muench would eventually become known by a name still familiar throughout the Northwest.

The story at this point must travel back to (where else?) Germany. Henry Weinhard was born 1830 in the Württemberg area, a breeding ground for brewers who immigrated to America. After learning to brew in his homeland, he headed for the shores of America in the same year Saxer began operations in Portland. He worked his way across the continent with brief stays in the brewing towns of Philadelphia, Cincinnati, and St. Louis before finally arriving in the Oregon Territory. Hiring on at Muench's Vancouver Brewery, he surveyed the area and its possibilities before striking out on his own. The first attempt to establish his own business was a partnership with George Bottler in 1857. Opening a small brewhouse on Couch and Front Streets, they gave it their best effort, but lack of profits folded the operation within the year.

Young Henry returned to Vancouver and resumed work for his old employer. Within two years, by saving and sweat, he was able to buy out Muench's brewery and, once again, be his own boss. This time it worked. By 1862 Weinhard was ready to set his sights on bigger game and sold the Vancouver operation to Anton Young. The Vancouver brewery would stay in operation through various sales and mergers until the late 1970s when, as producer of Lucky Lager, it finally shut down.

Weinhard crossed the river to Portland with a pocketful of capital from the sale of his brewery and in the same year of 1862 bought out Saver's Portland Brewhouse. Business went so well that by 1863 the Weinhard beer sales were rapidly outgrowing the tiny space on First and Davis. Searching for a new site, Henry selected and bought a parcel away from the city center on what is now Twelfth and Burnside. A good selection, for the brewery remains in that location to this day.

One of the more interesting stories involving the brewery occurred in September of 1888 after Weinhard had secured both his reputation and fortune. In that year a local businessman passed away and left the city funds to build a fountain. Thus it was that "Skidmore" fountain was erected to fulfill its benefactor's desire to provide for the thirst of laborers and horses. A newspaper clipping reveals what happened when, as the dedication drew near, Henry was moved by a combination of this gesture and civic pride. "He himself would bear the expense of whatever hose was necessary, in addition to the fire hose of the city, to connect his largest lager tank with the fountain and have the fountain spout free beer." What a great idea. Horses are known for their love of beer, and it's said laborers have also been known to partake. Unfortunately the city authorities turned down the offer, afraid the thirsty masses would puncture the hose to tap their own supply.

When Henry died in 1904 the business was passed on to his son-in-law, Paul Wessinger. Oregon was one of the states on the leading edge of Prohibition, and as such, it voted itself dry in 1916. Thus the Oregon brewers were faced with a total of seventeen beerless years. This monumental challenge was met by the wills of Paul Wessinger and his son Henry, who are credited with guiding the company through Prohibition. Their plan included marketing soft drinks flavored with raspberry, apple, cherry, and loganberry with names of R-Porter, Appo, Luxo, and Toko. Then as the end of the dry period neared, Henry Wessinger made a move that secured the company's future. That story goes back to the year of Henry Weinhard's death when Arnold Blitz ran the Portland Brewing Company at 1991 Upshur. Another of the Northwest's strong brand names, with its well-known "Edel Brau," the company sat out the bad years much as everyone else by making non-alcohol beverages. Then in the late twenties as the end appeared near, Blitz rebuilt the entire brewery operation. Across town, Wessinger reached the same conclusion. The attention repeal got in the 1928 presidential campaign was enough of an indication, and he approached Blitz with a proposal to merge. The deal went through in 1928, and as Prohibition ended, their combined strengths put the Blitz-Weinhard company in the position of a regional power.

The families involved stayed active in operations up until 1977 when the business was sold out to Pabst. Since then there have been two other buyouts: G. Heileman in 1983, and Bond, the Australian brewing giant, in 1988. But through it all the company's identity and products remained intact. To this day the Weinhard brand remains one of the most recognizable names in Northwest brewing. The city of Portland has always embraced its brewers, and over the years, despite its rather limited size, at one time or another more than twenty-four breweries have claimed to be its hometown beer.

All these breweries that survived Prohibition would take part in the most drastic change to ever occur in American beer. Brewers were always very careful and conservative in changing their formulas, but events were about to overtake and force them into actions they would have normally avoided.

The period of the late 1930s was not a wild beer party lasting from repeal to Pearl Harbor. True, once again beer could be had, but the nation was still mired in the Great Depression. Money was tight, and inefficient breweries dropped like flies. To compound the problem, there were food shortages. The effects of long-term drought in the Midwest were devastating to farmers as the "dust bowl" accounted for the death of farm after farm. The impact on the country's grain belt and the effects on agriculture were staggering. The resulting slump made recovery from the Great Depression even more difficult, and it was the second step in a process of change that would nearly destroy a fine heritage of brewing.

Another factor altering the nation's taste in beer can be traced to the Prohibition-induced consumption of soda pop. With the rise of industrialized America, polluted water supplies were an ever-present danger, and the national conscience retained its age-old fear of water. But now soda was one of the few alternatives. Compounding the shift to soda was another result of Prohibition, the preference for hard liquor, which could be more easily transported and smuggled than beer. Unfortunately, the quality of this Prohibition hard stuff was questionable at best. "Pick your poison" was often nearly the truth. In fact, the expression "the real McCoy" derived from a smuggling ship captain of that name who was renowned for bringing in a genuine product rather than the rotgut produced in backwoods stills or the widespread bathroom gin. Most Americans were faced with the unpleasantness of resorting to these vastly inferior liquors. In order to make the drinks more appealing, the modern cocktail was invented, and often using a base of soda, it started to shift the country's taste.

Grain shortages in the dust bowl increased the cost of doing business. Worse, funds were limited in the aftermath of the Great Depression. Thus, many brewers were forced to cut back on the grain in their recipes. No matter, the people had been drinking soda, and any beer at all tasted pretty good. Then came World War II. Though officially neutral for the better part of the war's first three years, the United States would assist the Allies through massive shipments of grain. The effect was to continue the shortage experienced by the brewers, and so the good citizens braced for war and continued to drink a lighter beer.

Involvement by the United States was unavoidable, and rationing continued the forced diet of lighter beer styles. Then the brewers, ever more aware of the power of advertising, realized a shift in their customer base had occurred. With many of the men off fighting the war, it was Rosy the Riveter they needed to please, and a light beer style was just the thing to win her over. As the war in Europe ended in April, and in the Pacific theater in August, returning American servicemen found Rosy had stocked the refrigerator with ice-cold bottles and cans of light, fizzy beer perfect for summer. The style would remain as the country implemented the Marshall Plan. Limited supplies of grain continued as America fed a recovering Europe.

By the time the war was over, the country had for more than thirty years resorted to light, highly carbonated beverages. American beer tastes had undergone an incredible alteration, and brewers who refused to change went under. Thus the national and major regional brewers had helped the country shift taste, and the majority of the population who bought in to drinking lighter beer joined in a vicious circle. The people guzzled down lighter and lighter beer and eventually earned the United States a worldwide reputation in brewing that was less than flattering.

CHAPTER 12

Other Significant Brewers

The Hop for his profit I thus do exalt,
It strengtheneth drink, and it flavoreth malt:
And being well brewed, long kept it will last,
And drawing abide—if you draw not too fast.

—THOMAS TUSSER, 1524–1580

Beers Outside the Major Brewing Centers But in the Public's Heart

Although most famous breweries were clustered in major cities, some small-town brewers carved out a share of the market in less populated areas. Sometimes the area grew up around them and other times it didn't. But what they have in common is that they grew large enough, and managed Prohibition with such efficiency, as to remain in business when the national brands gobbled up most everything else. On occasion these regional breweries expanded to make their own impact on the national scene while others were content to remain "the local brewer."

Once again the story begins in the East at the original Genesee Brewery, which began life just north of New York's productive hop-growing region in 1878 on the banks of

Rochester's Genesee River, not far from Lake Ontario. Starting rather late compared to most of the eastern brewers, it was still one of the first to distribute beer in the western part of the state and produced the well-regarded Liebotschaner brand. After eleven successful years it was the subject of a takeover by Bartholomay Brewing, which consisted of two additional breweries and malting houses of the region.

When people think of takeovers, they picture a practice originating in the 1980s with healthy doses of ugly subterfuge and bitter business fights. Actually the roots of takeovers stretch back to a popular practice among holding companies in the 1880s and 1890s. During that era many industries put together smaller companies to gain control of an area. Such alliances were constructed of breweries by buying up single plants to form one large brewing company. In the 1980s companies sold off the pieces to increase profit in the action. But back in the early days of Genesee, their backers were owners who respected the value of brand recognition. Because of their wisdom, the Genesee brewers were able to retain both their jobs and the Genesee name.

Throughout all this, down in the brewhouse worked Louis Wehle, who by his ability and industry eventually moved up to the position of brewmaster. In 1920 and throughout Prohibition he sought other income and toiled in the grocery and bakery business while his heart longed for beer. It's not hard to imagine him in his kitchen late at night. Then, at the time when light and shadows look extra harsh, sitting at his kitchen table with head in hands, he would think and plan to someday return to brewing. Success stories always seem filled with these images. Eventually the hero snaps to the realization of opportunity at hand and jumps to action. This is precisely what happened to Wehle. In 1932, anticipating repeal, he purchased the old plant and readied the brewery for production. By April 1933 he was once again marketing Genesee. The long-suffering, and thirsty, fans of Genesee began making up for lost time.

Next came the big squeeze by national brands, but Genesee still managed to hang on. The quick resumption of brewing helped in part; then, while its peers fell by the wayside, Genesee moved on with a strategy common among regional brewers that survived—Genesee stayed with what worked. It remained true to its market and relied upon their traditional sales areas of New England, New York, Pennsylvania, and eastern Ohio. Genesee didn't attempt to compete with the huge advertising budgets of the big brewers. Instead it concentrated on point-of-sale ads and promotions augmented by limited regional advertising campaigns. Genesee directed its efforts with the principle of knowing what it was and maintained a personality without trying to duplicate the products of the big brewers.

Its stable of brand names also remained relatively unchanged, yet it did offer a varied product line to suit customers. The bulk of its business has always been a beer the Northeast simply called "Genny." It's what the company termed a popular-priced mainstream beer, and so it remains, with the emphasis over the years being consistency. But the most famous Genesee product was the Cream Ale. Along with steam, this is closest to a unique American style, although some may liken it to a derivation of Kölsch. "Genny Cream" was introduced as a means of offering customers a beer in a lagerlike style. The cream beer imitates lager, even though it uses top-fermenting ale yeast, by adding a lengthy cold aging. This imparts a more crisp finish with a less fruity profile than ale.

This is not to say Genesee has avoided innovation. The product line of the 1980s included a Genesee light beer, a no-alcohol beverage, and the acquisition of the Fred Koch label (another Rochester brewer). Then in February 1992 the brewery took what might be its most unusual step over the past half century when it introduced a beer in the specialty craft category. The highly regarded "Michael Shea's Irish Amber" was formed as a subsidiary to Genesee and achieved a healthy success. Sticking with what works has always made Genesee think twice about growing too fast.

A bit farther west was a brewery that started small like Genesee. It, too, survived, but by taking bigger risks. In 1848 Bernard Stroh immigrated to the United States from Germany. As with many of his fellow brewers, it was the intolerable political climate of the Prussian uprising that caused him to leave his homeland. However, his path to America was a bit more indirect. His first stop was Brazil, where he laid plans for an eventual move to Chicago. All that changed when he finally started the last leg of his journey. During a scheduled stop in Detroit he "liked what he saw" and decided to set roots.

It was 1850 when Stroh interrupted his plans, and he immediately took up his old trade by building a very small brewery just off Detroit's Gratiot Avenue, in the German section of the city. This was yet another of those great American stories of pulling yourself up by your bootstraps. In keeping with the "rugged individualism" that characterized the period, Bernard Stroh worked nearly singlehandedly to establish his business. Working out of the small brewery for fifteen years, he slowly purchased land for a new facility on Gratiot Avenue. It was all too common to spot Stroh personally hand-delivering beer from his "Lion Brewery." But his effort soon paid off; sales were so strong, he was soon drawn away from deliveries by the pressing need to purchase more land, complete the brewery, and hire on additional staff, all of which he finished in 1868.

When he finally had a chance to lean back and take a much-deserved breather, he decided a symbol for the brewery was in order. Thinking back to his homeland, he borrowed the lion crest of Germany's Kyrburg Castle in Kirn. Bernard's considerations for the design were finished in 1870, and the same Stroh's coat of arms has represented the company's beer from that day to the very latest can or bottle rolling off the line today.

With success at hand, he decided to reward himself—by renaming the company B. Stroh Brewing in 1882. Unfortunately, Bernard didn't enjoy the name long because he died that same year. When you think about all the times this happened, it almost seems like naming a brewery after yourself was the kiss of death.

Bernard Stroh's two oldest sons assumed control at their father's passing, and operations continued on a regional level. One of the sons, Julius, is credited for a 1912 return to tradition. Many brewers of that era, Stroh included, had converted to the "modern" method of steam for heating their kettles. But Julius argued for a return to the old method of using a direct flame. Fire-boiling added a slight amount of caramelization to the beer, and "Stroh's fire-brewed Bohemian" became the beer's sobriquet.

Prohibition saw the company resort to the common practice of making near beer, malt extracts, sodas, and ice cream, with the latter so popular, it remained in production. This success with other products handsomely positioned Stroh to emerge from the dry years as a strong regional brewer. By the mid-1960s the company began a slow and systematic expansion, which led first to a spot among the nation's top ten, then on to acquisition of the once mighty Schlitz, and eventually to fourth largest in the country.

Another midwestern brewer would move things along in a similar fashion and with nearly the same results. Gottlieb Heileman began his Wisconsin brewing career with a partner named John Gund back in 1858 when they opened the City Brewery. The partners did well and only parted company when Gund sold out his share in order to start his own company, Empire Brewing. We needn't feel sorry for Gund, though. He achieved reasonable success with Empire, and the brewery operated until just after his death in the late 1890s.

As Gund was pursuing his own dreams, Heileman set his own sights even higher. Operation of the brewery was Heileman's alone, and under his guidance, and a program of slow and steady expansion, their beers became a success. The year 1878 brought Gottlieb's death, and his wife, Johanna, like Mary Elizabeth Hudelpohl of Cincinnati, assumed company leadership. Johanna ran the business with some assistance, but major decisions remained hers. One of those decisions, in 1902, was to file for copyright of "Old Style Lager" as the name of their major product. Old Style was the beer that grabbed attention, and a following developed in the region of western Wisconsin, Illinois, eastern Iowa, and southeastern Minnesota.

Johanna survived Gottlieb by thirty-nine years and on her passing in 1917 left a brewery on sound financial footing with a strong regional customer base. Better yet, she left company management to R. A. Albrecht, who had acted as Johanna's adviser since 1911. In fact, Albrecht deserves the credit for leading G. Heileman out of Prohibition. The dry period was handled in the same manner as the big brewers—by producing near beer. When it was over, the company established a course of modernization combined with the modest growth policy originally set by the founder.

But in 1959 Heileman launched a campaign of regional brewery acquisition that would eventually place it among the country's largest. The strategy was to search out favorably priced breweries that held regionally well-known brand names. Among the purchases from 1960 on were Wiedemann, Kingsbury, Blatz, Schmidt (of St. Paul), Sterling, Rainier, Drewry's, Grain Belt, Carling National Brewers, Lone Star, Weinhard, and Red, White & Blue. By 1987 G. Heileman was the fourth largest brewery in the United States. Then, in the middle of the takeover craze, Alan Bond, the Australian brewing giant, cast his eyes toward G. Heileman and saw a North American jewel. Assembling a financing package, Bond took over Heileman to gain greater access to a ready-made distribution network. The result of merging his new American company and his well-established Australian brewery holdings was creation of the planet's fourth largest brewing company.

Before long Bond's house of cards fell. As with many others in his situation, interest payments came due, and unable to meet these commitments, Bond lost control of the company. First he was forced into receivership by the Australian courts and then he resigned his post. In spite of this, Heileman remains in operation, a bit weakened by the whole ordeal but still producing some of the heartland's most loved regional beers.

Even farther west was another of these success stories, but this one would top them all. Adolph Herman Joseph Coors was born in Germany in 1847. Orphaned at age fifteen, and with no ties to his homeland, he headed for America in 1868, where he began working his way across the country. Making a stop in Chicago, young Herman Joseph took a job in a brewery and began an association that would be nearly indistinguishable from beer itself. Chicago was a rapidly growing city thrown up almost as fast as the timber could be cut to frame buildings. The quick pace of business and Chicago's great entrepreneurial spirit rubbed off on Coors, and before long he set his sights on the wide-open western sky with its equally open market.

Traveling ever westward, Adolph Coors found his way to mining country, and the abundance of wealth being taken from the mines told him he was in the right spot to begin his own business. The mines meant railroads to carry out the riches, and on the return trip trains carried back supplies and beer to miners with pockets full of cash and precious few things to spend it on. Thus Coors settled on Denver as a central area from which he could seek his own liquid gold mine.

Coors set up shop as a bottler in 1872, but within a year he was ready for bigger plans. After finding a suitable business partner, Jacob Schueler, he began searching the region for a good source of water located close to an area with commercial potential. What made sense was to concentrate the search on the western side of Denver, where water ran fresh and plentiful down the slopes of the Rockies and along the foothills. After an extensive survey and careful consideration, they finally settled upon a site with abundant underground springs. Even more appealing was the transportation potential offered by the Colorado Central Railroad, which would provide shipping to the mining areas west.

Despite steady growth and success, Coors's partner sold out his share in 1880, the single biggest mistake of Schueler's life. Even with competition from seven other brewers, Coors became a near overnight sensation, making Adolph Herman Joseph Coors a wealthy man.

But not every success comes along without a few bumps, and with Coors it was the same bump that upset all the other brewers' beer wagons. Prohibition came early to Colorado as it mimicked the actions of the other northwestern states and voted for the local option in 1916. By this time Coors was sixty-nine, the age when most of his peers would have chosen to retire; but he was more than ready for the challenge. The company developed a version of near beer along with a string of dairy products like cream and butter. Then in a very successful move, they got into making malted milk and rose to be the third largest producer in the country.

Adolph Herman Joseph Coors died in 1929, but under the

direction of his son Adolph Jr., the company continued along the course set by the founder. Coors remained a family-owned enterprise as most others evolved into corporate entities. (The family did tender a public stock offering in 1975 but limited the offering to retain control.) The greatest benefit for the company was originally a factor that restricted growth.

Coors beer wasn't pasteurized; rather, it was filtered. To assure the careful handling needed to maintain freshness, distribution remained in the western states. When travelers from the population centers of the East first tried Coors, especially when combined with the Mexican food popular in the West, they elevated it to a status of the mystical. Finally Coors expanded its distribution, but on its own terms and not until the company completed a carefully conceived plan. They first expanded their own bottling and canning works along with other related businesses such as ceramics, the material used in their filtering process. The reward of patience and perseverance was realized in the 1990s when Coors was firmly rooted in the number three spot among U.S. brewers.

Ever westward the pioneers pressed across the land, especially when all the good spots were already taken. And so it was in the beer business. The famous beer of Washington State owes its start to Butte, Montana, but its story begins across the ocean. Leopold F. Schmidt was born in Dornassenheim, Germany, in 1846, and in 1860 went to sea on a ship plying the coffee trade route. During a landfall in New York in 1866 he decided America suited him well and took a job working on Great Lakes steamers. By 1868 he was ready to move farther west, and making his way across a dusty landscape, he probably built up the powerful thirst that would shortly drive his life. He ended up in the Montana gold country, assumed work as a carpenter, and gained his citizenship. Everything seemed to go his way, probably because Leopold had a knack for business. Before long he was asked to apply this talent as manager of the Valiton Brewery. Within a year he left the firm to join another former Valiton employee in opening a new brewhouse. That partner was Mr. Sallie, the brewmaster, and he would give Schmidt the start of a thorough brewing education.

The beer bug bit hard, and hooked on the new occupation, Schmidt traveled back to Germany to attend the brewing academy at Worms. After completing his training, he returned to the United States with not only his formal brewing papers and up-to-date knowledge of the field, but also a proper German wife named Johanna Steiner.

Back in Montana, Schmidt started a family and built the brewery into a moneymaking facility that proved to be one of the most successful businesses in the Territory. The company called itself Centennial Brewing. After gaining statehood, the people called on Leopold to represent them in the new legislature. This was the move that would seal his fate. A new capitol was needed, and this wasn't a thing just to throw together; after all, the results of their decisions would be the foundation for the state's future. This momentous task prompted the lawmakers to designate a committee for the study of other state capitols. Appointed to this was Leopold Schmidt, who accepted this duty as seriously as any other aspect of business; and so in 1895 he packed his bags for a trip to the town of Olympia, Washington, to look over their government buildings.

It was fall when Leopold Schmidt entered an Olympia barbershop to get the haircut that altered his future. Once the barber heard of Leopold's mission, local pride took over. As he snipped, shaped, and shaved, he bragged about the area's water supply and the artesian wells recently drilled by the town's Talbott brothers. After the haircut, and intrigued by the enthusiastic endorsement, Schmidt looked to quench his thirst at the wells. One taste convinced him, and following a test from a lab, he was certain he found a truly great water for making beer.

Leopold moved rapidly. Selling his interest in the Montana brewery, he bought land at Washington's Tumwater Springs. He didn't even wait until spring for construction, and by the next July the brewery was ready. Calling it Capital Brewing, he made a high-quality lager with an especially clean taste. Schmidt then surprised the entire Northwest by charging 2.5 times what other brewers were asking for their beers. When questioned about the price, he merely told them the beer was made with such good ingredients and worth the price. It lived up to his claim and was so well received, he sold thirty-five hundred barrels in the first three months. This beer, named Olympia Pale Export, was Schmidt's ticket to the good life.

Over the years the company steadily expanded operations, and in 1905 the entire brewing operation was rebuilt. Schmidt pioneered the use of the new crown cap for bottling, which enabled him to pasteurize the beer and ship it to even farther-reaching markets. By 1908 the company was churning out as many as eighty thousand bottles a year. In 1914 Leopold died and his sons took over the business. Peter Schmidt faced the challenge of Prohibition by producing an apple beverage called Applju and a loganberry drink named Loju. Other products included jellies, jams, and dairy items. The company also utilized the facilities for cold storage and ice manufacturing. But by 1921 the family realized these best efforts were losers and closed the doors to wait it out.

In 1933 the Schmidts entered the world of repeal with a successful stock offering and rebuilt the brewery into a completely modern operation. Resurrecting the 1902 slogan "It's the Water," Olympia returned to business as one of the few to invest in new equipment. It was this ploy, rather than a quick return to sales, that ensured success.

Then in the mid-1970s the company began buying other regional breweries, including Hamms of St. Paul, Minnesota, and Lone Star of San Antonio, Texas. But in 1982 Olympia itself was bought out—by Pabst. When Pabst became a takeover target in 1985, Olympia was made part of General Brewing.

Washington would soon learn it was big enough to support even more brewing than this. Not far away from Olympia came Andrew Hemrich, who would start another famous Northwest brewery. He wasn't from Germany, but his father was, and as he grew up in Alma, Wisconsin, he learned to make beer in his father's brewery. In 1870, at age fourteen, he left to travel the West and spent the next twelve years in brewery jobs throughout Colorado, Nevada, Idaho, and Montana. It was in Montana, at Bozeman, just down the road from Leopold Schmidt, where Hemrich would get his real start in brewing by accepting a position as superintendent at the town's brewery. Two years later he had accumulated enough in savings to look for an opportunity of his own. Teaming up with a friend, John Kopp, he set out for Seattle in 1883 with a bag full of ideas for building his own brewhouse.

After acquiring land, construction began on a piece of property that is now Airport Way South and Hanford. The brewhouse was opened under the name Bay View, but the first batch of beer was named after another of Seattle's great vistas—Mount Rainier. Within two years Hemrich bought out Kopp and continued the business as a family effort.

June of 1889 was tough on the city, with a fire all but wiping out the downtown area. Luckily, the Bay View Brewery escaped the flames and Andrew Hemrich moved quickly to organize assistance from the brewery crew and provide free beer at the emergency centers. People may forget the volunteer efforts of a company's employees, but no one forgets free beer. This move would result in elevating Rainier to a special place in the city's heart. In 1892 the company took another step toward becoming the home-town beer when it merged with three other breweries to become the Seattle Brewing and Malting Company.

In 1910 Andrew Hemrich passed away and the business came under the direction of his brothers, all of whom had learned brewing under the tutelage of their father back in his brewery in Alma, Wisconsin. Already established as a giant in the region, the brewery and its operations remained much as Andrew had established.

Then in 1916 Washington adopted the same locally initiated Prohibition passed in the other Northwest states that year. The Hemrich brothers were secure in their position as the area's leading brewers, and rather than an attempt to limp along with questionable profits, they shut the brewery down and sold the Rainier brand name to a San Francisco brewery. Starting other businesses to hold them over, the brothers ran an icehouse and even a laundry while riding out Prohibition. On reopening the brewery at repeal, the Rainier brand name was still held by the California concern, so the Hemrichs marketed their beer under the name Apex and learned a tough lesson about brand recognition.

About this time the brewing family of Emil and Fritz Sick bought out the Hemrichs' interest and began negotiating to repurchase the Rainier label. The deal was closed in 1938 and Rainier came home to the Northwest. The next move was to purchase, tear down, and rebuild the old Bay View brewhouse. In fact, the modernization plan helped the company remain a viable regional brewer as the rest of the country's local beers were finding their way onto the endangered species list.

In the mid-1950s Molson of Canada became the majority shareholder of the Sicks' brewery; but the family continued to run the business until Molson sold its interest to G. Heileman in 1977. The Heileman purchase was part of its philosophy of expansion while utilizing the draw of locally established brands. In 1978 they succeeded in pushing Rainier over the million-barrel mark. By 1984 the sales would increase to two million. Success doesn't go unnoticed, and in September 1987 another buyout was announced, this time as part of the Bond takeover of Heileman. Fortunately Bond followed the same philosophy as Heileman and retained the Rainier name as a regional brewery. Today the brand remains as much a part of Seattle as Pike's Place or the Space Needle.

How all this impacts the American brew scene may not be all that apparent. These brewers who sat in regional population, but not brewing, centers went down one of four paths in the twentieth century, with each impacting on beer to this day. The unfortunate ones went out of business, and their legacy is lost to Americans. Another group, smaller than the first, survived by concentrating on their local product and the region that helped them grow. Yet another, and again, smaller, number of brewers would emerge on the scene as national breweries when their leadership successfully met the challenge of post-Prohibition beer life.

Finally, there was the fourth group. The descendants of these breweries would continue on by establishing a new and unique approach to brewing. As their sales fell through the latter part of the 1900s, they would prosper by doing business with a whole new way of brewing. This approach would reach to its past and call itself microbrewing.

By the late 1900s the United States was home to the largest brewer in the world and also produced the most beer, but despite this sea of foam, it was bereft of variety until the late seventies and early eighties which brought a revolution in beer.

In the fifteen years preceding the 1980s, American tourists, especially the baby boomers, "discovered" Europe. Their trips through the Old World reintroduced them to the variety and fullness of styles that had long since left the States. Also, those who crossed the ocean as part of the Cold War troop buildup acquainted themselves with Euro-brew. If these travelers were disappointed at first to find no American beer available, they were probably assuaged by finding that they enjoyed the local brews just as much. As these people returned home, they found few places carrying their European favorites. Unfortunately most of these imports suffered the ravages of shipping, so they just weren't the same as over there.

The devotees of the wine craze also had an impact on American beer tastes. Swirling, sipping, and evaluating wine opened American eyes to a whole new world of palatable sensations. At the same time it presented them with the basic skills needed for beer tasting. Eventually the price of the wine hobby hit home; it was great fun but could get rather pricey. An odd bottle of wine was great on occasion, but an everyday beverage was needed.

The common interest among these groups was the search for new varieties of beer. Available European beers were either oxidized and stale or had been made specifically for the American taste. Regional American breweries that survived were few and far between, with most trying to stay in business by duplicating the light pilsner style popularized by the national brewers. Clearly the choices were limited. What was a beer lover to do? The answer was part of America's long-forgotten heritage, and people were drawn to it naturally. They began making their own.

Many of the beer pioneers started in the same manner—with simple kits of malt extract and a bit of water boiled with some hops, mixed with cold water in a new plastic garbage can. Add yeast and wait for beer. Results weren't quite as good as what they anticipated, but the full body and fresh taste brought an alternative and a tease of what could be. Most weren't satisfied and their demands brought a measure of change and improvement to homebrew supplies. As the quality of the raw materials and the skills of homebrewers increased, their friends actually became sincere when they complimented the beer. The next step was fairly natural; after all, it was totally in keeping with the American character of capitalism to transform the hobby into a business. Their motivation was a mix of pride, ambition, crusading, and sense of history. Just as with all other pioneers, some would achieve varying degrees of success while others would fall along the wayside. No matter what their individual results, together they blazed a trail that would lead to the most rapid-growing segment of the beer industry, microbrewing.

One of the earliest microbrewers got involved because of a beer he had in college. At the time he was only interested in refreshment and he had no idea that what he was sipping started because of a lack of ice, but it would lead to a rebirth of American brewing.

It started with the gold rush of 1849 and the miners' thirst for lager beer, which couldn't be produced in the ice-free environment of San Francisco. What the miners invented was a hybrid beer using lager yeast at ale temperatures to produce an entirely new style called steam beer. Soon there were more than 150 steam beer breweries in California, Oregon, Washington, and Idaho. San Francisco alone had over 40. But following the advent of refrigeration, brewers were no longer limited to the steam style and many gradually changed over to a pure lager. Prohibition and a shift in the public's taste to lighter styles caused even more steam brewers to disappear. So by the late 1930s only one traditional steam brewer remained.

Anchor Brewing was born in 1896 on San Francisco's Eighth Street. Despite an adequate start, the post-Prohibition years left it limping along by sales to local taverns and restaurants. In addition to brewing a style that had fallen out of favor, the business was further hampered by selling only kegged beer as the country was embracing the take-home convenience of bottles. With the additional burden of outmoded equipment, it's amazing the company remained in business. As the 1950s came to a close, Lawrence Steese purchased the company and struggled to keep things running.

The rescue of the country's last steam brewery started

in the middle of the grain belt. Amana, Iowa, was home of the Maytags, a family with a prizewinning herd of livestock who developed a successful strain of American blue cheese and gathered a fortune from the appliance business. Son Francis Louis "Fritz" Maytag III traveled to California, at about the time Steese was buying Anchor, to attend Stanford University as both an undergraduate and graduate student. It was during graduate school, where he pursued Asian studies, that someone mentioned the last local brewery was about to go under. Fritz later recalled, "It was as if someone said, 'That's the last cable car and it's going out of business tomorrow unless you put up a few thousand dollars.'" And that's exactly what happened. Fritz found himself visiting the brewery at 541 Eighth. Meeting Steese resulted in a snap decision, and a commitment of $5,000 got Maytag involved in brewing.

Less than a year after buying in, Maytag was producing an all-malt steam beer, and as his involvement grew, he attended the Schwartz Brewing School in New York. Finally, in 1969 he obtained full ownership of the brewery. Recognizing the need for take-out beer, he started bottling Anchor for the first time in 1971. Then in the next year, once again driven by the historical significance, he brought out a porter.

Investing time and money while initially forgetting any hope of profit, Maytag turned the business around, and by 1975 he was ready to reintroduce America to styles lost to most of the country's beer drinkers. That year he unveiled Liberty Ale to commemorate the revolution. Later that same year Fritz came out with another long-ignored style in Old Foghorn, a barley wine.

In 1977 Fritz put his Maytag stock up as security and built a new home for Anchor on Mariposa Street. The new brewery even included the shallow panlike fermenters common to the original steam breweries. Within the first year in new quarters, Anchor doubled its output, and Maytag, along with the brewery, finally escaped from a perilous financial position.

Looking at Anchor's size now, it's easy to forget this was a microbrewery, but in fact, it was. When Maytag first entered the business, capacity was a mere six hundred barrels per year. But within twelve years of moving into the new facility, he increased it to over eighty-two thousand barrels.

The unfortunate part of the story involves Maytag's copy-righting the name "Steam," which effectively blocks other American brewers from identifying their products as this uniquely American beer. Despite this, Fritz is the true leader of the American microbrewery revolution and de-serves full credit and praise for the return to flavorful beers and the rescue of a near-vanished style. And he would often prove generous in the help he gave other start-up brewers.

Half a world away, events were unfolding that would have an equally significant impact on microbrewing. While Fritz Maytag was getting pulled into the workings of An-chor Brewing, a young navy technician was being trans-ferred to a Scotland navy base that was actually a submarine tender securely anchored in the middle of Scot-land's Holy Loch. There Jack McAuliffe assisted in the maintenance of Polaris "Boomer" submarines. During his free time McAuliffe would take the launch into shore and visit the surrounding towns of Dunoon, Gurock, and Gren-noch. The best of Scottish weather is summer, which most elsewhere would be likened to late spring, and the long winter is filled with cold, misty days. The warm and friendly pubs were an oasis that offered Jack strange beers whose warmer serving temperatures accentuated the full body and rich flavors. McAuliffe was nothing short of in-trigued, and throughout his stay he tasted, contemplated, and generally fell in love with the local beers and ales.

At the end of his tour of duty, Jack joined the ranks of other ex-servicemen who returned home to attend college. Eventually he settled into a job as an optical engineer in Sunnyvale, California. Although California is about as far from Scotland as you can get, his mind kept drifting back there, especially when he wanted a beer. By the time he moved to Sonoma in 1973, Jack realized his search for a decent, or any, English ale would be in vain. Facing a choice of doing without or making it himself, he opted for the more daring approach.

Several factors worked against McAuliffe. Aside from his lack of brewing experience, the venture was launched with limited marketing and dangerously low capital among the rising interest rates of 1976. With little more than driving ambition, Jack decided to do what no one had attempted for decades, the construction of a new small brewery.

One of Jack's problems—location—was solved when he rented one thousand square feet of excess warehouse space at Sonoma's Bafto Fruit Company. The next obstacle was a bit tougher—brewing equipment. At that time breweries were only a concern of the big boys, with big equipment and big pockets to dig into. It wasn't as though a person could just pick up a phone and order a small off-the-shelf brewing system. Jack's financial state would probably have prevented him from buying a ready-made system if any did exist, so he resorted to a skill picked up in the navy, scrounging.

Assembling parts and pieces ranging from old dairy equipment to junkyard pick-overs, McAuliffe began wiring, welding, and working on his brewery. Old stainless steel milk tanks were successfully converted to brewing duty in a move other microbrewers would follow. The next step was to hire Don Barkley, who graduated from UC-Davis with a degree in fermentation science. Jack finished construction and turned to marketing the beer. New Albion was selected as the brewery's name, which contained the dual reference to both Sir Francis Drake's name for the territory he claimed in the 1500s, and the country whose beer gave McAuliffe his inspiration. (Albion is an ancient name for England.)

First-year production at New Albion was 150 barrels, and soon McAuliffe was joining Maytag in resurrecting nearly extinct styles of ales. Sales never quite brought in enough to meet expenses because capacity was too low, so Jack made plans to move into a larger facility. Unfortunately everything came to an end in 1982 just before the anticipated move. An inadequate business plan and less than effective marketing led to its demise, not necessarily the beer or equipment. In fact, the equipment Jack assembled was good enough to provide many years production in the service of Mendocino Brewing in Hopland. Other microbrewers would soon follow McAuliffe's trail. Some, like New Albion, would falter, but others would bring the promise of fresh, flavorful beers to a very receptive America.

Sometimes ideas seem to strike like lightning. Originating from the same place, it strikes simultaneously in different spots. The microbrew revolution was no different. It seemed as though many caught the same idea at once. Forerunners of hand-crafted beer were a brave lot believing in a return to fuller-bodied, quality brews. A beer enthusiast's thoughts of these microbrewing pioneers usually turns toward California, and although generally correct, this would overlook one of the brewers who survived being "ahead of his time." Bill Newman of Albany, New York, was the East Coast's version of Brewing Pioneer.

Bill's story goes back to his roots and a father from London. In 1969 this combination landed him in Europe where he traveled extensively seeking out the local styles. At the same time he started following the efforts of Britain's Campaign for Real Ale (CAMRA) and fell in love with English-style ales. Beer wasn't the only thing he fell in love with in Europe, it was during his travels that he also met his wife, Marie.

Soon their beer trips were getting serious, and then fortune did them a good turn. Upon arriving in Heathrow in 1978, they discovered a *London Times* article on the opening of Godson's, the city's newest brewery. A tour and sampling was the final straw in getting Bill hooked. He took an apprenticeship with English microbrewing expert Peter Austin, and during his training Bill gathered as much as he could about mashing, brewing, marketing, and sales. Several months passed, and though Peter Austin could not sell his turnkey operation to Bill in the United States, Newman did come back with a set of plans to construct his own version in Albany.

The city itself helped out with some financial assistance, and Newman's was incorporated in 1979, making it one of the three oldest microbreweries in the country. Taking up residence in the city's industrial district, Bill located the brewery in a building that locals insist once stored the barrels for Schaefer Beer. Soon Bill had his own system running, using Ringwood yeast to produce an authentic English-style cask-conditioned ale. Patterned after the English system, the beers were sold on draft and in "growlers" for the carry-home trade. By the mid-eighties the brewery had risen into the top ten in the Great American Beer Fest's consumer preference poll, producing a winter warmer that author Michael Jackson listed as one of his favorite beers in 1987.

During its heyday the brewery not only made great beers but also served as an incubator for other micros. Remembering the benefits of his apprenticeship, Bill started a similar program in Albany. Throughout the mid-eighties over fifty brewers attended Newman's hands-on training programs, which spawned at least ten alumni who would go on to run their own breweries. The graduates are familiar to beer enthusiasts and include names like Jim Koch and Gary Heurich.

While all this was going on, Newman learned several tough lessons. First, the English style of brewing and distribution was not compatible with American drinking habits. Although the English consume 90 percent of their beer in a pub, Americans drink nearly the same percentage at home. In addition, American ale drinkers amounted to less than 10 percent of beer consumers. The final blow was the economic reality of capital requirements for a bottling line combined with the limits of a 10-barrel brewery. Survival meant finding another way of doing things. Thus, Newman's shifted to contracting his brew. Shutting down the brewery, Bill leased and shipped his equipment to Boston Brewing Company (the makers of Sam Adams).

Contracting the beer's production to another brewer allowed Newman to enter the bottle beer market. Albany Amber, the name of their flagship beer, was selected because amber-style beer had been associated with the region since the mid-1800s. Newman was one of the growing number of microbrewers who became more sales-oriented and began to pay more attention to image. In the change to contracting, Newman settled on a label that depicted an English symbol of a unicorn. With this in hand he was almost ready to restart his beer business.

The lesson learned with his ale made him switch to brewing a lager with alelike ingredients. Albany Amber used deep-roasted crystal malt, combined with Hallertauer and Cascade hops from Yakima to produce a smooth, malty beer that won a bronze at the 1989 Great American Beer Fest. Though it's generally classified as a Vienna, its alelike characteristics make it more of a style unto itself. Bill likens it to John Courage.

The second beer was "Saratoga," a Dortmunder export style. Fuller in body than a pilsner, it was developed as a deep gold beer using sweet malts with Hersbrucker and Hallertauer hops and a finishing hops of Saaz. The label has a vague reference to the unicorn by picturing a thoroughbred in a design that suggests the old days of the Saratoga racetrack, an Albany area landmark.

To contract out these beers, Newman searched for a micro that would produce the beer in small batches, resulting in fresher beer. After initially being contracted to larger breweries, Albany Amber was switched to Catamount Brewing of White River Junction, Vermont, a micro that followed in Newman's footsteps and where Saratoga was already in production.

Despite some of the hard times and the sorrow at watching other early micros go under, Bill never lost enthusiasm for the brewing business. He set plans for controlled expansion throughout the Middle Atlantic states and eventual construction of another brewery for reintroduction of his winter warmer and a pale ale.

Back in California, things were heating up, and as Maytag and McAuliffe were starting up, even more people poised themselves to jump on the beer wagon. Such was the case in 1977 when Paul Camusi listened to his buddy Steve explain how his brother had become a homebrewer. Paul was no stranger to beer, and with growing curiosity he arranged to find out just how Ken Grossman did it.

Ken was an avid homebrewer, and like most talented homebrewers, wondered how well the beer his friends praised could be made in a real brewery. When they got together, Ken walked Paul through the brewing process, and as they discussed hops and wort and pitching, they also found a wide commonality of interests. After their first introduction, conversations became more frequent and regular. The idea of a brewery became infectious and their enthusiasm built as though it were a mutual beer propagation network.

Many friendships and partnerships have been cemented over a beer, especially in the formation of microbreweries. Paul and Ken decided to give it a try, and Camusi moved to Ken's hometown of Chico. Developing a business plan was no easy task, and neither held enough capital to get started. Perhaps their young ages (twenty-six and twenty-four) were a benefit—there was nothing to fear, and how could they not succeed? With $110,000, mostly from family and friends, they set off to build their brewery.

Like McAuliffe and many of the other early microbrewers, they found very little equipment available to fit their needs. Equipment manufacturers wouldn't appear until the boom of microbrewery production took hold. So Camusi and Grossman found the path of least resistance, and cash, by gathering up pieces of old breweries, creameries, and dairies. It was common for most of the very early small brewers to obtain used equipment from the milk house. Dairies were a source of relatively cheap stainless steel tanks, which were adaptable, if not ideal, for brewing beer. Their big break came when Fritz Maytag replaced the original bottling line he installed at Anchor. Fritz offered the old line at a special rate to help the newcomers get on their feet.

Naming the brewery after California's famous Sierra Mountain range, Paul and Ken began operations from a small warehouse in 1981. Soon after, marketing and distribution was being conducted from the brewery's official vehicle: Paul's tiny Honda station wagon. Despite all the make-do and hardships, their hoppy "American-style" pale ale was instantly popular.

That first year in business they produced five hundred barrels. Encouraged by their reception, they decided to try a bit of variety, and Anchor's well-received Christmas Ale seemed a good enough example to follow. Thus, in 1982 they produced their first seasonal beer, "Celebration Ale," along with a porter. In 1983 the pale ale won a gold, and porter a silver, to start what would eventually amount to a treasure trove of medals from the Great American Beer Festival.

Rather than succumb to the euphoria of quickly gained fame, the two brewers reversed their field from the aggressiveness that got them started to a more tempered approach. They decided to address expansion in a slow, deliberate manner without overextending themselves. The gradual expansion brought sales to the five-thousand-barrel mark within their first five years, and on their tenth anniversary they moved into an all-new brewery equipped with one-hundred-barrel brew kettles and a production level of over twenty thousand barrels.

In the early nineties Sierra was brewing pale ale, porter, stout, Celebration Ale (holiday), Big Foot (a barley wine), and two lagers—a pale bock and a Summer Fest. Annual sales approached seventy thousand barrels in 1992, and the brewery's story was considered a model of micro-brewing.

Of course, every group, industry association, or trade has its share of colorful characters and pioneers. In the brewing renaissance this role is ably filled by "Buffalo" Bill Owen. Bill received an introduction to beer in that great drinking proving ground—college. Owens referred to it as "college, Friday night pizza and beer." It was also while in college, attending Chico State–California, that he began his homebrewing, and as a natural tinkerer, he was frequently adjusting and modifying his self-designed systems.

Following graduation, Bill joined the growing swell of Americans who would visit Europe and bring back a whole new perspective, and taste, for beer. On his return he embarked on a career in photography and continued to home-brew as the one means of obtaining the beer styles he craved.

Photography satisfied his creative side and he collected numerous awards along the way. It was also photography that brought him to a beer crossroads. The story has it that Owens was teaching a photography course in a local adult evening program when he noticed another class had even more people enrolled than his. Bill didn't look at this as a challenge, and he already knew how to home-brew. What he saw was dissatisfaction in mainstream American beer. After all, it was enough to drive these people to making their own. Opportunity wasn't just knocking, it was pounding a steady refrain. Owens didn't need a second invitation.

Homebrewers like Bill were the ones who persuaded the California legislature to modify the archaic three-tiered liquor law that prevented an alcohol manufacturer from selling directly to the public. Following the example set by Bert Grant in Washington, the lawmakers altered the restrictions to allow sales directly to the public in a restaurant setting. Bill used the time that passed during the legal machinations to complete plans for a brewhouse like those that dot the cities and towns of Germany. Owens's goal was to be the first brewpub in California, but he missed out by one month to Mendocino when he opened his Buffalo Bill's Brewpub during September 1983 in Hayward, California. These two brewpubs would be a model for hundreds more.

What Bill is most proud of is innovation. He counts among his accomplishments the publication of a short how-to book on building a small brewery, which sold over thirty thousand copies. He did it because, as he put it, "Homebrewing started the movement and as home brewers we all shared information and helped each other; so why not, we all need to grow up together." In the book Owens recounted his experience with step-by-step illustrations and procedures to duplicate his brewing system. In one of his more curious moves, he applied for state and federal copyright for the name *brewpub* but then allowed it to lapse. Perhaps his most cherished accomplishment was the introduction of his "Pumpkin Ale," a name he trademarked. Owens claims the beer was inspired by George Washington, and so great was his pride, he published the recipe in *American Brewer* magazine.

Bill's other well-known beer was christened "Alimony Ale." Watching his accountant suffer through a long and stormy divorce gave Owens the idea of producing the "Bitterest Beer in America" in recognition of the poor C.P.A.'s plight. The beer Bill devised had such a high hopping rate, some patrons claimed to have strained out hops with their teeth. Originally the Alimony Ale label contained a "personal ad" which read: "Steve, newly single (and paying alimony), is looking for an honest, full-bodied woman who can enjoy an honest, full-bodied brew and knows the meaning of parsimony." The label was in keeping with Owens's sense of humor, but the Bureau of Alcohol Tobacco and Firearms (BATF, which approves all labeling) wasn't amused. Bill opened a second brewpub in Fremont during 1988 and continued on with plans for eventually opening a microbrewery.

People speculated Buffalo Bill's nickname came from his

publishing, or his style of speech, and maybe from the way he talked about brewing, or even his ability to set up finances. In actuality it may be none of these; probably it's because Bill Owens became the brewing equivalent to another showman of the West, William Cody.

CHAPTER 13

Microbreweries

*I have fed purely upon ale; I have eat my ale,
drank my ale, and I always sleep upon my ale.*

—GEORGE FARQUHAR, 1678–1707

Anchor, Sierra, and the New Beer Pioneers

As more of these breweries started, and more people tried
the beer, word spread and it wasn't long until the city that
prides itself on timely stylishness needed to get in on the
new craze. New York is no place to let a new trend go
untried, and the Big Apple jumped on the brewpub bandwagon and rejoiced in the opening of the Manhattan Brewing Company. So well regarded were their brews that early
"beer experts" raved about the job being done down in
Soho. Unfortunately the first Manhattan brewery ran out
of enthusiasm and money, and its closure was a cause of
mourning among the city's beer drinkers.

One person who refused to believe the old Manhattan
would never reopen was head brewer Garrett Oliver.
Through meetings of the New York City Homebrewers
Guild, beer fests, and brewing contests, Garrett always told
the same story: "Hey, we're just looking for new owners."

Those who considered that simple statement a pipe dream were wrong. In March 1993 Manhattan was back in business.

Garrett started his quest for good beer in 1984 upon returning from a two-year stint in England. Fortunately, within a few months of returning home, the original Manhattan brewpub opened. Between this and homebrewing, which he started out of desperation, Garrett found salvation from mainstream beer. In the late eighties he heard of an opening at the Brewpub and showed up to announce his intention of taking the job. Then came the bleak day the brewery shut down. Garrett probably came the closest of any modern brewer to knowing what Prohibition must have felt like. During the brewery's dormant period he closely monitored the sale and remained active in the brewing/beer world. On reopening he resumed responsibility as head brewer.

The brewery sits well up on the third floor of an 1884 Con Ed power station. From Thompson Street the location was well marked by the brew kettle that emerged halfway outside the building as a decorated 3-D billboard. Inside, an English brewhouse was built on the third floor in an unusual configuration consisting of both a seven- and twelve-barrel mash tun. Though different, it allowed Garrett to perform a step infusion mash for both wheat and lager beers.

From the third floor, beers flowed down from the conditioning room directly to the bar, where they were drawn. One free-flow line was built and reserved for styles best served cold. The remaining four taps were installed as working beer engines (hand pumps), perfect for English ales. These engines produce a thick, creamy head for the top of a draft.

A brewpub offers a lot of latitude to the brewer, and Garrett took full advantage. Joining the regular brews of gold, amber and brown were specials of wheat, IPA, stout, and even doppelbock. Garrett observed, "As a brewer the best part about a brewpub is that after you finish a workday you can go downstairs and see people enjoying the beer as you have one yourself." The space to have that beer was set up as comfortable as possible, and the dining room retained the charm that made it so popular. Long wooden tables were matched with antique wooden chairs to give it a comfortable feeling, a place where people could relax and spend some time. The dominant feature of the room has always been the old copper-topped brew kettles, which, although only decorative, are effective in setting a proper brewhouse mood. Garrett's dream is for the owners to cut doorways in the back side of each and turn them into sunken booths.

Unfortunately, the same economic conditions that caused New York's original breweries to close have made the growth of brewpubs lag behind the remainder of the country. By 1993 there were only three working brewpubs and no microbreweries in the city. But with the enthusiasm Gothamites display for the city's specialty beer bars and beer festivals, it's just a matter of time, although most new brewers chose the more economical plan of establishing business outside the city.

Brewing was no stranger in the Catskills. By the mid nineteenth century this orchard and farming region of the central Hudson boasted twenty-two breweries, five of which were located in Kingston. Alas, the Volstead Act (AKA the Eighteenth Amendment, or Prohibition) and the postwar competition from the large national breweries did them in, with the last one closing its brew kettles in the 1950s.

The late 1960s brought Woodstock, however, and with it Nat Collins, who entered the Rainbow Farm Collective, filling the post of beekeeper. The flower children sitting in the bliss of communal spirit soon discovered there just might be a little something missing in their otherwise perfect marriage with nature. That one thing could only be—beer. So Nat's assignment was to convert the commune's fermentables, honey and grain, into a suitable beverage. Although he subsequently left to pursue a more conventional career, he continued to refine his homebrewing abilities. In the late 1970s he formed and ran his own construction firm, but all the while he dreamt of retiring and running his own brewery. By the late eighties he decided that time had come. Disbanding the firm, he took to the road and visited microbreweries and brewpubs, attended courses at the Siebel Institute, and became an AHA/HWBTA-recognized beer judge.

On returning to Woodstock, he started searching for an appropriate building to house his dream. This brings us to a Kingston foundry that first saw operation in the 1830s and where the gantry crane is still there up above the hung ceiling. Although Nat wanted to locate in Woodstock, the space in the foundry building and the cooperation from the city were too good to pass up. Now was the time that all the construction experience, and help of friends, came in handy as he cleaned and refurbished the building, which last saw duty as a garage. The equity of sweat, patience, and determination paid off in a six-thousand-square-foot brewhouse with a new poured slab floor, angled just right for clean brewery operations.

A firm believer in the old ways, Nat followed a traditional and time-honored brewing process. The beer produced by these efforts is an American lager called "Hudson Lager," so well made, it was selected to be served across the river at the prestigious Culinary Institute of America. It was a conscious decision to start with a lager because the local population patronized Bud and Miller, and Woodstock soon began making inroads in that market. Nat started cautiously, and despite the temptation to expand rapidly, he stuck with his original strategy. The first step was to add a bottling line, and then begin the introduction of other products—a pumpkin lager named Ichabod Crane Pumpkin Beer and a classic English porter he called Big Indian. It wasn't until 1993 that the brewery underwent its first expansion with the delivery of an additional primary fermenter and three more conditioning tanks. All this led to an eventual expansion to about six thousand to eight thousand barrels a year, with a total of ten to twelve employees. Nat continued along the slow-growth curve because handling was extremely important in an unpasteurized beer such as Woodstock. Overheating, chilling, and agitation would cause it to lose the flavor that makes it a unique full-bodied brew.

The most unique aspect of Woodstock's brews is the fine art framed in a diamond logo. The lager portrays a Hudson River sloop passing near what appears to be Storm King Mountain. The interpretation brings to mind the work of Bierstadt, Church, Cole, and Cropsey. In fact, each beer features a different scene portrayed in the style of the Hud-

son River School, which is very fitting since Frederick
Church lived just across the river.

As with other micros, Nat made public relations a part of
his business plan and opened the brewery for tours on Satur-
days and by appointment. The tour, which is handicap-
accessible, includes a full explanation of the brewing process
and ends in the tasting room. As you walk through you
may discover Nat has kept ties with his beginnings, for it's
not uncommon to see his homebrew equipment stuck in a
corner. Nat may even sheepishly tell you of his adjustment
to the new size of the operation and how the first time he
entered the mash tun for a cleaning, he took a cordless
phone along, just in case he got stuck inside the tank.

Yet another brewery would see the wisdom of locating
near, but not in, the big city. In this case, the birth of New
England Brewing can actually be traced to a vacation.
Back in 1988 Richard and Marcia King were traveling
about the Green Mountain State and stopped for a drink
that would change Norwalk, Connecticut. Sipping the beer,
they marveled at how fresh and full-bodied it seemed.
When they made an inquiry they discovered they had come
upon the Catamount brand. As they continued on their
trip through New England, they tried even more local beers
and wished they could get this sort of thing back home.

Following their return, they decided that maybe starting
a brewery was possible and got in touch with noted Connecticut beer enthusiast Ron Page. Ron was an accomplished homebrewer who introduced them to Phil Markowski,
who hired on as brewer. By February of 1989 they decided
to go forward with the idea of building a brewery and incorporated in April.

The choice of the first brew resulted from Phil's homebrewing attempts at steam-style beer. All involved with
New England wanted a product representative of America,
and after all, this was a style unique to the United States.
Starting with a one-barrel pilot brewery, they formulated
the recipe and had Atlantic Amber out in draft form by
February 1990. As in most infant microbreweries, the new
owners suddenly found themselves in fifteen-hour days as
they wrestled with success while maintaining quality.
Quality continued to be the guiding rule as they addressed
bottling, distribution, marketing, and packaging. The basis

of each decision was not rapid expansion or quick payback but pride in the beer.

As business grew, Ron Page submitted to the inevitable and joined Phil as brewmaster. By 1992 the brewery had come out with four products: the original Atlantic Amber, Gold Stock Ale, Oatmeal Stout, and Holiday Ale. Produced from English two-row and crystal malts, Atlantic Amber was so well thought of by brewing peers that it won a gold medal at the 1993 Great American Beer Festival. Gold Stock Ale was the brewery's effort to reproduce a classic New England stock ale. Made for real beer enthusiasts, this style beer was in the pale ale category but bigger and stronger for long storage. Oatmeal Stout was introduced as one of their seasonal beers, and as such was given a brewing season of January till April or May. In order to achieve the silkiness of an Oatmeal Stout, New England used eight different malt varieties, including additions of wheat and flaked barley. The fourth brew, Holiday Ale, was developed from English pale and crystal malts along with chocolate and roasted barley. As with other winter warmers, the formula included traditional ingredients of cinnamon, nutmeg, and vanilla beans, along with "dry hopping" of spices. First produced in 1990, the beer was sold in swing-top bottles until the brewery discovered the true cost of this decorative package. Marcia remembers that first bottling run on Thanksgiving eve with a smile. After resetting the bottling machine for filling and then hand-setting the tops along with the labels, Marcia recalls how they finished up at 3:00 A.M. and had fifteen guests show up for a noontime Thanksgiving feast. Needless to say, the swing tops wouldn't reappear until a new bottling line was installed.

Most micros will admit they would do some things differently if they could start all over, and New England Brewing is no different. They all agree it would have been great to be more prepared for success. Their first year had them change their brew kettle size three times. They also mention avoiding the use of individual tanks on casters, and of course, they would have more room, to avoid Ron and Phil's endless choreography of tank ballets in order to keep up with demand.

Then they got the opportunity to start over. The city was

working at redeveloping the downtown, concentrating on the seaport area. An old warehouse was available, and New England jumped at the chance to move in. Marcia, a Norwalk resident, couldn't say enough about the cooperation received from the town, including help with remodeling the warehouse by means of a facade-improvement grant. The best part of the move for beer lovers was the ability to mash by decoction, which, of course, means lagers and Oktoberfest beers, and the brewpub provides the opportunity to test-market new bottling possibilities.

Combining old warehouses with new brewing equipment has proven a popular combination, and so it was in the city located where the Mississippi nears the end of its journey to the Gulf. There, its path widens and slows, turning in a large, lazy arc. The French settled here because a town with three approaches covered by water could be easily defended; later this feature drew the Spanish. They're long gone, but the resulting French-Spanish culture, spiced further by the descendants of Acadia and Africa, created what is probably the most culturally unique town in America. That large bend in the river remains a landmark, and its shape suggests the city's official nickname as well as the name of the town's first new brewery in over seventy-five years, Crescent City.

Hot days and cool jazz are a perfect lead-in to cold beer, and the Big Easy was once the location of several breweries. The largest, Jackson, makers of JAX, closed years ago, and the once proud brewhouse has since become a vibrant urban shopping mall. It took the interest of a Bavarian brewer with a love of jazz to bring a beer of character back to the old town.

Wolfram Koehler would listen to his mother speak of his great-grandfather, Heinrich Huessner, a brewer from the village of Wiesenbronn. When it was time for him to seek a calling, he revived the family art by attending a technical university in Berlin followed by an apprenticeship in brewing. For the next several years he held the idea of getting away from chemistry and back to basic brewing. Thus a brewpub seemed to be the answer and he began looking for a suitable mix of location and backing. His search encompassed Spain, New Zealand, Aruba, Australia, and South America. In a chance meeting—the type that hap-

pens to many, but only those with initiative grab—he remembered an introduction to a New Orleans local whom
he met again at a trade show in Munich. Before long Wolfram was busy designing what would turn into a custom-
built brewery.

Inside an old warehouse at 527 Decatur Street Wolfram
began a construction project that maintained much of the
original structure, from old brickwork to refurbished cy-
press beams, and both the bar and staircase were re-
worked from salvaged wood. The patio flagstones and many
of the doors and windows were similarly saved. Wolfram
fully embraced his adopted city in the remainder of the
brewpub. On the walls he hung displays of work from local
artists and he brought in soothing live jazz, which included
nationally known musicians. Finally the tables were set
with a wide variety of tempting New Orleans dishes.

He located the copper-clad mash tun and brew kettle
behind the bar so brewing would take place within reach
of those at the taps. The space directly above the bar was
opened to display three five-hundred-gallon fermentation
tanks situated on the second floor, and five additional fermenters were placed out of sight on the third. Wolfram
termed it his brewhouse in reverse. He installed the grain
mill on the fourth floor, and dropped the crushed grain to
the mash tun on the ground level, then pumped the wort
up to the second or third floor for fermentation. The finished beer then traveled back down to the taps.

As to be expected, Crescent City followed the German
purity code of 1516, the *Reinheitsgebot*, in making of all
the beer. Perhaps the most interesting of the brewmaster's
stories was how he secured his yeast supply. It seems that
Wolfram Koehler had an old acquaintance who ran a large
brewery and yeast propagation facility in Costa Rica. The
lager yeast strain comes, of course, from Bavaria. Once a
month or so, Wolfram would board a flight for Costa Rica
with a Cornelius keg of beer. Over the weekend he and his
friend emptied the keg, and then sanitized and filled it with
a fresh supply of yeast before he boarded his flight back
to New Orleans, a very productive weekend.

At any time Wolfram would have four fresh brews on tap,
including a pilsner, a Vienna, and a Munich, with the
fourth beer reserved for a monthly special, most likely a

weiss beer in warmer months. The reception of the beers
so exceeded expectations that on the brewery's first New
Year's Eve the customers made their way through more
than twelve hectoliters (314 gallons).

Crescent City is representative of the far-reaching impact
of the brewery revival. By the early 1990s it was possible
to find a similar story in most of America's larger cities and
in the smaller towns as well.

Despite the South's early history of importing most of
their beer rather than constructing breweries, things
changed with the advent of the microbrewery movement.
People traveling to the microbrewing centers came back to
the South with a "me too" attitude. Consider Arizona. It's
not the first place to come to mind when thinking about
beer. Phoenix had its first brewery established in the mid
1800s. While there were soon upwards of half a dozen in
the area, they all disappeared with Prohibition and the
growth of the large national brewers. Phoenix grew from a
small outpost to a true city, with snowbirds (midwestern-
ers) returning each year to escape the ravages of harsh
corn belt winters. The other group to migrate there was
the cactus league of baseball spring training. Between the
winter activity and the hot Southwest summers, it was only
a matter of time before someone built a brewpub.

The region actually became home to multiple brewers. In
Tempe, Bandersnatch became known as home of the "beer
in your face club," where customers paid for the privilege
of getting a beer thrown at them. Scottsdale also had a
watering hole, Hops, a trendier place built to combine
Southwest earth tones in a modern angular design. In
Phoenix the brewpub originally opened as Barley's but in
a change of owners became Coyote Springs. The other
brewpubs are mentioned because Coyote owner Bill Garrard always encouraged people to try them all. His philosophy—"What's good for one of us is good for all."

Bill had the brewpub at the center of his mission to convert people over to the taste of real beers. Interestingly, he
did this in a method that would horrify the hard-core craft
brew enthusiasts. Alongside his own he featured mass-
market beers like Coors. Garrard explained, "My first task
is to get them in the door, then if they're drinking Coors,
I'll come over and ask them if they wouldn't like to try our

gold. I'll even buy them one just to get them to try it. Most times it will win them over."

As with most brewpubs, Coyote Springs was decorated to invoke a feeling of old-fashioned "real beer." This included a beautiful carved-wood backbar with a story as rich as the wood's texture. It was originally built in St. Louis but moved on to Butte, Montana, where it picked up a bullet hole. The next stop was Portland, Oregon, where it serviced the Barbary Coast Room of the old Hoyt Hotel. Following this it went into storage, then 110 years after it left St. Louis, it landed in Phoenix.

The brewmaster was an old hand to the Phoenix area. Clark Nelson came over from Bandersnatch to assist with the formulation of Coyote Springs' beers. Clark got his start in brewing early on. He had a grandfather who brewed beer and a mother who brewed root beer at home. After watching her several times, he decided to try his hand. In retrospect he thinks he might have used champagne yeast and too much sugar; several of the bottles exploded, and those that didn't got the family tipsy. But he didn't stray far from these brewing roots. Never liking the American standard-style beer, he began home-brewing. Even while serving on one of the nuclear navy's submarines, he brewed and produced, on a bet, a North Atlantic beer made out of Cheerios.

Coyote Springs named its beer after the brewpub school that leans toward simplicity. The beers are simply gold, red, amber, and brown, with an occasional specialty brew like oatmeal stout or bock. For years Phoenix offered visitors winter golf, spring-season baseball, summer vacation, or fall football, and by the 1990s there was year-round beer.

The spread of brewpubs and microbreweries further exposed the public to a range of beer styles that had been of limited availability in the United States. As people tried these beers they were not only converted to the new taste, they became proselytizers, introducing friends to the experience and hobby of seeking out new flavorful beers. The more beers these people tried, the more accustomed to fresh beers they became, and often the less tolerant they were of beers that didn't measure up. Among these apostles of the new beer was the same group that started craft brewing, the homebrewers. As time went by, the beer enthusiasts gained more knowledge of styles and taste and became even more demanding, almost militant, in the standards they would accept. The result was a continuing increase in the quality of marketed beer.

The craft brew movement showed the country's thirst for these beers could be satisfied in a variety of methods. Brewpub sales were usually restricted to the premises and proved that Americans would go out for a beer, if it was a beer of quality. But brewpubs could be expensive to open. Starting costs in the 1990s rose to between one and three million dollars, and the low profit margin of the restaurant business made food service experience essential.

The microbrewers had a trade-off with brewpubs. They had lower start-up costs, as low as $300,000, and a few got away with even less. In addition they weren't concerned with the brewpubers' worry of operating a restaurant. What they had to consider was using a distributor resulting in lower profits, or assume the difficulties encountered in making their own deliveries. Microbrewers delivering their own products learned the importance of prompt service. Tap and refrigerator space at the tavern or store represented a precious and volatile commodity. To earn and keep shelf space, a beer had to be a popular, quick-moving brand, and the brewery needed enough brewing capacity and delivery service to keep its designated space filled. Despite these and numerous other challenges, the microbrewers succeeded. But what about those with a great idea, market, and beer who weren't ready to own and operate a brewery? The industry would even provide an opportunity for them.

CHAPTER 14

The Rise of
Contract Brewing

Give me a bumper, fill it up;
See how it sparkes in the cup;
O how shall I regale!
Can any taste this drink devine
And then compare rum, brandy, wine
Or aught with nappy ale?

—JOHN GAY, "A Ballad on Ale"

The Boston Brewing Company
and the Best Craft Beers

Brewing beer without a brewery could only have originated in America. No brewery space? Lease it. No brewing equipment? Lease it too. No brewmasters, bottlers, or haulers? No problem, lease them all. This method opened the doors to hundreds of more beers than would have been possible if the industry were restricted to individual breweries, and the best part was, it benefited everyone involved.

Typical contract brewers were people who had marketing ideas for original beers and possibly were homebrewers who had run a few test batches. Without a brewery of their own, it must have seemed like an impossible task to get into the business. But perhaps they were sitting in their local taverns looking for an answer to this predicament. While nursing a beer, and wishing it were one of their own, the brewers mulled over the problem again and again. Finally they focused on the local taps that had been sitting there all that time. But the local brewery just may go under. They might be laying off some of the workforce soon. It was probably about this point that an idea began to form.

Brewing agreements that resulted from contractors and established breweries translated into regional breweries running closer to capacity. It also meant more efficiency, greater employment for the brewery workers, less capital outlay for the contract brewer, and more choices for the consumer. It was a situation in which nearly everyone, especially the beer-drinking consumer, wins. Some people would make disparaging comments about these beers; some purists believed they should have been brewed by the owners themselves. Truth was that many people who owned breweries had little more knowledge than some of the contractors. On top of that, a new beer may be given a try, but it would drop out of sight if the quality wasn't there. Those who sold well-made beer survived, and a good number of them even brought home medals from the Great American Beer Festival. If they had a decent beer and were aided by sound management, they prospered.

One of the most successful contractors got its start with the Bierbauer family in 1856. That year Charles Bierbauer began brewery operations on the site the brewery still occupies. In those days the tiny brewery produced lager-style beers, which had become the fashion of the day, but a series of events soon began that would transform their operations into a major brewing concern, starting with F. X. Matt's birth in 1859. His brewery training was conducted at the Duke of Boden Brewery in Rothä, Germany, his career was launched and then, at the age of twenty-two, he became another of the many immigrants to enrich America. Continuing his brewing, he found his way to Canajoharie, New York, just east of Utica. There he worked in the Louis Bierbauer Brewery owned by Charles's brother.

In 1885 Charles Bierbauer passed away and the business was merged into the Columbia Brewing Company. It was the smallest of nine breweries that called Utica home and produced barely four thousand barrels a year. Then in 1887 it became the West End Brewing Company, with F. X. Matt as manager.

F. X. guided the company as president until retirement in 1950. Even then he wasn't able to call it quits; he remained actively involved in the business until his death in 1958 at the venerable age of ninety-nine. His drive was responsible for both steady growth and successful weathering of Prohibition. The period of 1920–1933 was negotiated by shifting production to Utica Club brand soft drinks, malt tonic, malt extract, and other malt-related products. After repeal the Utica Club name was retained for beer, where it continues to this day.

As the 1980s arrived the brewery was, of course, headed by a Matt; in fact, three of them. F. X. Matt II served as chairman, Nicholas Matt as president, and Alfred Matt as director of marketing and sales. Together they represented the third generation to run the business. As the family confronted the brewing situation of the 1980s they adopted a unique approach that avoided the syndrome of placing all their eggs in one basket. Their plan was to continue production of their flagship beers, Matt's Premium and both Utica Club Pilsner and Cream Ale, while expanding these with variations of Utica Club Light, NA (a nonalcohol brew), and Matt's Light.

From this solid footing Matt's added the unique twist of contracting to keep operations running at near capacity. The manner in which the company conducts the contracting end of business is a case study in success. The key was the way Matt selected the beers they were willing to brew. By no means did they take in just anyone with the urge to slap a label on a bottle. They practiced extreme scrutiny. What their method ultimately produced was a list of contracts that reads like a Great American Beer Fest Hall of Fame. Among the beers they brewed were Brooklyn Lager, New Amsterdam, Dock Street, Olde Heurich, Harpoon Ale, and Prior Double Dark. Thus, the world of contract brewing has been good to Matt. The brewery runs at capacity, workers remain employed, and the public enjoys the benefits.

All this wasn't enough. Watching the barometer of public taste and demand, the brewery next ventured its own entry in the craft/specialty market. The Saranac line of Matt brews has since gathered its own awards, such as the 1992 gold medal for Saranac Adirondack Lager at the Great American Beer Fest's premium lager division. Then the company introduced additional styles of golden pilsner, and a black and tan. Nick Matt kept his finger on the pulse of how the beers were doing in a number of ways, but perhaps the most simple was just going to the store. He says he's likely to learn from what he doesn't find. At one point he couldn't find the black and tan in the store. The cause was simple: They weren't producing enough.

If old F. X. Matt were alive in the 1990s (and he almost was), he'd surely be smiling at the way his grandsons managed the business. Thanks to their foresight, New York can still enjoy its brewing heritage.

If in the early 1990s you asked the average beer drinker to describe a contract-brewed beer, you'd most likely get the same response as if you'd asked him to describe the theory of relativity. However, if you asked him to name a microbrewed beer, the one he'd most likely name would be Sam Adams. Boston Brewing and the company's beer heritage go back to Germany of 1840, five generations back from Jim Koch. Migrating to America, the oldest son of the family, Louis Koch, settled in St. Louis and established a brewery in 1860. Louis made good beer, but two of his neighbors, Lemp and Anheuser-Busch, were a bit more successful and forced Koch's brewery out of business.

Louis Koch's oldest son, without a brewery, took a job brewing for others, as did his oldest son. The tradition of eldest sons working in the brewing business passed down through five generations to the late 1900s, when Jim Koch looked as though he might break the trend. He graduated from Harvard with an M.B.A. and entered the business world as a management consultant. His father even advised him to stay away from the beer industry.

Jim did quite well in management, and for a while it looked as though he'd follow his father's guidance. But Jim's eye was always on beer, and as the 1970s and 1980s progressed, he came to the conclusion there was a niche for quality beer in America. As a business school graduate,

Koch realized there was more than one way to skin a cat. Other businesses leased excess equipment—airplanes, trucks, warehouses, cars, and factories. Why not a brewery? Thus, in the early 1980s Jim Koch started researching the possibility of making beer without a brewery.

As Koch looked to brewing's future, he reached to the past. The story Koch encouraged was that he revived his great-great-grandfather's recipe. The tale contains some truth, but a large amount of credit should be given to Dr. Joseph Owades, the brewing consultant who formulated not only Sam Adams but a significant number of beers for other contract brewers. In 1984 with formula in hand, Koch was ready and he began distribution of Boston Beer Company's Sam Adams Lager with the intent of selling five hundred barrels per month. He reached his initial goal in his first three months. For an aggressive businessman, this was all the indication of success Koch needed.

The growth of Sam Adams was nothing short of phenomenal and was reflected in Boston Brewing Company taking home the Consumers Preference Award at the Great American Beer Festival in 1985, 1986, and 1987. Well established by 1988, Koch began to think about an image problem: no brewery to point at. Searching the Boston area, Jim found a suitable home in what was the old Haffenreffer Brewery's bottling shop in Jamaica Plain. Leasing equipment from Bill Newman and putting all the pieces together, Koch had just what he needed to project the image of a company making beer in small, hand-crafted batches. With these moves Koch now had a facility to lead the public through. Its production amounted to less than 1 percent of Boston Brewing's output, but it allowed the company to experiment with other beers. A variety of products soon followed: Boston Stock Ale, Cranberry Lambic, Cream Stout, Wheat, Bock, and Lightship.

Koch championed quality, and to that end introduced easy-to-read freshness dating on his beer's labels. As freshness expired, Boston Brewing purchased back hundreds of cases a year. Jim even found a way to put a positive spin on this. He invited the city's bartenders to fill the tank of a dunking machine with the stale beer. Then in front of his employees he was ceremoniously "dunked."

By the early nineties Boston Brewing had expanded across the country. Beer with Koch's label was brewed under contract in three locations, and the annual production reached a quarter million barrels. Others were to follow his strategy.

In 1986 Steve Hindy was home in Brooklyn enjoying his good fortune. He could home-brew without worrying about getting caught. Better yet, if he ran out of his own supply, he could hop over to the store for a cold six-pack. It wasn't always so easy. He had been working as an Associated Press correspondent in the Middle East. Most of those countries' norms were governed by fundamentalist religious customs forbidding the manufacture or use of alcohol. Penalties for violation were at best severe. Despite this, most Middle East areas would unofficially ignore those living in the foreign compound and other infidels, as long as they kept their place, kept the alcohol under wraps, and didn't infect the local population.

It was under those constraints Steve Hindy, like many others, learned to brew. Some learned distilling through pamphlets like "The Blue Flame," and others took up wine making, but Steve was a beer man and he turned his kitchen into a brewery.

Politically events got hotter than Hindy's brewpot and he packed up his things—including his brewpot—and headed stateside. In Brooklyn you could easily get cold beer. Of course, it was beer brought in from somewhere else; the Brooklyn breweries had long vanished. Steve had grown rather accustomed to the fresh taste of his own beer, so his tiny kitchen in what was once one of America's leading brewing cities became Hindy brewery number two.

It was the summer of 1986 when he offered some of his beer to a neighbor in the apartment complex. Tom Potter gratefully sipped the beer and talked with Steve about the ghosts of once great breweries. Steve must have surprised Tom when he swung the discussion around to the possibility of a Brooklyn beer revival. Tom worked for Chemical Bank, and the cost of doing business in New York was all too real for him. Hindy then brought up the idea of starting their own brewery. Steve was enthusiastic, but Potter remained skeptical at best. Over time Hindy wore him down and eventually con-

vinced him to tag along to a microbrewery convention
that fall in Portland. The trip resulted in Potter catching
the bug; things were about to change.

Once back home in New York, Potter started working on
a business plan, and by May of 1987 he was beyond the
point of no return. The idea for a new beer had grown big
enough to demand attention full-time, and so Tom Potter
left his banking job to become a brewer. Tom started lining
up backers and in a stroke of perfect timing, closed the
financing a mere week before the Black Monday stock market crash of October 1987. With capital in hand, it was
only a matter of developing a beer. Hindy had ideas of what
he wanted, but an expert was needed to formulate a large-
scale recipe. The two partners found Bill Moeller, a retired
Philadelphia brewer who had beer running through four
generations of his family.

With Moeller and his credibility in tow, the newly formed
Brooklyn Brewing Company approached F. X. Matt in
Utica, New York, with a proposal for contract brewing.
Matt's didn't know what to think at first. Potter, Hindy,
and Moeller were proposing a beer that relied upon dry
hopping to achieve a big, flowery nose. The folks at Matt's
hesitated; dry hopping was a nearly forgotten practice.
Though initially reluctant, Matt's grew to like the idea and
challenge of making a real brewer's beer and they agreed
to give it a try. The finished lager was made with pale and
crystal malts and a mixture of Hallertauer and Cascade
hops, which gave it a malty taste and unforgettable hop
bouquet.

The next step was packaging and distribution. Hindy and
Potter wanted a design that simply stated Brooklyn's identity. The partners decided graphic artist Milton Glasser was
the one who could put it all together and initiated a courtship that made Glasser a limited partner as compensation
for his design work.

Fortune smiled again when another neighbor suggested
they wouldn't be taken seriously by the metropolitan beer
distributors and asked why they didn't start their own.
From a rented warehouse they began selling their beer,
picking up New York distribution for other contract brewers as they went along.

Eventually Brooklyn Brewing would carry up to 130 different beers. The strategy that developed was to carry a complete line of "gourmet" products. One of the strengths they developed was the role of consultant to the relatively beer-poor New York restaurant scene. Brooklyn brought them the knowledge and ability to put together a sound upscale beer list with the advantage of dealing with only one distributor. During all this they kept a careful eye on their own beer and steadily increased sales to fifteen thousand barrels by 1993, gathering tribute and medals from the Great American Beer Festival along the way.

On the other side of the state from Brooklyn, events were taking shape that would bring another contract brewer on the scene. Rochester, New York, was the home of Pete Slosberg in the 1970s when he developed an interest in homebrewing. Leaving behind his electronics marketing job, Pete headed for the greener pastures of California and graduate school. Slosberg took his homebrewing with him, and refining his technique, he started winning awards and contests with his beer.

Later, Pete settled into a job with a telecommunications firm in the silicon valley town of Palo Alto. It was perfect for Pete; California was both an electronic and computer center and incubator for new brewers. Over time Pete and a co-worker talked about getting a business to run just for fun when it dawned on them—what could be more fun than beer? In January 1986 Pete was contracting with the local Palo Alto Brewery. First-year production was 725 barrels, and even at this low figure, Slosberg realized the beer business was no part-time endeavor. Pete's was going to need a full-time president. The beer was gaining popularity and had received its first award from the Great American Beer Festival.

Two years after start-up was a critical time for the company, and several things occurred in rapid succession. Palo Alto Brewing Company went out of business, and Pete's switched to the August Schell Brewery in New Ulm, Minnesota. The other significant move was to hire Mark Bonzini as president. Bonzini had made his mark in the beverage world by guiding Seagram's wine coolers to a number one spot, knocking off the early leader, Bartyle and James. To add a little more confusion to an already unsettled situation, the company was the subject of a lawsuit.

When Pete first bottled his Wicked Ale, he used a picture of his dog on the label and included the Latin *"Cave Canem Nidentum"* or "Beware of the White Dog." Milly, unfortunately, bore a striking resemblance to Spuds McKenzie, the spokes-dog for Anheuser-Busch, and the brewing giant brought legal action against the tiny company. Trademark and copyright protection is a serious matter, and the makers of Bud and Spuds, though perhaps not gravely threatened, did feel obliged to keep such things in check. Eventually Anheuser-Busch dropped the case; it was okay for the founder to use a picture of his dog on both the label and bottle caps. By that time Pete and company had decided to make a change. New packaging was developed that featured a picture of Pete's great-grandfather Zadie Slosberg, who was himself an old-time homebrewer. The design was so well done, it received a 1990 Cleo award in advertising.

Despite the growing pains, Pete's Wicked Ale was welcomed wherever it was introduced. The beer gained additional recognition when it was voted best ale in America in 1987, 1988, and 1989 at the Great American Beer Festival. Then in 1992 Pete's was awarded a gold medal in the American Brown Ale category. But the success also brought new challenges. In July of that year he was no longer able to meet his capacity needs through his existing relationship at August Schell. Slosberg considered his options. Should he switch breweries? Did it make sense to remain a contract brewer? Would he be able to afford his own brewhouse? It was then the winds of providence shifted his way.

Not far from August Schell sat the old Jacob Schmidt Brewery in St. Paul, which had seen its most recent service as a G. Heileman facility. The once proud brewery had recently been rescued from its shutdown state by a group of local investors but was running well under its two-million-barrel-a-year capacity. The owners were looking for an arrangement to make operations more efficient while Pete wanted more control of his own destiny. They found a solution in each other's needs. It was thus Pete came to receive his brewing license, purchase some equipment, and for the first time hire his own full-time head brewer and staff to go along with it all. Thus Pete's

Wicked entered the transition phase of contract brewing with a foot in either world, and after 1992 Pete would look at the Minnesota Brewing Company as the brick-and-mortar part of Pete's brewing.

Pete felt he would know he had made it if he spotted what he considered a symbol of success. The moment finally came in 1992. While strolling through a parking lot in Oregon, Pete stopped and smiled. For there at his feet, pressed into the dirt, was a bottle cap from Pete's Wicked Ale.

On the other side of the country another contract beer would also make the transition to brewery, having experienced a beginning much like Pete Slosberg's and the other microbrewers'. Rob Nelson and Bob Clark were Georgia natives, beer enthusiasts, and homebrewers. Their first step toward owning a brewery sounds familiar to most accomplished homebrewers who at one time or another entertain a little fantasy. Welcoming in 1989 on New Year's Eve with a few too many homebrews, they started talking about owning a real brewing company. The next morning it was Bob Clark who remembered the whimsical plans and reminded Nelson of their solemn pledge to enter the beer business.

After some research and consideration, the two friends decided a brewery might be a little too ambitious a start and so, like Pete Slosberg, they settled on the idea of contracting their brew. That's when they discovered the road to success is strewn with potholes. They began with the obvious, lining up the finances. Rob laughed as he recalled the problems with getting a few dollars together. The investment community was intrigued with the idea of a hand-crafted beer; it had a certain appeal. But the money folks soon hit them with the age-old paradox: They didn't have any beer experience. Rob worked in the medical supply business, and Bob had a background in computers. Sure, financing could be lined up, but the two partners needed experience. Fortunately, they ignored the advice of experts, and went out on a limb. Putting their own resources and reputations on the line, they next decided the only way to make their kind of beer was at a facility that would let them use their own brewmaster. The answer was found by looking back almost one hundred years and a thousand miles away.

Established in 1898, the Dubuque Star Brewing Company was once the pride of Joseph Pickett and Sons. Pickett was once the brewer for Chicago's Edelweiss and Drewry's, but the brewery had fallen on hard times, and like others, it agreed to take on contract work. Unlike other contractors, they also agreed to allow Rob and Bob's Georgia Brewing Company to use its own brewmaster in making their Wild Boar Beer.

It's quite amazing they pulled everything together so quickly, but only ten months later, Rob found himself with Georgia Brewing's beer at the 1989 Great American Beer Festival. The partners were as surprised and delighted as anyone when they were awarded a bronze medal and also garnered fifth place in the last of the festival's consumer preference polls. The next year was difficult, but the thrill of the medal convinced them things were looking up. The 1990 Festival proved even more rewarding. When Rob heard they earned a gold in their second year, he phoned back to the East Coast to a sound-asleep Bob. Clark was happy to win but wasn't sure about being awake in the middle of the night. He'd get used to it soon.

Things seemed to be going Georgia Brewing's way. They were selling beer, getting new accounts, and gaining awards and recognition; they even ordered up loads of promotional items. Then they received a near disastrous call from Dubuque. The brewery was going out of business.

With success in sight, the two homebrewing buddies suddenly found themselves with their entire lives tied up in bankruptcy court. They were near devastation when they received a rescue call. The other beer contract brewed in Dubuque, Simpatico, had a proposal. If Georgia Brewing would commit to continued production at the brewery, they'd work up a financing plan that included a share of ownership. They told the two partners to think it over and give them a ring back. The way Rob tells it, they spent a couple of minutes considering and dismissing any negatives of the plan and then several more deciding how quickly they could respond without looking anxious. Later that day they returned the call and became part owners of a real brewing company.

Asked what the biggest difference was between contracting and owning, Rob responds with two observations. On a positive note, he says they can more easily schedule when a batch of Wild Boar would be brewed. On the downside, he recalls that as contractors, when the brewery crew would tell them a part broke, he'd respond with, "Well, go buy a new one." But after becoming an owner, he changed it to, "How can we fix it?" The challenges are new and things are a bit different when you own a brewery, but Rob says he wouldn't trade the feeling he gets looking at that old Iowa brewery building for anything.

The number of beer drinkers in America is actually a much smaller percent of the population than some people may imagine. The United States is nowhere near able to claim the position of number one beer drinking nation per capita. However, if consideration is limited to the amount consumed among those who do drink beer, the United States can claim the distinction of first. What did this mean to the micro/craft brewers? In the early 1990s, not much. The market projections for the percentage of consumption attributed to micro/craft beer was but a small portion of the country's annual beer production. But with all that in mind, craft beers did represent the fastest-growing segment of the beer sales.

Estimates calculate that every reasonably sized town could support a small brewery, just as they did in the past. But this scenario is not likely to be fulfilled without a major change in America's drinking habits, customs, and tastes. Most of the country's beer drinkers have been heavily influenced by the megabrewers with their large advertising budgets. It seemed as though the beer drinkers were caught up in a "more is better" attitude. At the soul of the craft beer movement is the idea that more may not necessarily be better, and, in fact, it is generally less. The craft brewers have a job of education. They must work together to introduce the public to the broad spectrum of taste in beer.

Be assured if a significant market opens for more full-bodied beers, full of the taste of malt and hops, the big brewers will have their version on the street in no time flat. They're running a business. Why didn't these breweries come out with a super premium beer when the craft brewing craze hit? Part of the reason was a market share too small to worry about; another was overcoming the stigma of a big brewery producing a good beer, a problem shared with some of the larger wineries. All things considered, the craft beer movement will prove a very interesting trend to watch.

CHAPTER 15

The Modern
Brew-in-the-Home
Movement

You can have some home-brew, if you want to,
you know.

—THOMAS HARDY

*Dear Tom, this brown jug that now foams with
mild ale,
(In which I will drink to sweet Nan of the Vale)
Was once Toby Fillpot, a thirsty old soul
As e'er drank a bottle, or fathom'd a bowl;
In bossing about 'twas his praise to excel,
And among jolly topers he bore off the bell.*

—FRANCIS FAWKES, 1720–1777

Beer Lovers Go Back to Their Roots

The revival of homebrewing in the 1970s and 1980s can
be attributed to the same factors that initiated the microbrewery movement. Americans who traveled to England
enjoyed ales there ranging from the thirst-quenching milds
and browns up through pale ales to the porters and stouts.

In Germany they relished crisp pilsners, malty Munichs, old-style Kölsch from Köln (Cologne), and some fortunate wanderers even discovered the smoky richness of Rauchbiers in Franconia. Perhaps the biggest treat was reserved for those visiting Belgium with its complex Trappist ales, ancient lambics which were even flavored with fruit, and refreshing Saisons. Americans found there was a world of beers as diverse as the countries and cultures that made up the world. Coming home to America, they found that what they thought was a solid beer-loving country was really a land of monotony.

So like the Pilgrims and countless others, they turned back to the kitchen to refire the brew kettle and devise their own versions of these products. Those early days of the 1970s were rather rough. Recipes called for a hefty amount of corn sugar, making the beer cidery. Yeast was often contaminated and led to infections, sourness, sulfury notes, and incomplete attenuation. Malt extract was, at best, of mediocre character. Homebrewers were also plagued by inexact methods of priming, which could produce either flat beer or an occasional bomb. Nearly everyone has heard a story about exploding homebrew bottles. The army could use them as land mines if it were only possible to set the timing. Undaunted, the homebrewers pushed on; even their failures were interesting. If it wasn't perfect beer, they were at least getting variety.

As more people took to the brew kettle, there was just one problem. It was illegal, an unexplained glitch resulting from an oversight in the laws enacted during repeal. Then in 1979 Congressman Barber B. Conable (R, New York) was persuaded by homebrewers to introduce a provision legalizing brewing beer in the home. Time went by, the number of brewers increased, and the quality of homebrew got better and better. In part it might have been the practice and knowledge they gained while making their beer. Another factor, though something of a chicken-or-the-egg argument, could have been the increase in microbrewing pulling the homebrew ingredients up, although some homebrewers claim it was the other way around. Or it might simply be that with increasing frequency, they demanded more quality in the materials they purchased. And as competition increased between suppliers, there was a healthy capitalistic move toward a higher grade of materials. Finally, brewers and manufacturers began to respond to the needs of the homebrewer. For example, hops were packaged in smaller lots and a variety of yeast strains were marketed.

It's always been hard to think of modern homebrewing as a hobby. Although performed on a smaller scale, the ingredients, techniques, and methods were made to replicate the larger breweries. As the numbers swelled, the suppliers began manufacturing all types of specialized equipment. Soon there were scaled-down roller mills, extralarge brewpots, wort chillers, counterpressure bottle fillers, kegging equipment, lauter tuns, and yeast culturing kits. Old glass water cooler bottles (carboys) became a hot commodity as these brewers gobbled them up for duty as primary fermenters. With all the improved equipment and supplies, the brewed-at-home beers had a remarkable leap in quality. By the 1990s blind judgings often placed the better examples as equal to, and occasionally superior to, many of the microbrewed beers.

No matter how good the supplies, the made-at-home beers would not have improved without an increase in brewing skill. Several factors can be credited with the education that took place.

Publishers and booksellers always observe public trends, and as the beer movement picked up, the keepers of the printed word took notice. Magazines and books ran off the presses in hopes of cashing in on part of the craze. To their surprise, it stuck, and fifteen years after it was legalized, homebrewers were still increasing in numbers. The how-to books provided part of the answer. Each new manuscript seemed to increase the level of sophistication, and many homebrewers studied enough to be able to hold their own technical discussions with brewing academy graduates. Authors Pat Baker, Dave Miller, Dave Line and Charlie Papazian explained in simple terms how a batch of beer was made. Along the way they described troubles encountered and how to combat them. Then they provided technical knowledge of the items within a brewer's control and how each of these affected the finished beer.

The next significant event took place in Boulder, Colorado, when a person educated in the workings of the atom got sidetracked by beer. Charlie Papazian was an avid amateur brewer who found himself teaching a homebrew class after hours for a local community college. Papazian wrote a guide on how to make beer, and with growing interest and anticipation, watched the country's beer taste evolve. He might have become a brewer, but the night course may have steered him aside. For instead, Charles Papazian took up the cause of homebrewing education.

His writing was a good start, but the ambitious, energetic Papazian took a large step further and created a full-time position for himself by founding the American Homebrewers Association in 1978 as a nonprofit educational association. Within a few years of its origin, the Association was looking over a quickly changing beer-scape. The microbrewing industry was gaining strength and the ranks of homebrewers and beer enthusiasts were multiplying rapidly. To further educate the beer-loving masses, the Association started the Great American Beer Festival in 1982.

The Beer Festival served several purposes. It met its initial goal of education through the vast numbers of people attending to sample, speak with brewers, and take notes on their favorite beers. But before long the GABF took on an additional role as a beer competition. At first there was some criticism because the winners were identified by a popular vote. It wasn't a very sophisticated method: attendees were given tickets to exchange for samples. The number of tickets each brewer collected determined the "best" beer. Unfortunately this turned into a popularity contest of sorts. Brewers sponsored giveaways at their booths or staffed them with models. This practice was somewhat questionable, but some beers such as Sam Adams benefited. The Boston Brewing Company won the poll three years in a row, skipped attending one year, and then won again on their return. This was the basis for the advertisements that Sam Adams was voted "best beer four years running." Although slightly deceiving, it was effective. Eventually the organizers discontinued the popular vote and even went so far as to prohibit distribution of any promotional items the brewers didn't regularly give away.

Within a short period the Great American Beer Festival established a panel of judges to rank the beers in a blind competition. Gold, silver, and bronze medals were awarded to those beers that most faithfully represented a style. The competition was another of those factors that helped improve the quality of America's hand-crafted beers. The festival was so successful, it became one of the most well-attended beer events in the country.

A year after the initial Great American Beer Fest, the Institute of Brewing Studies was formed as an offshoot of the American Homebrewers Association to "provide education and service to the growing craft-brewing movement." Further changes to the Association came in 1986 when the Association of Brewers was adopted as the corporate name under which the AHA, Great American Beer Festival, Brewers Publications, and Institute for Brewing Studies became divisions. Brewers Publications was founded as one of those divisions to publish books for home and professional brewers and beer enthusiasts. Along with descriptive and scientific information on beer and its components, Brewers Publications produced a series of books on classic beer styles. The Association got into the magazine business with five yearly issues of *Zymurgy* (the word for the study of fermentation), directed at homebrewers, and *New Brewer*, aimed at the craft-brewing members of the Association.

In 1993, fifteen years after it all began, the Association of Brewers proudly looked back on sixty-seven total issues of *Zymurgy*, an additional fifty-eight issues of *New Brewer*, thirty-six books in print, eleven consecutive Great American Beer Festivals, ten microbrewers' conferences, and AHA membership of more than sixteen thousand.

This wasn't the limit of the Association's crusade for better beer. Teaming up with the trade group of homebrew suppliers, the Home Wine and Beer Trade Association, the two groups began sponsoring homebrewed beer competitions, which resulted in further improvements in both the brewer's techniques and quality of ingredients.

About 1985 Pat Baker was looking over the annual competitions and was pleased to see steady growth in the number of participants, entries, and quality. But there was something nagging at him. Judging seemed a little inconsistent at times, and the score sheets returned to the entrants didn't always provide helpful feedback on how to improve their beers. Sitting down at a typewriter in July of 1985, Pat wrote a letter that would overhaul the entire process. At prior competitions and get-togethers he had been talking to a core of people about starting a program for judges. His letter to Sue Kenny and Grosvenor Merle-Smith summed up those conversations, and with Baker's additional thoughts on structure, the framework of the Beer Judge Certification Program was established.

To serve as a judge, participants would have to pass a grueling three-hour written exam on beer, brewing, styles, and faults, and successfully evaluate four beers. Judges were ranked, based on a combination of test score and experience gained in the program in levels running from Recognized up through Certified to National and Master. The program was also successful in bringing standardization to the manner in which competitions were run, the scoring systems used, and an improvement in suggestions to the brewers who entered beer. The feedback was another part of the influences that brought such remarkable improvement to the homebrewed beers during the 1980s and 1990s. No longer did friends of homebrewers turn their noses up at the offer of a homebrew; instead people began asking for handouts, which, of course, led to homebrew lessons and further increased the number of Americans who were heading back to their roots.

Another influence that increased the quality of homebrewed beer was the formation of homebrew clubs. Many were formed under the guidance of the American Homebrewers Association's AHA Registered Club program, and served not only as the center of beer social functions but also as educational forums. For example, the New York City Homebrewers Guild, established in the mid-1980s, arranged to meet at one of the city's local beer bars, where, once a month, members would taste and discuss the style merits of the special of the month.

At first the Guild served more as a drinking club. Meetings were called to order by the loudest bellower, more often than not an ex-president of the Guild. As the club evolved, the focus centered more on brewing. At each meeting a guest speaker from a commercial brewery, an author, or some other person associated with the beer industry would deliver a short talk on selected topics, followed by a question-and-answer period.

Soon the speech segment was joined by an in-house

judging session. The registration of homebrewed beers by a competition coordinator took place during the speech. After the question-and-answer session would be a blind judging of beers brewed by the members; these were evaluated by the club's certified judges. Beers were critiqued on official score sheets and returned to the brewers before the ink was dry. The meeting was then opened for brewers and judges to discuss the merits and problems of the beer along with possible solutions to any brewing or style faults. The postscoring confrontations no doubt provided judges with immediate lessons on how to present criticism in polite and constructive writing.

Clubs provided other services such as the New York Guild's Beer Judge Training course. They also sponsored trips to breweries and hosted mini beer festivals along with regular homebrew competitions. All these events brought in even more members and created additional brewers and beer enthusiasts, and on occasion the club would serve as an incubator for new microbrewers.

By the early 1990s homebrewers were an active and influential part of the beer scene. They got friends involved in beer tastings, cajoled their associates into trying craft-brewed beers, negotiated with loved ones to visit brewpubs, and actively recruited new members in the unofficial order of the mash shovel. The homebrewers further raised their voices for higher-quality brew materials and volunteered criticism, sometimes less than diplomatically, to commercial brewers whose products occasionally didn't quite measure up. And of course, from their ranks came the brave souls who left the comfort and security of old jobs to try their hand at professional brewing. As they proselytized and brewed, they developed another insatiable thirst—for more knowledge about their avocation—and so they turned to the printed page.

CHAPTER 16

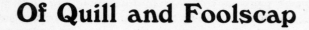

Of Quill and Foolscap

There let him browse, and deep carouse,
Wi' bumpers flowing o'er
Till he forgets his loves or debts,
An' minds his griefs no more.

—ROBERT BURNS

The Beers, the People, the Pen, and the Papers

As the microbeer movement gained strength and adherents, "brewspapers" directed at the beer enthusiast soon appeared. Some, of course, established their periodicals just to profit off a growing potential readership. But many entered the publishing world simply because they liked beer, others because it was a means to somehow be connected to the new brewing industry, and still others because it seemed like a fun thing to do.

Regardless of their reasons for taking on the risk and headaches of launching a new magazine, the results were the same: The printed word was one more contributor to the growth of the microbrewery industry. The "brewspapers" sold ads to the brewers, brewpubs, and distributors of craft beers. Free copies of the paper—which included beer reviews, brew stories, locations, maps, and features on the breweries—were distributed free to the patrons of pubs and stores that carried these new beers. As people read about other beers, they would give them a try and introduce them to their friends. Gradually subscriptions grew and provided a more solid footing. Regional beer tabloids found audiences across the country as microbrewery pilgrims read up on areas of prospective touring and brewery trips became nearly as common as visits to wineries.

Papers weren't the only format. Magazines sprang up to fill the role of nationwide reporting. The magazines looked for new angles to cover, and the world of beer became broader than merely opening a chilled bottle. Articles soon spread beyond the arena of brewery descriptions. There were biographical sketches, historical pieces, beer stories, essays, book reviews, coverage of proposed legislation, and even regular columns on beer cuisine. The education of their readers paid off. As the beer enthusiasts grew more knowledgeable and demanding, the quality of writing improved. By the early 1990s there was a beer paper in every region of the country, and some even began competing in overlapping markets.

All About Beer is considered the first of the beer magazines. It began as one of a group of specialty magazines developed by McMullen Publishing Company of Southern California. In its early years the magazine broadly covered the beer industry and beer drinking with stories as likely to address the latest news from Anheuser-Busch as it was to report on the newest micro. It was a scattered approach to be all things to all beer drinkers. Purchased by Mike and Bunny Bosak, the magazine gradually shifted its focus toward the growing import and craft brew audience.

The Bosaks signed up beer personalities to churn out regular columns and filled the remainder of the glossy pages with articles by freelance writers and press releases from large brewers. As the industry developed, so did the magazine, with occasional ups and downs. Some articles were timely and informative, and one of the most popular was a regular panel review of guest beers. But the magazine also accumulated files of stories that were sometimes dated, including some that ran after a brewery had closed. And writers were sometimes frustrated by slipped or incorrect bylines. Despite its flaws, the Bosaks were developers of the first beer magazine available coast to coast, and they provided a name to build on.

In 1992 Daniel Bradford took control from the Bosaks and began an aggressive project to reshape the magazine. His idea was to elevate the level of writing, sharpen the graphics, and place more emphasis on craft brews. Bradford's relationship with beer went back to Boulder, Colorado, where he taught history at the university. In his lean days as a student Dan financed his schooling by hustling part-time on the fringe of the book and magazine industry. This prompted a friend to suggest working as a book agent. It was Bradford who cut the deal for Charlie Papazian's homebrewing book, and his connection with Papazian drew him deeper into the world of beer.

Fortunately for Bradford, the book agent business was supplying less than a full-time income, because he would accept a position as marketing director at Papazian's new Association of Brewers. This was in 1984 when Bradford's experience with promotions would help with the Great American Beer Festival. Dan's involvement as director gathered him even more experience in layout and publishing, and before long he was assisting with the development of *The New Brewer,* the Association's trade magazine.

Bradford's combination of beer and magazine experience kept growing. Then in 1991 Dan got married. When his bride accepted a job offer in Durham, North Carolina, he bid good-bye to the Rockies and the Association of Brewers. As he settled into life on the East Coast, sources told him *All About Beer* might be available. Dan listened to suggestions, and when he heard the pitch for the fourth time, he decided to surrender. The first few steps proved a blur in Dan's memory, but next thing he knew, he had a wife, a new home, a new baby, and a magazine to run. He described getting involved as

> a good idea, and so now instead of producing various special events I produce six special events a year called a magazine. I'm really into the public education aspect and to battle the "fascist neo-prohibitionists"—it's the way to maintain our right to enjoy a part of our heritage.

Embracing a mission to do just that, *All About Beer* brought beer drinkers the latest updates from the craft-brew world along with encouragement for responsible drinking.

The glossy pages of *All About Beer* covered the broad picture of the entire country. What was left untouched, as microbrewing rapidly expanded, was a market for local brewery news. Earliest in the movement was California, and the activity there attracted the attention of a couple from British Columbia contemplating a move to the sunshine state. Bret and Julie Nickels settled into California life during 1987; drawing on their previous job of promoting a beer-related restaurant chain, they entered the realm of microbreweries.

In 1988 they published their first issue of the *Celebrator* and released it at a fund-raiser for the Lyon Brewery Depot, which had burned down. The brewers in attendance scooped up the copies to take back for their customers. The Nickelses built up the paper as a two-person operation, writing, editing, publishing, selling advertisements, and distributing. After two years of facing deadlines and struggling with the problems of an unsettled distribution system, the Nickelses reluctantly decided to sell.

The *Celebrator*'s white knight was Tom Dalldorf, who ran a wine store café in Hayward during 1979 and began carrying the microbrewed beers as they appeared on the scene. Being located in the same town as renegade brewer Bill Owens may have had an effect, but whatever the reason, when Tom heard the paper was up for sale, he jumped at the chance. One of Dalldorf's first moves was to computerize the editing and layout, abandoning the old cut-and-paste method that made publishing a bimonthly migraine.

Tom began his stewardship of *Celebrator* with a circulation of forty thousand in August of 1990 and in quick succession added a core of feature writers, cleared up distribution problems, and expanded throughout the West Coast. The coverage also changed as Dalldorf added stories on beers from the Rocky Mountains along with brewery updates from throughout the United States. He even included beer travel pieces on classic beer treks in Europe and the Far East.

The story of the *Celebrator* even came complete with a happy ending for the original owner. After two years away from the paper, Bret Nichols returned to serve as editor in chief. Tom continued to operate the magazine out of Hayward and could regularly be spotted talking beer in Buffalo Bill's Brewpub.

Another of those magazines that started life elsewhere was *American Brewer*. Its origin was in Portland, Oregon, where Fred Eckhardt, a local writer, set up the periodical as a micro and homebrew magazine with the name *Amateur Brewer*. In 1987 it was sold out to micro pioneer Bill Owens of Hayward, California. Owens couldn't resist tinkering, and nearly everything but the subject changed. The name evolved to *American Brewer,* with a writing style that mixed tongue-in-cheek humor and sarcasm with a love of fun. Bill's background in graphics came into play as he also changed the look. It was in this forum that Bill proudly offered his Pumpkin Ale recipe to the world.

Operating out of an office consisting of a modified closet and a table in the back of his brewpub, Bill would line up advertisers and dictate articles on a cordless phone while stirring the mash at one moment and pulling a draft the next. Just when it seemed his life couldn't get any crazier, Bill discovered he could actually carry two portable phones. Perhaps this was when he got the idea for yet another magazine. He just didn't have enough irons in the fire.

The idea fermented slowly, though (for Bill), during 1989–1990 as he toyed with several ways to pick up a second cover. Along with Bradford, he was one of those who considered purchasing *All About Beer* from the Bosaks. Finally he decided to start one from scratch. At some point during his planning Alan Eames sent Bill a copy of the European *Beer the Magazine,* and Bill fell in love with the big, colorful, flashy layout. As Bill put it, "A look of class." It was an upscale magazine about upscale beer, and his mind raced with the possibilities; perhaps there was a niche for a beer version of the *Wine Spectator,* with a large, glossy tabloid format.

People starting new microbreweries have often benefited

from using business school students who developed the business plans and marketing studies as class projects. This concept wasn't lost on Bill Owens and he arranged for the help of some graduate students from Harvard. With a plan in hand and four to five months of heavy marketing and sales, Bill unveiled the first issue of *Beer the Magazine* in August of 1993. The rush to put out the first issue was a typical Bill Owens move, and it would be more than five months until the second appeared. But quality tells, and the United States soon had two national beer magazines to inform and educate the public.

Through the hoopla and commotion, Bill continued to operate his world brewing and publishing empire off the back corner table of his brewpub. Finally this was even a bit much for flamboyant Bill and he refurbished a small office just across the street.

Just as with the microbrewery movement, things originated on the West Coast, but as activity in the field finally came east, so did the idea of a "beeriodical." Unlike microbrewing, it didn't begin in New York, but rather up the coast in Boston.

At some point most American families have been touched by the beer business, and in a great many, especially in New England, the brewing of beer was as much a part of the home as a family meal. Don Gosselin was one of these. Gosselin's family had always brewed at home; it was a part of a Yankee way of life and heritage. His granduncle even gained some notoriety as a big name in Prohibition homebrewing, and Don learned the art from his own father while still a senior in high school.

In 1988 Gosselin was involved in running a Newton, Massachusetts, business named the Barley Malt and Vine Inc., a homebrew supply shop. Looking for ways to promote the business, he started a newsletter that dealt with beer and how to brew it. During 1988 the shop received numerous compliments on the newsletter, and by 1989 Don had latched on to the idea of printing a New England brewspaper. Thus *Yankee Brew News* was born with a slant toward regional beer news. When the paper debuted it was the first brewspaper east of the Rockies. To say this was forward-looking is an understatement. At that time there were only ten microbreweries and brewpubs in New England to cover, but within five years that number would grow four times over. It seemed as though a new place was opening every other month, and in fact, this was true. There was a lot of action to report on, and it kept the readers and pages full of new information.

It was almost inevitable for Gosselin to limit the paper to New England brew news. Folks up in that section of the country have a strong sense of regionalism. As Don says, "New Englanders will even pay a premium for items made in New England. They look at the rest of the country with a curious glance and a bit of amusement." Those few attempts to cover areas outside the Northeast drew negative reactions and caused Gosselin to abandon any ideas of becoming the *USA Today* of beer.

Distribution was built up by supplying the paper to taverns, restaurants, and package stores that wanted to build up their sales of microbrewed beers. The retailers looked at *Yankee Brew News* as an easy and inexpensive way to educate their customers about the trend toward handcrafted beers. Subscriptions built slowly, but Gosselin was pleased to see a fair percentage of orders coming from outside the Northeast. Don figured this was the part of the beer wave that spun off beer hunters, people who would go to New England for vacation and look to return the next year armed with brewery information. As more beer lovers picked up, and passed on, copies of the *Yankee Brew News,* circulation began to pick up, and a base of over fifty thousand was reached by 1994.

Several minor changes were made to coincide with the larger reader base, changes that New Englanders would rather call adjustments. Gosselin slightly expanded the coverage to eastern Canada and northeastern New York. Then he increased the printing frequency from a quarterly to a bimonthly, something Don wished he had done even sooner. "There's just too much to cover and our readers like their beer news just as they like their beer—fresh!" Don knew the paper turned the corner when it was no longer necessary to push hard for advertisers. Instead of the paper reaching out to sell them, they were calling the *Yankee Brew News* for space.

Gosselin's idea of fresh beer news is exactly what led to formation of the country's first beer monthly. A group of beer lovers in the New York area started in September 1994 *The Beer & Tavern Chronicle* to provide even more timely news to beer readers with as big a thirst for beer news as for the beverage itself.

The story of *The Chronicle* is one in which things happened to come together correctly as a partnership of talents made for a publishing team that might not have been successful if any of them attempted an independent venture. One piece of ownership came from Liz Branch and John Murphy. Liz had experience in selling advertising and, along with John, ran a delivery service. Eventually their mutual love of beer led them to open a homebrew business, The Little Shop of Hops, in an unused portion of their New York City store. A monthly newsletter they developed and the success of the shop translated to a distribution of more than six thousand newsletters. As they worked on deadlines and mailings, they eventually thought they would have been just as well off publishing a magazine.

The business of running a homebrew shop brought them into contact with a New Jersey shop owner named Tom Clark. Tom got into the business by going to school. In college he attended a semester at Wruxton in the United Kingdom, and adjacent to the school was the Hook Norton Brewery, where Tom soon developed a taste for Old Hooky ale. A return to the United States and a continuing thirst for full-bodied beer directed him to a management internship at Old World Brewing in New York.

Beer had definitely entered his blood; he was working in it during the day, homebrewing at night, and eventually opened Red Bank Brewing Supply in 1991. His second store, Brunswick Brewing Supply, came soon after in 1993. Not even this satisfied him. He was traveling and studying beer all over the United States and Europe, and eventually began distributing beers for Minnesota Brewing, Cold Spring, and August Schell while planning to open a microbrewery.

Eventually an acquaintanceship between Clark, Branch, and Murphy grew into a business relationship. One of their efforts, Brew Kettle Inc., entered them into the arena of hosting beer festivals. Over beers and during business meetings they continued to toy with the idea of starting a periodical that would focus on the New York market. But they needed editors.

Where to look if you needed partners and editors to start a new beer publication? How about in a bar? It was at regular meetings of the New York City Homebrewers Guild that Liz and John met a homebrewer, beer judge, writer, and author named Gregg Smith. In the spring of 1994 they brought out their plan and asked about spare time for the new business. It sounded great, but the plans to go monthly made it obvious that another person experienced in layout was needed, a fellow colleague with a similar background to join the team. Thus Rob Haiber came to fill the spot of coeditor. Finally all the pieces were in place and the partnership, with a special mix of sales, advertising, writing, editing, and distribution, came together in America's first beer monthly, containing columns on beer bars, style profiles, interviews with brewers, homebrewing tips, and beer history. As with other writers, they soon found that news, updates, information, and beers came their way freely. What a great business. But it also meant the strange "work" of frequenting bars and breweries to collect stories, sell ads, and perform PR duties. It even got to the point that occasionally the last thing they wanted was a beer.

At their best the periodicals give readers informative descriptions of the industry and timely updates on activities and beer fests.

The development of beer papers in every region of the country was a sure barometer of the increasing number of craft-brewed beers. These papers specialized in stories about the micro and small contract breweries, and their circulation growth was a direct reflection of the beers' success.

The magazines and papers found their place as an educational tool, a sounding board for the industry, a travel guide for enthusiasts, and a forum for hobbyists. As time went by, better and better writers became beer enthusiasts, and when they turned their talents toward the brewspapers, there was a steady increase in the quality of articles. The ranks of brew scribes grew so large that by the mid 1990s writers formed the North American Guild of Beer Writers, with the objective of generating even greater improvement in beer journalism. All these efforts led to a more educated consumer, which drove both a further expansion of microbrewing and an increase in the quality of those beers.

Appendix I

The Top Ten Brewers and Their Beer

1877

1. George Ehret, New York, NY
2. Ph. Best, Milwaukee, WI
3. Bergner & Engel, Philadelphia, PA
4. P. Ballantine & Sons, Newark, NJ
5. Conrad Seipp, Chicago, IL
6. H. Clausen & Son, New York, NY
7. Flanagan & Wallace, New York, NY
8. Jacob Ruppert, New York, NY
9. Beadleston & Woerz, New York, NY
10. Jos. Schlitz Brewing Company, Milwaukee, WI

1895

1. Pabst Brewing Co., Milwaukee, WI
2. Anheuser-Busch Brewing Assn., St. Louis, MO
3. Jos. Schlitz Brewing Co., Milwaukee, WI
4. George Ehret, New York, NY
5. Ballantine & Co., Newark, NJ
6. Bernheimer & Schmind, New York, NY
7. Val. Blatz Brewing Co., Milwaukee, WI
8. Wm. J. Lemp Brewing Co., St. Louis, MO
9. Conrad Seipp Brewing Co., Chicago, IL
10. Frank Jones Brewing Co., Portsmouth, NH

1973

1. Anheuser-Busch, Inc.
2. Jos. Schlitz Brewing Co.
3. Pabst Brewing Co.
4. Adolph Coors Co.
5. Miller Brewing Co.
6. Falstaff Brewing Corp.
7. F. & M. Schaefer Brewing Co.
8. Stroh Brewery Co.
9. G. Heileman Brewing Co.
10. Carling Brewing Co.

Large Brewers—1993

1. Anheuser-Busch
2. Miller Brewing Company
3. Coors Brewing
4. Stroh Brewing
5. G. Heileman Breweries
6. Pabst Brewing
7. Genesee Brewing
8. Latrobe Brewing Company
9. Evansville Brewing
10. Yeungling

Top Contract Brewers—1993

1. Boston Beer Company, MA: The Sam Adams brands—Lager, Lightship, Boston Ale, Wheat, Octoberfest, and Double Bock
2. Pete's Brewing Company, CA: Pete's Wicked Ale, Pete's Wicked Lager, Pete's Red, Pete's Wicked Winter Brew
3. William & Scott Company, CA: Rhino Chaser Lager and Ale
4. New Amsterdam Brewing, NY: New Amsterdam Amber, New Amsterdam Ale, Winter
5. Brandevor Brewing, WA: Simpatico, Wild Boar
6. Brooklyn Brewing, NY: Brooklyn Brown, Brooklyn Lager, Chocolate Stout

7.   Dock Street, PA: Amber, Bohemian Pilsner
8.   Neuweiler, PA: Ale, Black & Tan, Lager
9.   Mill Bakery, Brewery and Eatery, FL: Hornet Tail Ale, Red October
10. Atlantic City Brewing, NJ: Diving Horse

Top Craft Brewers—1993

1.   Anchor Brewing, CA: Steam, Porter, Our Special Ale, Liberty, Foghorn, Wheat
2.   Sierra Nevada, CA: Pale Ale, Big Foot, Wheat, Porter, Stout, Celebration Ale
3.   Red Hook Ale Brewery, WA: Redhook Ale, Ballard's Bitter, ESB, Blackhook Porter, Wheat Hook
4.   Full Sail Brewing Company, OR: Pilsner, Golden, Amber, Brown, Porter
5.   Widmer Brewing Company, OR: QLT Bier, Hefe-Weizen, Marzen, Weizen, Oktoberfest, Bock

Top Microbreweries—1993

1.   Pyramid, WA: Wheaten Ale, Hefe-Weizen, Amber, Pale Ale, Brown Ale, Sphinx Stout, Snow Cap, Bock
2.   Bridgeport, OR: Bridgeport Ale, Blue Heron Pale Ale, Pintail Ale, Double Stout, Old Knucklehead
3.   Mendocino, CA: Peregrine Pale Ale, Blue Heron Pale Ale, Red Tail Ale, Eye of the Hawk, Black Hawk Stout
4.   Rockies (Boulder), CO: Amber Ale, Wrigley Red, Porter
5.   Catamount, VT: Gold, Amber, Porter, Wheat
6.   Abita, LA: Golden, Amber, Turbo Dog, Andygator
7.   Frankenmuth, MI: Pilsener, Dark, Oktoberfest, Bock, Weisse, Old Detroit, Perry's Majestic
8.   Oldeburg, KY: Premium, Bock, Stout, Summer Beer
9.   Portland, OR: Oregon Honey Beer, Portland Ale, Mount Hood, McTarnahans Porter, Stout
10. Rogue, OR: Water Front Lager, Golden Ale, Rogue Ale, Red, Mogul Madness, Old Crustacean Barley Wine, Shakespeare Oatmeal Stout, Mexicali, Rogue 'n' Berrie

Top Brewpubs—1993

1. Sudwerk, CA: Lager, Pilsner, Märzen, Dark Lager
2. Gordon Biersch, CA: Export, Märzen, Dunkle
3. Tied House, CA: Pale, Amber, Dark
4. Rock Bottom, CO: Draft, Arapahoe Amber, Red Rocks, Falcon, Molly's Titanic, Black Diamond Stout
5. Wynkoop, CO: Wilderness Wheat, Märzen, IPA, ESB, Special Bitter, Scottish Ale, Sagebrush Stout
6. The Walnut, CO: Swiss Trail Wheat Ale, Big Horn Bitter, Old Elk Brown Ale, Devil's Thumb Stout
7. Goose Island, IL: Golden Goose Pilsener, Lincoln Park, Mild, Best Bitter, Honkers Ale, Winter Warmer, Oatmeal Stout, Imperial Stout
8. Cambridge, MA: Golden, Pale, Amber, IPA, Porter
9. Marin, CA: Albion Amber, Mount Tam Pale Ale, Irish Red, Old Dipsea Barley Wine
10. Silo, KY: Derby City Dark, Red Rock Ale, Lager

Appendix II

Noteworthy Cities and Their Noteworthy Breweries

Albany

Albany Brewing Co.
Peter Ballantine & Sons
Beverwyck Brewing Co.
James Boyd's

Dobler Brewing Co.
Hedrick Brewing Co.
John Taylor & Sons

Baltimore

Carling National Breweries
Dukehart Brewing Co.
Gottlieb-Bauernschmidt-
  Strauss Brewing Co.

Maryland Brewing Co.
National Brewing Co.

Boston

Boston Beer Co.
Haffenreffer & Co.
Massachusetts Breweries
  Co., Ltd.

New England Breweries,
  Ltd.
John Roessle Brewery
Rueter & Alley

Brooklyn

Consumer's Park Brewing Corp.
Peter Doelger Brewing Corp.
Edelbrew Brewery, Inc.
George Ehret
Nassau Brewing Co.
Piel Brothers Brewery
Rheingold Breweries, Inc. (S. Liebman)
F. & M. Schaefer
John F. Trommer's Brewery
F. W. Witte Brewing Co.

Buffalo

Magnus Beck Brewing Co.
William Simon Brewery

Chicago

Best Brewing Co. of Chicago
Birk Brothers Brewing Co.
Michael Brand Brewing Co.
Busch Brewing
Canadian Ace Brewing Co.
Chicago Breweries, Ltd.
Peter Hand Brewing Co.
John A. Huck Brewery
Keeley Brewing Co.
Lill and Diversey
Manhattan Brewing Co.
McAvoy Brewing Co.
Schoenhofen-Edelweiss
Conrad Seipp Brewing Co.
Sieben's Brewery
United States Brewing Co.

Cincinnati

Burger Brewing Co.
Foss-Schneider Brewing
Gerke Brewing
John Hauck Brewing Co.
Herancourt Brewing
Hudelpohl Brewing Co.
Kauffman Brewing
Christian Moerlein Brewing Co.
Red Top Brewing Co.
Schoenling Brewing Co.
George Wiedemann Brewing Co.
Windisch-Muhlhauser Brewing Co.

Cleveland

Cleveland Brewery
Cleveland & Sandusky
  Brewing Co.

John M. Huges
Schmidt & Hoffman

Detroit

Columbia Brewing
Detroit Brewing Co.
E. & B. Brewing Co.
Goebel Brewing Co.
Kaiser & Schmidt
  Brewing Co.

Philip Kling Brewing Co.
Koppitz-Melchers
  Brewing Co.
Pfeiffer Brewing Co.
Stroh Brewery Co.
Tivoli Brewing Co.
E. W. Voight Brewing Co.

Louisville

Central Consumers
  Brewing Co.
Falls City Brewing Co.

Frank Fehr Brewing Co.
John F. Oertel

Milwaukee

Banner Brewing
Val. Blatz Brewing Co.
Capitol Brewing
Cream City Brewing Co.
Adam Gettelman
  Brewing Co.

Independent Brewing
Miller Brewing Co.
Pabst Brewing Co.
Jos. Schlitz Brewing Co.

New York (Brooklyn breweries are listed separately)

Beadleston & Woerz
Bernheimer & Schmid

Flanagan, Nay & Co.
Jacob Ruppert Brewery

H. Clausen & Son
Peter Doelger Brewing Corp.
George Ehret's Hell Gate
    Brewing Co.
James Evrard Brewing Co.

F. & M. Schaefer
    Brewing Co.
Conrad Stien
Tracey & Russel

Newark

Peter Ballantine Brewing
    Co.
Christian Feigenspan, Inc.

Gottfried Krueger
    Brewing Co.

Philadelphia

Louis Bergdoll Brewing Co.
Bergner & Engel Brewing
    Co.
John F. Betz & Son, Inc.
Esslinger Brewing Co.
Liebert & Obert
William Massey & Co.
Henry F. Ortlieb Brewing
    Co.

Francis Perot's Sons
    (Malting Co.)
F. A. Poth & Sons, Inc.
C. Schmidt & Sons, Inc.
Robert Smith Ale
    Brewing Co.

Pittsburgh

C. Baeuerlein Brewing Co.
Darlington & Company
Duquesne Brewing Co.
Eberhardt & Ober
Ft. Pitt Brewing Co.
Independent Brewing Co.
Iron City Brewery
Philip Lauer Brewery

F. L. Ober
Phoenix Brewing Co.
Pittsburgh Brewing Co.
Straub Brewery
Z. Wainwright
M. Winter Bros.
    Brewing Co.

Rochester

American Brewing
  Company
Genesse Brewing Co.

Standard Rochester
  Brewing Co.

San Francisco

Anchor Brewing Co.
National Brewing Co.
New Albion Brewing Co.
San Francisco Breweries,
  Ltd.

A. Schuppert Brewery
John Wieland
  Brewing Co.
Wunder Brewing Co.

St. Louis

American Brewing Co.
Anheuser-Busch, Inc.
Columbia Brewing Co.
Empire
Falstaff Brewing Corp.
Gast Brewing
Griesediecks Brothers
  Brewing
Home Brewing
Independent Breweries Co.
William J. Lemp
  Brewing Co.

National Brewing
Louis Obert Brewing Co.
Phoenix Brewery
St. Louis Brewing
  Association
Joseph Uhrig
  Brewing Co.
Wainwright Brewing Co.
Julius Winkelmeyer
  Brewing Association

Syracuse

Bartels
Greenway Brewery
Haberle Brewing Co.

Moore & Quinn
Zett

Bibliography

Anderson, Will. *The Beer Book*. Princeton, NJ: The Pyne Press, 1973.

———*From Beer to Eternity*. Lexington, MA: The Stephan Greene Press, 1987.

Barbor, Thomas. *The Encyclopedia of Psychoactive Drugs*. New York, NY: Chelsea House Publishers, 1986.

Baron, Stanley. *Brewed in America, A History of Beer and Ale in the United States*. Boston: Little, Brown and Company, 1962.

Barrows, Susanna, and Room, Robin. *Drinking, Behavior and Belief in Modern History*. Berkeley, CA: University of California Press, 1991.

Batterberry, Michael and Ariane. *On the Town in Old New York*. New York: Charles Scribner's Sons, 1973.

Bayles, W. Harrison. *Old Taverns of New York*. New York: Frank Allaben Genealogical Co., 1915.

Berkin, Carol A., and Wood, Leonard. *Land of Promise: A History of the United States*. Glenview, IL: Scott, Foresman & Company, 1987.

Bowen, Catherine Drinker. *John Adams and the American Revolution*. Boston: Little, Brown and Company, 1950.

———*Miracle at Philadelphia*. New York: Book of the Month Club, 1986.

————*Yankee from Olympus—Justice Holmes and His Family*. Boston: Little, Brown and Company, 1944.

Brown, John Hull. *Early American Beverages*. New York: Bonanza Books, 1966.

Butcher, Alan D. *Ale & Beer: A Curious History*. Toronto: McClelland & Stewart Inc., 1989.

Clark, Peter. *The English Alehouse: A Social History 1200–1830*. New York: Longman, 1983.

Dedman, Emmett. *Fabulous Chicago*. New York: Atheneum, 1981.

Digby, Joan and John. *Inspired by Drink*. New York: William Morrow and Company, Inc.,

Downard, William L. *Dictionary of the History of the American Brewing and Distilling Industries*. Westport, CT: Greenwood Press, 1980.

Doxat, John. *The Book of Drinking*. London: Triune Books, 1973.

Eames, Alan. "Turning a Page." *All About Beer*, November 1994.

Earle, Alice Morse. *Stage Coach and Tavern Days*. New York: The MacMillan Company, 1900.

————*Customs and Fashions in Old New England*. Williamstown, MA: Corner House Publishers, 1983.

Erikson, Jack. *Brewed in California*. Reston, VA: RedBrick Press, 1993.

————*Star Spangled Beer*. Reston, VA: RedBrick Press, 1987.

Farb, Peter, and Armelagos, George. *Consuming Passions: The Anthropology of Eating*. Boston: Houghton Mifflin Company, 1980.

Fennelly, Catherine. *Life in an Old New England Village*. New York: Thomas Y. Crowell Co., 1969.

Finch, Christopher. *A Connoisseur's Guide to the World's Best Beer*. New York: Abbeville Press, 1989.

Fleming, Alice. *Alcohol, the Delightful Poison*. New York: Delacorte Press.

Forget, Carl. *Dictionary of Beer and Brewing*. Boulder, CO: Brewers Publications, 1988.

Foster, Terry. *Pale Ale*. Boulder, CO: Brewers Publications, 1990.

————*Porter*. Boulder, CO: Brewers Publications, 1992.

Gies, Joseph and Frances. *Cathedral, Forge, and Waterwheel: Technology and Invention in the Middle Ages*. New York: Harper Collins Publishers, 1994.

Grossman, Harold J. *Grossman's Guide to Wines, Spirits, and Beers*. New York: Charles Scribner's Sons, 1955.

Grun, Bernard. *The Timetables of History*. New York: Simon & Schuster, 1975.

Haiber, William Paul and Robert. *A Short, but Foamy, History of Beer*. La Grangeville, NY: Info Devel Press, 1993 .

Jackson, Michael. *The New World Guide to Beer*. Philadelphia: Running Press, 1988, reprinted 1989.

————*The Pocket Guide to Beer*. New York: Simon and Schuster, 1991.

————*Michael Jackson's Beer Companion*. Philadelphia: Running Press, 1993.

Kitman, Marvin. *George Washington's Expense Account*. New York: Simon and Schuster, 1970.

Kochan, James. "A personal index of military records." Morristown, NJ: Curator National Historical Park, 1994.

Lathrop, Elise. *Early American Inns and Taverns*. New York: Arno Press, 1977.

Lender, Mary Edward and Martin, James Kirby. *Drinking in America; A History*. New York: The Free Press, 1982.

Levin, Phyllis Lee. *Abigail Adams*. New York: St. Martin's Press, 1987.

McLaughlin, Jack. *Jefferson and Monticello*. New York: Henry Holt & Co., 1977.

McNulty, Henry. *Drinking in Vogue*. New York: the Vendome Press, 1978.

Mee, Charles L. *The Genius of the People*. New York: Harper & Row Publishers, 1987.

Meier, Gary and Gloria. *Brewed in the Pacific Northwest*. Seattle, WA: Fjord Press, 1991.

Mendel, Jeff. *Brewers Resources Directory 1990–1991*. Boulder, CO: Brewers Publications, 1990.

Mendelsohn, Oscar. *The Dictionary of Drink and Drinking*. New York: Hawthorn Books Inc., 1965.

Miller, Dave. *Brewing the World's Great Beers*. Pownal, VT: Storey Communications Inc., 1992.

Morini, John. *America Eats Out*. New York: William Morrow & Co., 1991.

Morison, Samuel Elliot. *The Oxford History of the American People*. New York: Oxford University Press, 1965.

Muscatine, Doris. *Old San Francisco*. New York: G.P. Putnam's Sons, 1975.

New York Times, "Bond Brewing Group Put in Receivership." December 30, 1989.

Paymasters Account, "Lidgerwood Collection of Hessian Papers," May 31, 1777.

Phillippe, Louis. *Diary of My Travels in America*. New York: Delacorte Press, 1976.

Pierce, Bessie Louise. *A History of Chicago*: New York: Alfred A. Knopf, 1957.

Prial, Frank J. "The Man Who Rescued a Brewery." *New York Times*, July 11, 1984.

Protz, Roger. *The European Beer Almanac*. Moffat, Scotland: Lochar Publishing, 1991.

———*The Real Ale Drinker's Almanac*. Moffat, Scotland: Lochar Publishing, 1991.

Rae, Simon, ed. *The Faber Book of Drink, Drinkers, and Drinking*. London: Faber & Faber Limited, 1991.

Randel, William Pierce. *Centennial: American Life in 1876*. New York: Chilton, 1969.

Rice, Kym S. *Early American Taverns: For the Entertainment of Friends and Strangers*. Chicago: Regnery Gateway, 1983.

Robertson, James D. *The Great American Beer Book*. New York: Warner Books, 1978.

Ross, Phillip E. "Bid for Heileman Spurs Stock." *New York Times*, September 5, 1987.

Ruggo, Barry. "Boston Brewing's Image Center." *Ale Street News*, February 1993.

Smith, Gregg. *The Beer Enthusiast's Guide*. Pownal, VT: Storey Communications, 1994.

———"Beer in the Civil War." *All About Beer Magazine*, April/May 1993.

———"Upstate New York, Regional Breweries." *BarleyCorn*, July/August 1993.

———"Bill Newman, Godfather of New York's Microbrewers." *BarleyCorn*, January/February 1993.

———"New England Brewery Warms Norwalk." *Yankee Brew News*, Spring 1993.

———"Woodstock Brewing Company." *Yankee Brew News*, Winter 1992.

———"Crescent City Brewhouse." *All About Beer*, September 1992.

———"Manhattan Reopens Quietly." *BarleyCorn*, July/August 1993.

Smith, Page. *A New Age Now Begins*. New York: McGraw-Hill Book Company, 1976.

————*The Shaping of America*. New York: McGraw-Hill Book Company, 1980.

————*The Nation Comes of Age*. New York: McGraw-Hill Book Company, 1981.

Tousey, Thomas G. *Military History of Carlisle and Carlisle Barracks*. Richmond, VA: Dietz Press, 1939.

Tunis, Edward. *Colonial Living*. Toronto: Fitz Henry & Whiteside Limited, 1957.

————*Frontier Living*. New York: Thomas Crowell Co., 1961.

Van Doren, Carl. *Benjamin Franklin*. New York: The Viking Press, 1938.

Wagner, Rich. "Brewing in the 17th Century." *Zymurgy*, Spring 1992.

Wheeler, Graham, and Protz, Roger. *Brew Your Own Real Ale at Home*. St. Albans, UK: Camra Books, 1993.

Wigely, Russel E. *History of the United States Army*. New York: McMillan, 1967.

Wilford, John Noble. "Trade or Colonialism? Ruins May Give Answer." *New York Times*, May 25, 1993.

Yenne, Bill. "America's First Brewmaster General." *All About Beer Magazine*, April/May 1992.

Zymurgy, Summer 1993. "Everything You Always Wanted to Know About Beer."

INTERVIEWS:
Bill Owens, November 16, 1993 (unpublished)

Patrick Baker, December 4, 1993 (unpublished)

Marcia King, January 5, 1994 (unpublished)

Daniel Bradford, January 15, 1994 (unpublished)

Don Gosslin, January 30, 1994 (unpublished)

Pete Slosberg, February 2, 1994 (unpublished)

Bob Brewer, address to New York City Homebrewers Guild, March 15, 1994 (unpublished)

Pete Slosberg, September 12, 1994 (unpublished)

Rob Nelson, September 17, 1994 (unpublished)

GREGG SMITH is a beer historian, Great American Beer Festival judge, and a past member of the Beer Judge Certification Committee. He has been ranked as a national judge by the Beer Judge Certification Program. Mr. Smith travels extensively researching, writing, and speaking about beer and brewing for magazines such as *All About Beer, Beer the Magazine, New Brewer, Yankee Brew News,* and *Brew.* He is managing editor of the *Beer & Tavern Chronicle* and director of the Mountain Brewers Beer Festival.

Index

Thirsty for an Exotic Home Brew?

Anxious to Get Started on Your Own Home Brewery?

Let *Brewing Expert*
CHARLIE PAPAZIAN
Show You How With:

THE NEW COMPLETE JOY OF HOME BREWING
76366-4/$11.00 US/$13.00 Can
Learn first-hand about the history of beer;
discover the secrets of brewing world class styles of beer;
and find out how to add "spice" to your favorite blend

THE HOME BREWER'S COMPANION
77287-6/$11.00 US/$13.00 Can
Special advice on fermenting, yeast-culturing and
stovetop boiling; helpful trouble-shooting tips;
and answers to the most often asked questions

—*And Don't Miss*—
BEER:
A History of Suds and Civilization
from Mesopotamia to Microbreweries
by Gregg Smith
78051-8/$11.00 US/$15.00 Can